SAY GOOD NIGHT,

GRACIE!

How to Order:

Quantity discounts are available from the publisher, Prima Publishing & Communications, P.O. Box 1260SB, Rocklin, CA 95677; telephone (916) 624-5718. On your letterhead include information concerning the intended use of the books and the number of books you wish to purchase.

U.S. Bookstores and Libraries: Please submit all orders to St. Martin's Press, 175 Fifth Avenue, New York, NY 10010; telephone (212) 674-5151.

Say Goodnight, Gracie!

The Story of
George Burns & Gracie Allen

Cheryl Blythe and Susan Sackett

Prima Publishing & Communications
P.O. Box 1260SB
Rocklin, CA 95677
(916) 624-5718

Cover design by the Dunlavey Studio
Interior design by Nancy Etheredge
Typography by Com Com

Prima Publishing & Communications
Rocklin, CA

Library of Congress Cataloging-in-Publication Data

Blythe, Cheryl.
   Say good night, Gracie! : the story of George Burns and Gracie Allen / Cheryl Blythe and Susan Sackett.
      p. cm.
   Reprint. Originally published: New York : Dutton, © 1986.
   ISBN 1-55958-019-4
   1. George Burns and Gracie Allen Show television program.
   2. Allen, Gracie, 1906–1984. 3. Burns, George, 1896–
   4. Comedians—United States—Biography.   I. Sackett, Susan.
   II. Title.
   [PN1992.77.G463859   1989]
   791.45'72—dc20   89-10818
                                                         CIP

89 90 91 RRD 10 9 8 7 6 5 4 3 2 1

Printed in the United States of America

This book is dedicated
with love
to Gracie Allen
(1906–1964)

CONTENTS

Photo sections follow pages 112, 144, and 176.

ACKNOWLEDGMENTS

A number of people were instrumental in the creation of this book. The authors appreciate the time given us by the following:

Herb Browar, who gave up an afternoon of football to recount his wonderful memories of "Burns and Allen" and McCadden days. We'd also like to thank Herb for his photos.

Ralph Levy, for taking time out from his busy schedule to share so many of his stories with us. Also, special thanks for his photos.

Jack Bannon, our guinea pig who gave us our first interview. Thanks for all the additional information on Bea Benaderet and for the lovely photos of her.

Paul Henning and his charming wife, Ruth Henning. Thanks for the fascinating stories, the hot coffee and tea, and a beautiful Sunday morning in the loveliest home in Toluca Lake.

Al Simon, who graciously invited us into his beautiful Beverly Hills home to reminisce about the days of "Burns and Allen" and especially McCadden Productions.

Robert Easton, for a most entertaining as well as informative afternoon spent among the thousands of books crammed into every corner of his home. Thanks also to June Easton for serving us a "proper" English tea. Also thank you for the photographs.

Rod Amateau, a busy director, who took a break from his work to have lunch with us and give us some valuable information.

Larry Heath, an equally busy film editor, for allowing us to join him and his son at their weekly lunch while sharing stories about the "Burns and Allen" sound track.

Fred de Cordova, the executive producer of "The Tonight Show Starring Johnny Carson," who was kind enough to share a few moments with us.

Dwayne Hickman, for providing us with additional information.

Sharon Cookenboo and Carl Dutton of KHJ-TV Channel 9 in Los Angeles, for their efforts in locating information for us.

Dr. Robert Knutson and Ned Comstock for letting us live each Saturday at the USC Archives of Performing Arts, and for their invaluable assistance and patience.

Audree Malkin of the UCLA Theater Arts Library, for her assistance in script research.

Richard Arnold, for his cheerful help with our research.

Allan Burns and Gene Roddenberry, Cheryl's and Susan's respective full-time employers, for their understanding and friendship.

Bill Whitehead, our editor at Dutton, for his enthusiastic support, making this such a joy to write.

Bart Andrews, our agent, for many, many reasons.

And, of course, our continuing gratitude to the two people who made it all possible:

GEORGE BURNS *and* GRACIE ALLEN.

PREFACE

She called him "Nattie" and he called her "Googie." For thirty-eight years they lived together, played together, slept together, and, most important for us, worked together. Their love affair with each other was surpassed only by the love affair their audiences had with them. For Nattie and Googie were one of America's favorite television teams: George Burns and Gracie Allen.

Ice cream cost a nickel; a movie set you back fifty cents. A flight from New York to Los Angeles took eleven hours. "The Tennessee Waltz" was the number-one song. And for $500 you could put a down payment on a house—or you could buy this newfangled thing called a "television set."

It was 1950—the start of the decade that would later be called "fabulous." On Thursday, October 12 at 8:00 P.M., CBS presented "The George Burns and Gracie Allen Show." America's most popular stage and radio couple had made the daring transition to live television.

Their gamble paid off. Unlike so many shows that moved from radio to TV and failed ("The Fred Allen Show," "The Great Gildersleeve," and "Easy Aces"), George and Gracie's show was an instant hit. Their eight-year run produced two years of kinescopes, plus 239 filmed episodes that are still airing in syndication today. And during the past twenty years, "Burns and Allen" has also aired in Canada, England, Italy, Australia, Philippines, Hong Kong, Bermuda, Egypt, and Rhodesia/Zimbabwe.

Perhaps the reason for the continuing popularity of "Burns and Allen" thirty years later is that it wasn't meant to be social commentary. The humor was timeless. We tuned in each week to be enchanted by Gracie's inside-out logic and the resulting complications. Is it any wonder then that *People* magazine noted, "The show holds up remarkably well over the years; it is still funny because its stars are funny"?

Most likely if this show were pitched to the networks today, they would try to make George the long-suffering husband who ultimately loves Gracie *in spite* of her befuddlement. As it stands, George loves Gracie *because* of it. We were never forced to watch George roll his eyes and bemoan his fate. He loved Gracie just as she was and would never change her. He genuinely enjoyed her.

A simple example: Gracie has just offered an hors d'oeuvre to a guest. He eats it and, gesturing with the toothpick, asks Gracie what it is. Speaking as one would to a child, she says simply, "It's a toothpick." The guest then leans over to George and whispers, "The hostess is really a fruitcake." George confides, "She's my wife." The embarrassed guest, trying to recover, comments, "Good hors d'oeuvres." As Gracie walks away, the unflappable George grins at the camera and says, "Good fruitcake, too."

George Burns and Gracie Allen developed a format that has never been successfully duplicated in the hundreds of television sitcoms that followed: George and Gracie played themselves doing a weekly television show, although we seldom saw the show they did. Nearly all the stories took place at home, where assorted neighbors, studio personnel, and other visitors dropped by.

What made this format unique? George Burns was the only actor in a television comedy who comfortably stepped in and out of character—from *playing* himself on his show to *being* himself talking to the viewing audience. We all eagerly awaited those moments when George would turn to the camera and tell us what he thought Gracie might do next.

In addition, drawing on their popularity as a vaudeville team, they were able to incorporate their routines into the show's closing by sharing with us those wonderful stories about Gracie's "family." Uncle Harvey was a favorite:

GEORGE: Your Uncle Harvey, he's a real genius, isn't he?

GRACIE: Um hmm. But very few appreciate him. Except the men at San Quentin.

GEORGE: Oh, the fellows at San Quentin. They love him?

GRACIE: Yes. Do you know that he figured out a way where they could break rocks without working?

GEORGE: What was his plan?

GRACIE: Well, you wrap the rocks in packages, mark them "fragile," and send them through the mail.

And, of course, there was the classic ending. Cigar in hand, George would turn to his wife, grin, and deliver that famous line:

"Say good night, Gracie."

Smiling warmly at the audience, she gave a little bow and always obliged with "Good night."

ABOUT THE AUTHORS

Cheryl Blythe has worked in television and movie production for twenty years. Among her credits are "The Carol Burnett Show," "The Mary Tyler Moore Show," M*A*S*H, and "Victor/Victoria."

Susan Sackett worked as assistant to the producer of "Star Trek—The Motion Picture" and its sequels. She is the author of three books on "Star Trek," and continues to work with the show's creator while pursuing her writing career.

1

THE TRAIN TO

JERSEY

From the ages of seven to twenty-seven, I was lousy... but I was lucky to have vaudeville. As bad as I was, there were theaters that were even worse, where I could play and work on my acts.
—GEORGE BURNS

To begin the story of George and Gracie, we must go back to 1922, when vaudeville was in its heyday. One night, a seventeen-year-old Irish girl named Gracie Allen accepted the invitation of a girlfriend to catch an act at a theater in Union Hill, New Jersey. One of the performers was an acquaintance of Gracie's friend who was looking for a new partner. After his act, Gracie was taken backstage to meet the twenty-seven-year-old comedian. His name was George Burns.

What were the circumstances that led these two people to be in the right place at the right time?

Nathan Birnbaum was born on Monday, January 20, 1896, at 95 Pitt Street on New York's Lower East Side. He was the ninth of Louis Phillip and Hadassah Bluth Birnbaum's twelve children. Later the family moved to the third floor of a three-room flat in a tenement at 259 Rivington Street. His father worked for the local clothiers and helped out the neighborhood rabbi in the synagogue.

George once joked about his parents' relationship: "When my mother and father got married, my mother wanted to go to work, but my father put his foot down and said, 'No, dear, I will not allow it.' So my mother stayed home and raised twelve children, and did all the washing, cooking, scrubbing, sewing. My father was a gentleman of the old school. He didn't believe a wife should work."

But Nathan's father died when the boy was barely seven, and suddenly his mother had to support the family. Fortunately, her late husband's employers offered her "homework" —finishing dresses, overcoats, etc. Every little bit helped.

Shortly after his father's death, young Nathan acquired a new surname. The Birnbaums lived about ten blocks from the Burns Brothers coal yard. Being rather poor, Nat and his pals would help themselves to all the coal they could stuff in their knickers. As they waddled down the street barely able to walk, people from the neighborhood would shout, "There go the Burns Brothers." And so Nathan Birnbaum became Nathan Burns.

About six months later he got the rest of his name. An older brother named Isadore had a nickname; not Izzy, as you might guess, but for some reason his friends called him George. Young Nathan was crazy about this brother, and decided that if George was good enough for him, then George would be his name too.

The show business bug bit George Burns almost from the start. He attended P.S. 22 and once had the lead in a school play—"The Life of Peter Stuyvesant." But his formal education was cut short for economic reasons, and he left school after the fourth grade. Nearly seventy years later, on November 23, 1977, he received an honorary diploma from P.S. 22, recognizing his life credits earned during his many decades in show business. "Now that I've graduated," Burns joked, "I'll be able to make a living."

Actually, George began making a living at the tender age of seven. As he tells it, "I sang with four kids, the PeeWee Quartet. We sang on ferryboats and in yards and on street corners. On ferry boats we found out how to make money. On the Staten Island ferry you'd pay five cents, you'd ride up and down, and if a fellow and a girl liked each other, they'd pay ten cents and ride up and down on the ferry for hours. The PeeWee Quartet would sing in front of the people who were making love, and they didn't want to hear us sing—they wanted to make love. So they paid us not to sing. We made more money not singing than we did singing."

At the age of fourteen, George became part owner in a dance school—BB's (Bernstein and Burns's) College of Dancing. Unfortunately this establishment was quickly closed by the police, who labeled it a den for delinquents.

Next George turned to vaudeville, doing a little singing and dancing, but he really didn't have his career goal clearly in mind. He recalls, "I worked with a seal, I did a roller skating act, I was a monologuist. I did anything I could think of to stay in show business." One time he even did a dog act. He remembers waiting in a booker's office for a job and hearing a call come in for a dog act. The job paid $10 for a single performance. When the booker got around to asking George what he did, without hesitation he immediately replied, "I got a dog act!" George then rounded up two stray dogs and took them along. He placed them on the stage to do whatever they wished while he and his partner danced.

Soon after that, he was performing in a ballroom dancing act with Hannah Siegal, whom George renamed "Hermosa Jose" after his favorite cigar of the moment. They received a call from a booking agent who offered them thirty-six weeks on the road. They were supposed to leave on a Monday, but Thursday of the preceding week, Hermosa's father decided he wouldn't let her go with George unless they were married. George wasn't about to cancel thirty-six weeks, so he married her. They both were in love with show business—but unfortunately, not with each other. Exactly thirty-six weeks later, they were divorced. And while they were at it, they broke up the act.

For a while George worked as a single under a variety of names. "After playing a theater I would have to change my name," says George. "The booker would never give me another job if he knew who I was." (It didn't occur to him to change the act.) One time George met a man named Eddie Delight, who had just had two thousand business cards printed saying, "Eddie Delight, in Vaudeville, 1922." The cards outlasted Eddie's vaudeville career; George inherited the cards and promptly began working as Eddie Delight. When the cards ran out, George worked under such names as Billy Pierce, Jed Jackson, Captain Betts, Jimmy Malone, and Buddy Links. "It didn't make any difference to me what my name was, just so I was on the stage. That was all I cared about."

Not an immediate success as a single, George formed several partnerships. One act was Brown and Williams (he was Williams), a song-and-dance act. They even tap-danced on roller skates. Another time he formed a trio with two friends, Hymie Goldberg and Nat Fields. Working under the name of "Goldie, Fields, and Glide" (George was Glide, after one of his favorite dance steps), the three young men entertained at clubs on the East Side.

In 1922, George was doing an act called Burns and Lorraine—working under his own name for a change—when his partner, Billy Lorraine, decided to leave the act. George sought yet another new partner, and this became the turning point in his career.

He was about to meet Gracie Allen.

At the time George and his boyhood chums were stealing coal, Grace Ethel Cecile Rosalie Allen was born in San Francisco on July 26, 1906, just a few months after the famous earthquake. Her father, Edward Allen, was a minstrel song-and-dance man who ran a dance school out of their home. Gracie's first stage performance was at the age of three, when,

dressed in a man's top hat and tails, she sang an Irish song.
She refused to wear the red beard that went with the outfit.
As Gracie once put it, "Out I went with the long tails drag-
ging on the boards behind me and, over my arm, the red
beard. . . . I was the only one to get a write-up in the paper—
'la petite Gracie,' they called me."

Gracie showed early promise as a performer, exhibiting
her prowess at highland flings, and when she was only four,
winning a cup for a sword dance. By this time her father had
made her part of an act, the Allen Sisters, and Gracie danced
with her three older sisters, Pearl, Hazel, and Bessie. She
attended the Star of the Sea Convent School, but it was clear
that Gracie was not going to be a scholar. Every afternoon
she'd come home from school, dress up, take her ten-cent
allowance, and go downtown, walking from one theater lobby
to the next, looking at the pictures out front. Whenever her
mother needed her to run an errand, she never confused Gracie with street names; rather she would simply say, "It's a
block from the Orpheum." Then it became easy.

At fourteen, Gracie rejoined her three sisters in vaudeville, playing theaters in the San Francisco area. When she
completed school around the time of her eighteenth birthday,
Gracie and sisters Bessie and Hazel joined Larry Reilly &
Company. Gracie played a colleen, singing with a thick Irish
brogue that she later had a terrible time losing. When the act
was booked into Hoboken, New Jersey, and she saw the mar-
quee proclaiming "Larry Reilly," it got her Irish up. Even
though her billing was only "& Company," it meant the world
to her. When Reilly refused to add it, she quit.

Luckily, Gracie discovered that Hoboken was just a short
train ride from New York City. Weary of what seemed an
insecure livelihood in the theater, she enrolled in a New York
secretarial school to learn the secrets of shorthand and
typing.

It was while Gracie was studying stenography that her
friend Rena Arnold persuaded her to take a short trip back to
New Jersey to catch a vaudeville act playing in Union Hill.

Burns and Lorraine were doing a comedy routine with song and dance, and when Gracie learned that the act was going to split up, she went backstage to see Lorraine about a job. Instead, she decided to team up with the other partner—George Burns. "It was a choice of secretarial school, teaching dancing back home in San Francisco, or me," said George. "She didn't have train fare home, and hated to type, so my irresistible charm won out."

Burns had just met Allen.

2

LAMB CHOPS

GRACIE: *Remember when we met in vaudeville? I was just Gracie Allen then. Little did I think that you'd marry me and change my name to "Burns and Allen."*

The new team of Burns and Allen first played the Hillstreet Theater of Boonton, New Jersey, for only five dollars a day. And they didn't have an easy time getting their act together.

Gracie had planned for them to continue the act she had always done. Unfortunately, her scenery got lost during the return trip from Canada, and new backdrops and props would cost them three hundred dollars. No problem—George had written an act for himself and a partner that didn't require any new scenery.

George had naturally given himself all the funny lines, and Gracie was relegated to playing "straight man." But the audience laughed at all of Gracie's supposedly straight questions, and greeted George's funny answers with silence. At first he thought the audience must be out of their minds, but then George began to feel the same thing the audience did—

Gracie's personality. As George put it, "The girl . . . was struck by something magic in front of an audience. They adored her."

When they returned to their dressing room George made the decision that would see them through three-and-a-half successful decades. Before the next performance, he tore the act apart, giving Gracie all the jokes and taking the straight lines for himself. Said George, "It broke my heart, but I was young, hungry, and not a dope." That night they were a hit.

George rewrote a lot of their material to take advantage of Gracie's naturalness. Although much of Gracie's own conversation was worked into their routines, George created the bulk of their material from scratch. "I knew entrances, I knew exits, I knew how to switch a joke. . . . I was able to think of it, and Gracie was able to do it. That made us a good team."

But although George occasionally tossed in a funny line for himself (and found that the audiences now laughed harder at him than ever before), Gracie was the star. "They loved her," said George. "You know, there was nothing sexy about Gracie—no big bust or anything like that. She was just a dainty, nice, darling Irish girl with blue-black hair and a quick delivery and great, great style."

From the very beginning of their working together, George never allowed Gracie to resort to pratfalls, funny faces, or funny hats. And George's only prop was a cigar. Yet it was this now famous cigar that nearly ruined it all. For a while George expressed his exasperation with Gracie's "dumbness" on stage by blowing smoke in her face. But audiences had become very protective toward the lovable little screwball, and George learned, "You couldn't touch Gracie. When I walked on the stage with Gracie I used to find out which way the wind was blowing so the smoke from my cigar wouldn't go in Gracie's face. I had to be very careful."

Burns and Allen were not immediate headliners. At first they were what is termed a "disappointment act," which meant that they waited by their telephone for something to happen to an already booked performer. A missed train, a sudden illness, or a broken leg—any calamity would do. When that happened, the disappointed theater manager called in Burns and Allen to replace the act. "We were fortunate," said George. "There were lots of broken legs. . . . We were fighting for our livelihood, and though we never wished anyone bad luck, whether someone tripped or not sometimes meant whether we ate or not."

Their first big break came in 1925, when they were booked on the Orpheum circuit—the "big time"—sixteen weeks at four hundred dollars a week, more money than either of them had ever known. Best of all, Gracie was at last going to realize her life's ambition—to play the Orpheum in downtown San Francisco, where she'd spent so much time daydreaming as a child. It was to be the culmination of the successful cross-country Orpheum tour—until something happened that changed the course of both their lives.

On the eve of their San Francisco opening, Gracie suddenly doubled over in pain. She was rushed to the hospital with an appendicitis attack. George was at her bedside every minute—morning, noon, and night—with flowers. He had been bitten by the love bug some time ago, but didn't think he had a chance because Gracie had a boyfriend back home.

George knew that this was the girl he wanted to marry. "All my life I'd been in love with show business, and now, for the first time, I loved something more." Gracie wasn't so sure. She stalled; George persisted. Weeks went by. Finally, on Christmas Eve, George gave her an ultimatum: either they'd get married, or he'd split up the act. Gracie later referred to it as "Black Christmas." At 3:00 A.M. the next morning Gracie phoned George. "You'd better buy the ring," she announced. "How did you finally make up your mind it was me and not the other fellow?" a confused but elated George asked. "It was you who made me cry," she said. "I figured if you could make me cry, I must be in love with you."

Even George's mother was in love with Gracie, having met her one night when George brought her home to dinner.

The night before the wedding George phoned his mother in New York to tell her the good news. He was slightly hesitant because his mother came from an Orthodox Jewish background, and Gracie was an Irish Catholic. "I'm going to Cleveland tomorrow to marry Gracie," he began. Mrs. Birnbaum said, "Gracie's a lovely girl." "You know, Mama, she's not Jewish, she's Catholic." George's mother shot back, "If they'll have you, that's fine!"

On January 7, 1926, two weeks after "Black Christmas," they were married by a justice of the peace in Cleveland. She was nineteen and he was almost thirty. On their wedding night, George's pal Jack Benny thought he would play a joke on his newlywed friends. He phoned the Burnses long distance from San Francisco at 3:00 A.M. "Hmm?" answered a sleepy voice. "Hello, George?" began Jack. George snapped back, "Send up two orders of ham and eggs," and the phone was slammed down. George always knew how to handle Jack's practical jokes.

Six weeks after their marriage, Burns and Allen were playing New York's Palace Theater. Their act became known as "Dizzy," named for Gracie's character, now honed to perfection. The routine went something like this:

GEORGE: You're dizzy.
GRACIE: I'm glad I'm dizzy. Boys like dizzy girls and I like
    boys.
GEORGE: I'm glad you're glad you're dizzy.
GRACIE: I'm glad you're glad, I'm glad, [etc.]

Now you know why it was called "Dizzy."

Toward the end of the act George would say, "Music," and they would dance. Then he'd say, "Stop," and they'd tell a joke:

GEORGE: How long has your sister Bessie been married?
GRACIE: They've been married seventeen years and they have
    sixteen children.

GEORGE: Bessie and her husband have been married seventeen years and they have sixteen children?
GRACIE: Well, he was in the army one year.

Then George would say, "Music," and they'd dance right off the stage.

They had done this routine the first week they were together, and it fell flat on its face. When they performed it at the Palace, however, it was a smash. Years later when they were doing "The George Burns and Gracie Allen Show" on television, they would occasionally treat the audience to this routine.

About a year after their marriage, they hit the top in vaudeville with a skit called "Lamb Chops."

GEORGE: Little girl, do you care about love?
GRACIE: No.
GEORGE: Do you care about kisses?
GRACIE: No.
GEORGE: Well, what do you care about?
GRACIE: Lamb chops!

It may sound like silly dialogue, but by 1929 they were making big bucks touring on vaudeville's Keith circuit. Later that year they were invited to London, where they played for twenty-one weeks, delighting audiences at Victoria Palace and at London night spots like the Trocadero Restaurant, the Embassy Room, and Chez Henri nightclub. The English audiences adored them and would chime in on the punch line, "Lamb chops!" Once George, trying to break the monotony, changed the line, and the audience hollered, "We won't 'ave it!"

The British loved them. Burns and Allen went on to do a twenty-six-week engagement on BBC radio—a new medium for the comedy team. They were an instant hit and millions of staid Englishmen went around dazed for weeks, trying to quote Gracie.

Burns and Allen were on a roll. Earlier that year, they had made their film debut for the incredible sum of seventeen hundred dollars. It was the ultimate disappointment act— they substituted for an ailing Fred Allen in a Warner Bros. Vitaphone one-reeler. It was a nine-minute spot, but their standard street-corner flirtation act did not fit the sets that had been prepared for Fred. So they improvised.

When the camera started rolling, Gracie came on the set and began looking under ashtrays, in boxes, behind curtains, and in drawers. George asked, "What are you looking for?" She answered, "The audience." George pointed, "The audience is right there, in the camera. We're supposed to talk for nine minutes. If we do that, we get seventeen hundred dollars. Can you talk for nine minutes?" Gracie confidently replied, "Ask me about my brother." George did, and she began to talk. Nine minutes later she was right in the middle of a joke when George looked at his watch and said, "Thank you, ladies and gentlemen. Our nine minutes are up, and we just made seventeen hundred dollars."

By the end of the "Roaring Twenties," they were doing even better than that. As the nation's foremost vaudeville team, they were earning salaries close to two thousand dollars a week. The once unknown team of Burns and Allen seemed to have it all. But new heights awaited them. Network radio beckoned.

3

RADIOACTIVITY

> ATOMIC SCIENTIST: *Do you know any-*
> *thing about radioactivity?*
> GRACIE: *Of course, my husband and I*
> *have been in it for years. We*
> *started with Guy Lombardo.*

Looking back, it's hard to believe that George and Gracie
were turned down after their first American radio audition in
1930. An important NBC executive told them, "From my
knowledge of what the public wants, I can tell you that it
would not accept you as a regular feature. For one thing,
Gracie's voice is too squeaky—absolutely unfit for radio."

Meanwhile, the team's stage career continued to soar. A
year later they were appearing at the Palace in New York on
the same bill with Eddie Cantor and Georgie Jessel. Cantor
was one of radio's top stars, and after seeing Burns and Allen
work, he spoke to George. "I really enjoyed the act. In fact,
I'd like Gracie to do a spot on my radio show." "That's terrific," replied George. "When would you like us on the show?"
"No, I don't mean you," answered Cantor. "Just Gracie."
Undaunted, George wrote a Burns and Allen routine in which

13

Cantor played straight man to Gracie. Squeaky voice or not, the audience loved her as she practically stole Cantor's show from him.

Eddie Cantor may have been the first to present Gracie to the American radio audience, but credit for bringing the team of Burns and Allen to the airwaves—only one week later —goes to Rudy Vallee, who had an incredible knack for recognizing new talent. (Among his discoveries were such stars as Milton Berle, Edgar Bergen, and Alice Faye.)

Their appearance on Vallee's show led George and Gracie to CBS radio's "The Robert Burns Panatella Program," where on February 15, 1932, they joined the Guy Lombardo Orchestra as headliners, with Guy and George playing straight men to Gracie:

GUY: My brother Carmen played "Stars and Stripes Forever."
GRACIE: That's nothing. My brother held a note for twenty
         years!
GUY AND GEORGE: Twenty years?!
GRACIE: The bank wouldn't make it good.

During their appearances on Lombardo's show, CBS devised a publicity gimmick to help build the program's audience. Gracie was to conduct an on-air search for her long-lost brother. It had nothing to do with her real brother; it was just a running joke on the radio show—until the public took up the game. Everyone was either hunting for her missing brother, or *was* her missing brother. Stores across the country advertised in the local newspapers, "Do your shopping here. You'll find excellent bargains—you might even find Gracie Allen's missing brother."

The press took the publicity stunt to their hearts, as if they'd thought of it themselves. Gracie was photographed looking for her brother at all the famous New York sites—the Empire State Building, the Statue of Liberty, Coney Island. And she began to pop up, unannounced, all over the radio dial —in the middle of soap operas and dramatic shows, even murder mysteries—there would be Gracie, asking if anyone had seen her brother. Meanwhile, Gracie's real brother, George Allen, who was working as a clerk for Standard Oil in San Francisco, practically had to go into hiding. He was terrified of the press and spent a lot of time dodging eager reporters.

In the middle of this campaign, George and Gracie were to guest on Rudy Vallee's show on NBC. The powers at this rival network warned her not to mention the search for her sibling, fearing that she'd take the audience back to CBS with her. At the last minute, the dialogue about the missing brother had to be written out of the script, but when they went on the air, Vallee grabbed the wrong script and mentioned her brother. NBC was so incensed by the free publicity this gave its competition that they pulled Vallee's show off the air, which of course generated even more publicity.

At the end of ten days, CBS stopped the campaign while it was still going strong because they were afraid the public would tire of it. It was an immensely successful publicity gimmick, and Burns and Allen became more popular than ever.

By 1933 their popularity was at an all-time high, and CBS awarded them their own show, which ran for seventeen consecutive years. "The George Burns and Gracie Allen Show" (also called "Maxwell House Coffee Time" and, for a short while, "The Adventures of Gracie") featured many now famous stars in regular roles, such as Richard Crenna as "Waldo" and Mel Blanc as "The Happy Postman." Another featured role went to Clarence Nash as "Herman the Duck." (Nash at the time was just getting started in the duck-voice business over at Walt Disney studios, doing a new character named Donald.) Other regular cast members included Gale Gordon and Hans Conried.

Their bandleaders throughout the years were Jacques Renard, Paul Whiteman, Ray Nobel, and Meredith Willson, and they also had various announcers, including Harry Von Zell, Ted Husing, Toby Reed, Truman Bradley, Jimmy Wall-

ington, and Bill Goodwin. The show's unique format allowed
many of these usually anonymous people to join George and
Gracie in their routines.

The program's basic format consisted of Burns and Allen
comedy sketches, songs, and even vaudeville routines. On
many occasions Gracie, harking back to her days as an Irish
singer, would delight the audience with her lovely voice.

Although based in New York, the show took to the road
every few weeks, making for an exhausting schedule as they
trooped all over the map. Always performed live, the broadcasts originated from such widely scattered venues as In-
dianapolis, St. Louis, Chicago, Boston, Philadelphia, Washington, Baltimore, Atlantic City, Toledo, Cincinnati, Kansas City,
and, of course, Hollywood.

In 1934, while living at New York's Essex House Hotel,
George and Gracie adopted their first child, a girl, Sandra
Jean. At about the same time, the couple's motion picture
career was getting under way in Hollywood, so it seemed only
natural that when they decided to buy their first home they
settled in Beverly Hills. A year later they adopted a son,
Ronald John Burns. The four Burnses lived in that house at
720 Maple Drive all their years together.

Even while they were still with Guy Lombardo, movie
offers had begun to pour in. In 1930 they began filming a
series of "shorts" for Paramount Studios in Astoria, Long
Island. These were so well received that the team was invited
to Hollywood to do their first feature film, *The Big Broadcast
of 1932*. George reminisced about this appearance in a 1984
interview on NBC's "The Today Show": "We brought in our
own stuff in that movie. They said, Bring in five minutes of
stuff and we did 'Burns and Allen.' Everybody who was in
radio at that time was in the movie. And there was a kid in
there [who was] coming along. His name was Bing Crosby."

Other *Big Broadcast* films followed—one in 1936 and
another in 1937. In all, George and Gracie made twelve features for Paramount, including *Six of a Kind* (1934) with
W. C. Fields, *College Swing* (1938), and *The Gracie Allen*

Murder Case (1939), in which Gracie starred sans George. In 1939 they made *Honolulu*, in which Gracie proved how versatile she was—joking, singing, and demonstrating some nimble tap dancing. Gracie again soloed in a couple of pictures—*Mr. and Mrs. North* (1941), and *Two Girls and a Sailor* (1944). But this ended Gracie's enthusiasm for making movies. She hated getting up at 6:00 A.M., putting on makeup, and she hated the long hours it took to memorize her lines. She also felt self-conscious with all the cameras and lights.

It seems odd that a woman who had chosen show business for a career could feel so ill at ease in front of an audience, especially an invisible one. Yet even in radio, she had a fear of the microphone. She once told a reporter: "My hands are cold and clammy, my face is hot, and sometimes I fumble lines miserably. George loves that because the audience loves it. They think, 'Oh, that dumbbell, isn't she priceless—she can't even read the script.' "

The audience did love it. Throughout the years, the main appeal of their show was Gracie's giddy, fast-talking scatterbrained characterization. She'd say things like, "George tells me I have been on the radio for nearly six years now, but whenever I turn on the radio in our house I never get me." And the audience would roar.

George tended to limit himself to setting up Gracie's non sequiturs, a job his peerless timing enabled him to do brilliantly. And although Gracie was the acknowledged star of the show, she seemed to have little interest in it off microphone. It was George who supervised the writing, saw to it that the high quality was maintained, and established the program's overall direction.

In numerous interviews, George has explained why Gracie's humor worked so well: "Gracie's conversation on a radio broadcast often illustrates the way your mind might work underneath the surface of an intelligent, ordered conversation. It's obvious, for instance, that Gracie is an exaggerated caricature of a familiar and amusing type of scatterbrained woman. . . . But there's a deeper appeal. If you listen to

Gracie's prattle on the radio, you may notice that her logic is faultless, though usually mistaken.

"Gracie gets her laughs—we hope—because we often *think* the way Gracie *talks*, but we pride ourselves that we never talk the way Gracie thinks."

To wit:

GRACIE: I've just been reading in the papers that the Los Angeles police are hunting for a Chicago gangster. But why should they want one from Chicago? Can't they be satisfied with a hometown boy?

With their format well established, everything seemed to be going along smoothly until 1942—when the show temporarily lost its audience and its sponsor. George was the one who finally put his finger on the problem: Gracie and George were too old for the type of jokes they were doing at the time. Gracie's character was flirting with the announcer, and she and George were doing boyfriend-girlfriend insult jokes. "Now, you can insult your girl, but not your wife," George realized. "Everybody knew we were married and had growing children . . . you have to have truth in a joke just the way you do in anything else to make it any good. If it's basically dishonest, it isn't funny." George made a major format change and now portrayed them as the married couple they really were, and the show resumed its usual high ratings.

Gracie's character lent itself beautifully to publicity, and George and the network exploited it to its fullest potential. One of the most successful publicity gags was in 1940, a presidential election year. Guess who became a candidate for president? Right. Gracie's slogan was, "Down with common sense. Vote 'for Gracie," and her party was the Surprise Party. She had wonderful answers to the questions posed to her by the press. For example, when asked if she would recognize Russia, she apologized: "I don't know. I meet so many people. . . ." On the national debt: "It's something to be proud of; it's the biggest in the world, isn't it?" On foreign relations:

"They're all right with me, but when they come, they've just got to bring their own bedding."

She actually had a presidential train, complete with campaign platform, private rooms, dining rooms, and bathrooms with tubs. The front of the train was emblazoned with a kangaroo, the mascot of the Surprise Party, because of the campaign motto: "It's in the bag."

And, although Franklin Roosevelt and Wendell Willkie had little to fear from the Surprise Party candidate, Gracie actually received a few hundred write-in votes.

In 1942 George dreamed up another stunt for Gracie—the Piano Concerto for Index Finger. On the radio program she kept talking about this concerto, and everyone was waiting for her to play it. Finally Paul Whiteman, the music director at the time, helped write the concerto, and Gracie later performed it as a guest soloist with Whiteman at Carnegie Hall. She also made appearances with Arthur Fiedler conducting the Boston Pops at the Philharmonic and the Hollywood Bowl, and with Albert Coates conducting the San Francisco Symphony. Fifteen years later, in 1957, the gimmick was still going strong. Gracie Allen's Concerto for Index Finger was performed in a concert by the Atlanta Pops Orchestra, directed by Albert Coleman. It was the first time the musical selection was performed without Gracie at the keyboard. History does not note the name of the lucky finger owner who took over the chore.

Gracie's name was constantly in front of the public. She wrote a daily column syndicated in ninety newspapers. During the war years, Gracie exhibited her surrealistic paintings in art galleries for the benefit of the Red Cross. Also during that time, Burns and Allen continued do their radio show from military bases all over the United States, entertaining the troops and promoting the war-bond effort.

Year after year, George thought of new ways to keep Gracie in the public eye. In 1949 Gracie starred in a National Safety Council featurette to promote household safety. Their "scare" slogan became "Don't Be a Gracie," which meant

don't pick up a telephone with wet hands and don't get
clunked on the head by a falling bottle from an overcrowded
medicine cabinet.

As bizarre as some of them may have seemed, all these
publicity gimmicks paid off nicely. For nearly twenty years
the team of George Burns and Gracie Allen dominated radio,
winning the loyalty of 45 million listeners each week. They
were reaping the astounding sum of nine thousand dollars a
week and were finally able to ease up on their work schedule.
George at last found plenty of time for golf and bridge, while
Gracie happily indulged in gin rummy and canasta.

But this easy life-style was about to change dramatically.
George had set his sights on a new medium: television.

4

FROM

THE TOP

GEORGE: *Gracie, what do you think of television?*
GRACIE: *I think it's wonderful—I hardly ever watch radio anymore.*

In 1950, George Burns and Gracie Allen brought their act to television. George has downplayed the difficulty with his usual modesty. "We talked in vaudeville, we talked in radio, we talked in television. It wasn't hard to go from one medium to another."

Nevertheless, it was not an easy thing to do. Television is not "radio with pictures." George had watched other radio shows make the transition and fail, and he was not about to have that happen to them. "We're not going to make the mistake Fred Allen made," he told his writers. "We can't get by with just funny lines. We have to give them stuff to watch, too." But what?

William Paley, founder and chairman of CBS, was a big fan of George and Gracie, and was anxious for them to bring him a concept for a television show. As enthusiastic as George

21

was about the possibility, he was at a loss for a format. He
wanted their show to be different. He told Paley over lunch,
"I don't know how to do it. I'm a straight man. Gracie does
the jokes. What part do I play?"

Paley, and anyone else who knew George socially, realized just what a brilliantly funny man he was in private. Jack
Benny often laughed so hard at George's jokes that he would
slap his thigh uncontrollably. Paley recounted in his book *As
It Happened*: "People around [George] enjoyed rating jokes
by the number of times Jack Benny slapped his thigh. I think
the record was an eight-slap rating for one of George Burns'
punch lines."

It was at that decisive lunch in 1948 that Paley suggested
to George, "Why don't you start the program in front of the
curtain and do a monologue with your cigar and tell some
jokes. Then, when the curtain comes up, the two of you go into
your usual kind of routine. Perhaps halfway through the program you could come out and do another monologue leading
into another routine. . . . Make up a character, a story line, not
just a string of jokes, and come show me what you've got."
From this brief conversation came one of the best-loved, long-
est-running television series of the fifties.

George took Paley's concept and ran with it. He would
keep the domestic-comedy aspect of the radio show—he and
Gracie as themselves, at home—and add the most unusual
formula ever to work on television. Taking a cue from the
Broadway play *Our Town*, George decided to incorporate the
idea of a narrator periodically stepping out of the show to talk
directly to the audience—as he put it, "sort of step over the
line and let them in on it." George continued to develop his
format, and two years later the network requested a pilot.

George was ready—but Gracie wasn't. She was nervous
about memorizing new lines, scared of the cameras, and ada-
mant in her response to George: "This is one thing that I will
not be pushed into." George begged her to listen to his ideas.
He knew if they were to survive in the industry, they would
have to make the move to television. All he asked of Gracie

was to let them do one test. He promised her no tricks; they'd
shoot her from all sides, good and bad, so she would see the
absolute worst that could ever happen. If she didn't like it,
then it was no deal. George smiled to himself. In addition to
Gracie never realizing just how talented she was, she never
knew how pretty she was, either. The test, of course, was a
success. Sid Dorfman, a writer for both their radio and television shows, recalled Gracie's performance in a recent *Emmy*
magazine story: "When you saw this woman . . . you saw the
screen coming alive, and you knew something was there."

Enter Ralph Levy, a young Yale graduate, who had spent
three years with CBS–New York directing hourly network
variety shows and major sporting events, including the first
televised World Series. Following his New York success, he
was transferred to Hollywood with a team of four engineers
to open the West Coast division of CBS Television. Together
they launched the network's first West-to-East broadcasts.
His first effort was "The Ed Wynn Show," live from Hollywood; then came "The Alan Young Show"; both won Emmy
awards.

While on a well-deserved holiday in Mexico, Ralph's first
vacation in two years after what he referred to as a "crusher
schedule," he received a call from Harry Ackerman, the man
in charge of the CBS West Coast operation. Ralph remembers
that call vividly. "He asked me to come back the next day
because Burns and Allen had agreed to go on television and
he wanted me there at the first meeting. I told him I was on
vacation. He said, 'Well, George plays golf in the afternoon,
this meeting has to be in the morning.' I was really furious
that he thought I was going to come back. I didn't know
George, but I didn't like him already!" Orders were orders,
however, and Ralph hopped the next plane to Los Angeles.

George's offices were in the old Hollywood Plaza Hotel.
At their first meeting there, Ralph listened to the concept for
the new series and was horrified. Nothing about it fit any
proven formula for successful television. The horror seemed

mutual on George's part. How could this young college kid
understand anything about his business? Exeter and Yale did
not prepare one for working with Burns and Allen. Eventually, though, they each decided to give the other a fair chance,
and it was agreed that Ralph would direct the test film.
George eventually acknowledged Ralph Levy as "one of the
smartest young men in television."

The film was shown to the Carnation Company. Easy
sale. They bought it and remained the sponsor for the series'
entire eight-year run.

The first order of business was writing the premiere episode. While they were still working on the radio show, George
and his writers drove to Palm Springs to do some intensive
writing. Paul Henning, George's head writer, remembers this
session as a drastic change from radio. "In radio, George
didn't have too much of an active hand in the writing. Although he approved the material, he pretty much left it to the
writers. When it came to television, you really had to work
and use your imagination. This is where George came into his
own." Together, George and his writing team perfected a
format that was to last eight years.

It all seems so simple in retrospect. First, "Burns and
Allen" *admitted* it was a television show. The premise involved George Burns and Gracie Allen doing *another* television show we rarely saw. The show we *did* see revolved
around George and Gracie's home life. Second, we all knew
George and Gracie were real people; they never pretended to
be anyone they were not. Yet without a second thought we
suspended reality to accept their fictional neighbors, the Mortons. And third, we bought the idea that when George stepped
out of the plot to talk to us, sometimes he knew what was
going on in the story even when he hadn't been in an "all-
telling" scene—and sometimes he didn't. Did we say simple?
In addition to all of this, the early shows were a cross between
a sitcom and a vaudeville show, with guest singers and danc-
ers who entertained us between the first and second act of the
show. Can you imagine trying to sell this to a television network today?

George has often said, "Radio was like stealing money. You didn't even have to open a door. You just stood there, held a piece of paper in your hand, and you read it." There were no props to worry about. On cue, a sound-effects man slammed a window or dropped a glass, opened a creaky door, or even made footsteps. As George put it, "You did nothing and you got paid for it." He and Gracie were going to have to make drastic adjustments for the transition to live television.

In order to do a competent job, George refused to do a live show more than once every other week. They had spent many long years in vaudeville perfecting seventeen minutes of material. Now every two weeks they would have to memorize twenty-six minutes of *new* dialogue. This would be especially difficult for George.

Contrary to what a lot of people think, George was not an ad-libber. With the first episode, he formed a habit that would be with him the rest of the series. Everywhere he went he carried pages of the latest script. He would often be seen walking down Sunset Boulevard talking to himself, practicing his lines, much to the bewilderment of fellow pedestrians. It wasn't uncommon to see him in his car, stopped at a Beverly Hills traffic light, reading script pages. His lines were done with extra-large type so he could see them at a glance during these impromptu rehearsals. His diligence paid off, because when he went before the cameras every word, every nuance was perfect.

The time was getting close. The majority of the staff were housed at the Algonquin Hotel in New York, and there the writers worked around the clock. Sets were being built on the stage of the old Mansfield Theater, at 256 West Forty-seventh Street. In order not to block the audience's view of the show, the cameras were placed on two high platforms in the audience, although a third camera did remain on stage to catch George's monologues.

Knowing what he wanted in a supporting cast, George hired Bobby Friar (now artistic director of the Ahmanson

Theater in Los Angeles) as casting director. George was used to hearing good "cold readings," and radio actors were his first choice. These were people he could count on to be great the first time and maintain that spontaneity at the actual performance. Stage actors, on the other hand, needed rehearsal to perfect their delivery. But they had one advantage over radio actors—they knew what to do with their hands. Too often radio performers would try out for the Broadway stage, give brilliant readings, and on opening night, still have no idea how to make use of their hands. They were too accustomed to having that script in front of them.

Bobby and George reached some compromises. Bea Benaderet, who had worked with George and Gracie on their radio show, was the perfect Blanche Morton; stage actor Hal March would be Harry. Bill Goodwin, George's announcer on radio, would continue in that same role on the TV series. The script called for an "encyclopedia salesman," and this guest role went to veteran actor Henry Jones. The Singing Skylarks would provide the mid-show break. Rehearsals began.

On Thursday evening, October 12, 1950, the Mansfield Theater audience sat in keen anticipation. Backstage, artists were putting the final touches on makeup, technicians were hurriedly checking camera cues, while the cast nervously ran through their lines one last time. Gracie, especially, was concerned about following the chalk marks on the stage floor so as not to miss a camera shot, as well as remembering all her dialogue.

Suddenly there was no more time to worry. It was 8:00 P.M. and the countdown began: "And five . . . four . . . three . . . two . . . one. . . . On the air!" The conductor hit the downbeat with his baton, and television viewers sat back as the orchestra struck up the familiar opening chords to "Love Nest"—George and Gracie's theme. With love and adulation, the studio audience began applauding in expectation of the evening to come. The viewers at home were welcomed by Carnation Evaporated Milk, and were greeted with George's now familiar pose by the proscenium:

Hello, everybody. I'm George Burns, better known as
Gracie Allen's husband. . . .

He talked to us about being a straight man:

I've been a straight man for so many years that from
force of habit I repeat everything. I went fishing with a
fellow the other day and he fell overboard. He yelled,
"Help! Help!" so I said, "Help? Help?" And while I was
waiting for him to get his laugh, he drowned.

He finished his opening monologue by suggesting we all take
a look at where he and Gracie live. "Okay, boys, take it away."
    The curtain drew back to reveal a modest living room and
kitchen, with picnic-cloth fabric on the kitchen table, and frilly
curtains on a window that looked into a tree-filled backyard.
A natural rock fireplace dominated one wall of the living
room, with an odd assortment of chairs for any guests who
might drop in.
    The plot was simple: Gracie and Blanche wanted to go to
the movies, and George and Harry wanted to go to the fights.
George made up a card game that would exclude Gracie
and Blanche, hoping they would decide to go to the movies
without them, so the boys would be free to go their own
way.
    A few minutes into the show, it was time for a commer-
cial break, but instead of stopping the story, the commercial
became part of the show, as a disheveled Bill Goodwin came
rushing into the living room:

BILL: You know that little two-seater plane that I fly?
GEORGE: Yes.
BILL: I'm sitting at the controls this afternoon and all of a
    sudden I realize I'm out of gas.
GEORGE: What did you do?
BILL: I grabbed the microphone and called the tower. I said
    "Goodwin to tower, Goodwin to tower. . . . Do you read

me?" They said, "Tower to Goodwin, go ahead." So I said, "Do you use Carnation Evaporated Milk?"

GEORGE: That's what you said?

BILL: Every time I get near a microphone, I can't think of anything else to say. That Carnation Evaporated Milk is so great. . . .

And he continued with his product pitch.

After Bill finished, instead of leaving by the front door, he simply stepped over the little ledge at the front of the set and started to walk away. Just in case we might forget that we were watching a television show, George called out, "Wait a minute, wait a minute. Go out the way you came in. Use the door." An appropriately embarrassed and slightly befuddled Goodwin stepped back over the ledge, walked through the living room, and went out the front door. George then turned to the audience, took a puff from his cigar, and said:

Now, wasn't that better? You see, we've got to keep this believable. Now, back to the plot. It's now two hours later . . .

Interwoven through all of this were George and Gracie's vaudeville routines—nonsense runs of dialogue that had nothing to do with the plot, but established a style that would prevail throughout the run of the series. Take this example of an encyclopedia salesman's encounter with Gracie:

SALESMAN *(pointing to a picture of George):* These books would make a wonderful birthday present for your father here.

GRACIE: That's not my father. That's my husband.

SALESMAN: Oh, forgive me.

GRACIE: Oh, my father wouldn't mind, although he's a much younger man.

SALESMAN: Younger than your husband?

GRACIE: Yes, when I met George he was thirty. But when I met my father he was only twenty-four.

Halfway through the show, George introduced the Skylarks, then returned to the story at hand, trying to outsmart Gracie with his "Kleebob" card game. He should have known better. Gracie understood the nonsense rules right away, played out George's hand, and won the game. And off they went to the movies.

All too soon it was over. George and Gracie stepped out in front of the curtain. Holding hands, they smiled at the audience, George delivered that famous closing line, "Say good night, Gracie," and, graciously, she complied.

The orchestra began playing the closing theme, and while viewers at home watched end credits, the theater audience in New York applauded, wishing there would be an encore, but aware it would be two whole weeks before George and Gracie returned.

Friday morning, the newspapers ran the critics' comments. Had Burns and Allen been able to pull it off? *The New York Times* review said it all in the headline:

BURNS AND ALLEN BOW ON TELEVISION
Radio Comedians Successful in Transition to Video
Gracie as Zany as Ever

. . . As might be expected, there is no plot in "The Burns and Allen Show." It's primarily Gracie, constantly breaking out with some uproariously funny lines that would be downright corny if spoken by anyone but Gracie Allen. Most of the lines, however, are in keeping with her character, which makes her act delightfully acceptable.

As for the difficult transformation of a successful radio show into one for television, *The Times* went on to say:

Burns and Allen have made a transition which seems effortless. This observation, no doubt, attests to how hard they and their production assistants have labored to make the change. Some personalities don't get away with the move so successfully.

The young man from Yale had done all right, too.

Produced and directed by Ralph Levy, this program has all the intimacy, charm and relaxed atmosphere that any video show needs to make it a hit.

The comments concluded with:

While Gracie is the main part of the show, a lot of her appeal comes from the unobtrusive, almost unnoticeable work of George Burns, a philosophical man who remarked at one point in the show: "If she made sense I'd still be selling ties."

The debut was over. Everyone could relax. In a story in the October 22, 1950, *New York Times*, George and Gracie admitted they hadn't been at all confident about how things would turn out:

"We came in without any fanfare," said George. "It didn't help when we heard everybody talking about NBC's new television comedy stars." . . . Gracie admitted to being "petrified" in her video debut. "Why, I had butterflies in my stomach all during the show," she revealed. "All I could think about was, 'What's my next line?' I haven't memorized anything for twenty years."

Apparently all the worrying had paid off. When *Variety* came out a week later with its review, it had nothing but glowing remarks to add:

Carnation Milk fell heir to one of the TV delights of the season when "The Burns and Allen Show" debuted. ... It was relaxed; it had humor; it skirted all the cliché routining and production furbelows; it was original and imaginative in its concept; and above all it was designed primarily to project the talents of a comedy team schooled in show business with an appreciation of all the values that the term implies. In short, Burns and Allen have clicked with one of the best shows of the year.

5

ON THE COAXIAL

CABLE

The last two B & A kines are as good as film and at times indistinguishable from live.
—JACK HELLMAN,
Daily Variety *(January 18, 1951)*

The premiere show was a success, and for the next two months, the Algonquin Hotel became home and headquarters for the transplanted Californians. Because television shows originating in New York got more publicity than shows done in Hollywood, five more episodes would have to be done from the Mansfield Theater before everyone could return to the warm West Coast. Paul Henning recalled that they were all hoping to get home in time for Christmas.

New York was good to them. Almost every week there was another story in *The Times*, praising their efforts. For instance, on December 3, 1950, Jack Gould noted:

Their show is high-spirited farce which crackles with more good old-fashioned laughs than are to be found in the whole crop of pseudo-satirical offerings to which video is becoming increasingly addicted.

In order to earn those "good old-fashioned laughs," the writers worked long, hard hours. Every morning Paul Henning, Sid Dorfman, Harvey Helm, Willy Burns (George's brother), George, and Ralph Levy would get together in a suite at the Algonquin and kick around ideas, looking for a basic story line. It was always a simple, one-sentence premise: "Gracie dents the fender on the car and doesn't want George to know," "Gracie takes up a hobby," "Gracie plans a surprise party," etc. Once this was established, the writers would divide the work. George might write the monologues with Willy, or assign another writer to do them. The other writers would split into teams to work on Acts One and Two.

After a script was completed, everyone would regroup to have an informal reading of the material. Then decisions would be made as to what worked and what didn't. The final product was always a combined effort—no one person ever took full credit for creating a "Burns and Allen" script.

A kinescope was made of each episode by setting up a 16 mm camera in front of a small, high-intensity monitor that received the live images as they were being broadcast. Duplicates of this film were then shipped across the country for viewing by the West Coast. Not only did the West have to contend with these poor quality "kines," they didn't get to see them until two weeks after the live shows had aired in the East.

In March 1953 Gracie wrote a story for *Woman's Home Companion* lamenting the fate of the original jokes written for their live shows: "Every day a couple of our gags would be used by someone else on the West Coast, and by the time our show came over, [the joke] was dead. George finally wrote to one of the comedians who was using our stuff and asked him to please let it get out of our mouths first."

Their two months in New York were almost over. If there was any residual concern over the transition of a radio show to video, the reviews continued to dispel it. In his column, Jack Gould wrote:

While they are still the daft couple . . . their stage characters assume added credibility upon being seen. Where on
the radio their roles often leaned to repetitious caricature, on the screen their engaging nonsense is enhanced
by the warmth of their personalities.

Not about to rest on their laurels, everyone constantly
looked for ways to improve the show. In order to tighten the
stories, the variety acts were axed. (Those early specialty
numbers twice featured Bob Fosse, then a young tap dancer.)
Additional emphasis was placed on the show's visual
humor. Invariably, these moments were given to Gracie. For
example, while visiting with Blanche, Gracie is sewing lace
onto a doily. She calmly sits, holding the needle and thread in
one hand, the doily in the other. Blanche watches for a moment, then notices Gracie is doing it all wrong—she is holding
the needle still and pulling the doily away from it with each
stitch. Finally, Blanche can stand it no longer and asks what
we are all thinking:

BLANCHE: Wouldn't it be easier if you sewed the other way?
GRACIE: I'll try it.

And she promptly switches the hands holding the needle and
doily, and sews exactly as before.

As Paul Henning had hoped, they all did make it home for
Christmas, but they immediately went back to work, with
Live Show #7 airing December 28. CBS Studios in Hollywood
was their home base, and now New York would have to wait
two weeks for each episode to air. Nearly a year later, on
October 11, 1951, George and Gracie happily announced:

GEORGE: Gracie, this is our first show on the coaxial cable.
GRACIE: Really?
GEORGE: Yes. To install, it cost millions of dollars.
GRACIE: Then we better say good night. We can't afford it.
GEORGE: Well, I can't afford it either. Good night.

Thanks to that small strand of wire laid across the country, now everyone would see the kinescopes without the delay caused by shipping.

The recent TV "blooper" shows have made it a regular practice to search the vaults for kines from the fifties, hoping to find classic outtakes. They would be hard pressed to find any from "Burns and Allen" episodes other than an occasional boom shadow. George, Gracie, and the supporting cast's performances were flawless. According to Ralph Levy, "George may once have fumbled a little joke or something, but not Gracie. She was just perfect. She was a perfectionist. I never saw her blow a line anywhere."

Also, the timing on a live show had to be accurate to the second. The "Burns and Allen" stage manager would stand by and cue George, who always had a 60-second, 30-second, and 15-second joke prepared for every eventuality. If worse came to worse, he would simply say, "We're a little late, folks, good night."

The show was still performed in front of a live audience, and in keeping with the system they'd established in New York, the stage remained uncluttered so that nothing obscured the view. Levy's feelings were, "We put on a show as if we were putting on a theatrical show. There were no cameras in the way. . . . A camera cannot embellish comedy the way it can drama. It can only preserve what's in front of it. I like the audience at home to feel that the camera is just someone else sitting out in the audience."

As necessary as the studio audience was for the actors' pacing, there was one area in which they became more of a hindrance than an advantage—the dress rehearsals. These took place the day before the broadcasts. Ralph Levy explained the problem: "It dawned on us quite a bit into the season that different audiences laugh at different things at different times of the day. George would tell a joke and get a big laugh in the dress rehearsal and, knowing it was coming, on the night of the show he would stop and pause—and there was nothing. Or vice versa—he would get no laugh at a dress rehearsal and, knowing that, he'd step on his own joke on the real show. So we cut that out altogether and never again had an audience at the dress rehearsal. It really threw the actors too much."

After the "dress," everyone convened in CBS's fourth-floor conference room to work on the script, taking out what didn't play and polishing what did. Levy remembers one show in particular that was way too long. He suggested cutting a whole page of script, since he didn't find its only joke particularly funny. It involved Gracie's Uncle Louis taking saxophone lessons by mail and blowing the notes into an envelope to send to the correspondence school. At the conference, Levy found out that George himself had written that particular joke. A real battle ensued, culminating with George storming from the room and slamming the door. An anxious moment passed, then George reentered, faced Ralph, and bellowed: "You and your prep school education! I want you to know something—Gracie's Uncle Louis grew up to be the greatest saxophone player in the United States!" Ralph had to laugh, and the joke stayed in the script.

During those early years, "The Burns and Allen Show" was making innovations in live television. To avoid a stagnant look to the series, "Burns and Allen" used a variety of permanent sets. These included the front porches of the Burns and the Morton houses (312 and 314 Maple Drive, respectively), the Morton dining room, and the Burns patio, kitchen, and living room, with a staircase that led up to the second-floor bedrooms. Gracie had a slightly different impression of her home than we did:

REAL ESTATE AGENT: I presume the bedrooms are upstairs.
GRACIE: Yes, except when you're upstairs. Then they're on the
    same floor.

In the front of each interior set was a cutaway brick wall about eight inches high at the center that gradually angled upward to the side walls. The actors in the show would always use the doors to go in and out of the sets, but George would frequently step over the little wall when he spoke his asides to the audience. Then the camera would go past him, into the set, and resume the story.

One of the most ambitious ideas for a set in any live show was George and Gracie's swimming pool. We saw only a corner of it, but it was a brilliantly created illusion. The pool itself was a tank only eighteen inches deep that could be rolled out onto the stage. When it was filled with water, clever lighting provided an appropriately sun-dappled surface.

Because of the immediacy of live broadcasting, there was no way George could *really* go swimming, but that didn't concern the writers. In one of the early episodes, the script called for George to slip on a roller skate left on the patio and fall into the pool. A "Whoops!" was heard and "George" flipped into the water with a loud splash. A few moments later he reappeared, dry as a bone. George took impish delight in using occasions like this to talk to us directly:

> Dried off pretty quickly, didn't I? This California sunshine is wonderful.

In fact, the idea of George falling into the pool seemed so hilarious that the writers used it again at the end of the show, with George's double doing another flip into the water.

If that wasn't enough to stretch our credibility, in another episode George had to dive into the pool to rescue Harry Morton. And, once again, moments later there he was, bone dry. This time he mischievously winked at the viewers:

> You don't believe that was me in the pool, huh? *(He takes out his cigar and wrings water from it.)* Convinced? Well, I'm not going to fool you. On television we have to do things quickly so you've got to have a double, someone who looks exactly like you, so while George Burns is getting dry, I'm supposed to say a few words. . . .

6

THE WORLD

ACCORDING TO

GRACIE

GRACIE: *My mind works so fast. When I think of something I say it. Lots of times I say it even before I think of it.*

Dogs smoke pipes. Chickens prepare sandwiches. Buffaloes read newspapers. The Land of Oz? Hardly. These are simple, everyday occurrences as far as Gracie Allen is concerned.

Syndicated columnist Harriet van Horne came closest to describing this character in her article of May 5, 1953:

> Had Alice been able to take a companion with her to Wonderland, Gracie Allen would have been ideal. The Mad Hatter would have welcomed her with outstretched paws and trembling whiskers. . . . She'd have understood the customs and conversation in Wonderland better than the natives. "I feel taller in winter," remarked our Wonderland girl in last night's show. Pressed for an explanation of this phenomenon, she offered what should be obvious to anyone who thinks deeply. She feels taller because the days are shorter. . . .

The plots start off very simply but by the time Gracie has illuminated them with the moonbeams of her own special lunacy, there are six plots rolling at once. A kind of bedlam follows. Everyone is confused, distraught and all at sea except Gracie. She is the child who hums a little tune and goes on playing with his ball, unaware that the roof is falling in. In all of us, there ought to be a dram or two of Gracie Allen contentment. Life would be so much prettier. . . .

Every plot of "The George Burns and Gracie Allen Show" centers on Gracie's misinterpretation of the world around her and the resulting confusion. As George once said, "She is completely earnest about what she is doing and saying, and I think it is the fact that she is so kind to the rest of the world for its lack of understanding of what is perfectly clear to her that makes people love her. She is right and everybody else is wrong, but she doesn't blame them—she just gently tries to explain to them, patiently, and puts up with everybody."

For example, in one episode, George has been sneezing uncontrollably, so Gracie decides to consult a doctor:

GRACIE: What causes sneezing?

DOCTOR: Well, sneezing is usually merely symptomatic of an underlying cause. It may be a momentary irritation of the mucous membrane, it could be a psychosomatic manifestation, or it may be due to an infection in the respiratory system.

GRACIE: My goodness!

DOCTOR: I'm afraid that's a little difficult to understand.

GRACIE: Well, say it again slowly and I'll try to explain it to you.

Gracie has the greatest confidence in her intelligence. She puts salt in the pepper shaker and pepper in the salt shaker. Why? "Because everybody gets them mixed up and now when they do, they'll be right." Another time she is seen sorting

George's socks. Patiently, as if explaining the obvious to a child, she deals with her husband:

GEORGE: Gracie, what are you doing?
GRACIE: I'm seeing if they've got holes in them.
GEORGE: But then you turn them inside out and do the same thing.
GRACIE: I wanted to see if the hole goes all the way through.
GEORGE: Well, I just thought I'd ask.
GRACIE: If you don't ask, you don't learn.

George not only accepts these explanations, he expects them. Anticipating the usual Gracie reaction, he sometimes gets a surprise:

GRACIE: Where're you going?
GEORGE: I'm going down to the store to get some cigars and stamps.
GRACIE: Oh, who're you going to mail them to?
GEORGE: I'm going to smoke them myself. (*After a long pause*) Aren't you going to ask me why I'm going to smoke stamps?
GRACIE: Why should I? I've done one or two silly things in my life too!

Actually George takes great delight in Gracie, especially when she causes other people chaos. In one of his asides to the audience, he comments:

She's a real diplomat . . . she's always been very subtle. I'll never forget one time, we were at a party and the hostess was fishing for a compliment. She said, "Would you believe I'm forty-five years old?" Gracie said, "Of course I'd believe it. You're so honest, I'd believe it if you said you were sixty." Those are the little things I like about Gracie.

Sometimes Gracie's multifaceted character is prone to spouting proverbs:

It is the duty of every woman to spend more than she can afford so that her husband will go out and earn more than he's able to.

Or, how about this bit of logic:

Shorter cars use so much more gas. With a short car you have to travel much further to go the same distance.

And, in case you're still working on that one, try the corollary to it:

The longer a car is, the closer it will be to where it's going.

In one episode when Harry Morton gets a new secretary, Blanche is sure he is chasing her around the office. Gracie believes that instead of getting angry, Blanche should appeal to Harry's finer nature:

GRACIE: You say "Harry, what about our children?" and see what he says.
BLANCHE: He'll say we haven't got any children.
GRACIE: Then you say, "Yeah, how about that?" Never let them get the last word, Blanche.

George is the first to admit that Gracie's character on television is much the same as it was in radio and, in many ways, even in vaudeville. He understands her humor perhaps better than anyone. He once stated: "To her everything is a little nuts, and after listening to her you think maybe she's right. There are many women in real life who do and say the things that Gracie does. No matter how wacky she gets, there's always a touch of reality and truth in her. With-

out those touches, the show would've flopped long ago."
   One of the most charming aspects of Gracie's humor is
her literalness. In the fifth dimension of her childlike mind,
everything is taken at face value. Dogs really do smoke pipes;
she may think this is silly, but after all, she's not the one who
said it!

*On the train home from visiting her mother in San Fran-
cisco, Gracie is chatting with her fellow passengers:*
MR. GARLAND: Yeah, it's going to be great, sitting in my own
   easy chair with my dog at my feet, reading my paper and
   smoking my pipe.
*(Everyone waits for Gracie to say something, but she
doesn't.)*
MR. LINDSTROM: Mrs. Burns—aren't you going to ask him
   why he lets his dog smoke his pipe?
GRACIE: Of course not. If his dog is smart enough to read the
   newspaper, why shouldn't he smoke the pipe?

   Dogs aren't the only animals who are capable of human
traits in Gracie's world. In one scene, George describes a
conversation Gracie and the woman in front of her had while
standing in line Christmas shopping:

GEORGE: This woman said she was visiting here from New
   York State, and that her husband ran a Buffalo newspaper. Then Gracie said, "That's wonderful. How did he
   teach them to read?"

   Then there are those chickens mentioned earlier—the
ones who make sandwiches:

*The delivery boy, Bobby, has to leave. He tells Gracie why
   he is in such a hurry.*
BOBBY: Mrs. Vanderlip is waiting for a chicken to make sandwiches.
GRACIE: She'll wait a long time. It took me two years to teach
   our canary to sing.

Gracie is responsible for one of the most picturesque animal images ever:

GEORGE: What are you looking for in the Sears catalogue?
GRACIE: I'm looking for sweaters for cows.
GEORGE: Sweaters for cows?
GRACIE: Um hmm, you know they must be very scarce. Fred told me that he had forty Holstein cows and only twenty-two jerseys.

Most people could safely argue that Gracie is not the mental powerhouse she believes herself to be. Perhaps this is one of the most endearing things about her. The audience senses this and feels protective toward her as they would toward an innocent child. We don't really laugh *at* Gracie as much as we indulge ourselves in relishing her idiosyncrasies, and it's perfectly safe to do so because George encourages her:

GRACIE: Oh, by the way, I got a letter from Uncle Harvey. If we go up to San Francisco, he's going to give me the Golden Gate Bridge. He bought it, you know.
GEORGE: What did your uncle pay for it?
GRACIE: Thirty-two dollars. It cost millions but the man who sold it wanted to claim a loss on his income tax.
GEORGE: Yeah, it's probably scratched a little. We'll run up there next week and pick it up.

Perhaps nothing puts George's patience to the test more than Gracie's adventures in cooking. In a word, she can't, but that doesn't prevent her from giving it her all. Some of the best humor in the entire series comes from her attempts at the culinary arts. Combine this with her literal mind and we get:

GEORGE: Gracie believes everything she reads. She fried fish the other day and I had to buy her a new dress. The recipe said "Roll in cracker crumbs."

Gracie's intentions are always noble, if her results are a little less than perfect:

GEORGE: I'll tell you why Gracie has to get a new toaster. She wrecked the old one. Last night I asked her to fix me some hot chocolate, and she did, but it seems the Hershey bars kept melting before they popped out. It took me two hours to scrape the nuts off the ceiling.

Watch what happens when Gracie's cooking combines with her knack for numbers:

Gracie is counting slices of toast:
GRACIE: Let's see. Four, five, six, seven, eight, nine, ten.
TAX MAN: You must like toast.
GRACIE: Oh, this isn't to eat. You see, it takes thirty seconds to make a piece of toast, so by the time I make ten pieces, I know my five-minute eggs are done.

In fact, one of the most unusual areas of Gracie's mind is her creative use of mathematics:

GEORGE: She worked out a system where we wouldn't have to pay any tax. If you owe the government five thousand dollars, you make out your return for ten thousand. The government owes you five, and you owe them five, so you're even.

The IRS has yet to respond to this.

Anything to do with numbers, money, or banking opens up whole new avenues of confusion for Gracie. Her checking account manages to keep Mr. Vanderlip the banker (played by Grandon Rhodes) on his toes:

VANDERLIP: Tell Mrs. Burns a check is intended only as a means of transferring money from one person to an-

other. Not recipes and song lyrics, the latest gossip or
ten-day diets.

GEORGE: She writes all that on her checks?

VANDERLIP: Not only that, she signs them "Guess who?"

Often simple day-to-day household life presents problems
for Gracie. She is mystified by electricity. . . .

PHILLIPS THE GARDENER: Mrs. Burns, there's nothing wrong
    with that electric clock. You didn't have it plugged in.

GRACIE: I don't want to waste electricity so I plug it in when
    I want to know what time it is.

. . . the laundry . . .

HARRY VON ZELL: Whatcha doing?

GRACIE: Just going through the laundry and making out a list.

HARRY: Gracie, you make out your laundry list after it gets
    back?

GRACIE: Um hmm. It's the only way. I've been doing it for
    years and I've never lost a thing.

. . . and even the telephone . . .

*Gracie is working around the house. She passes the tele-
phone, picks up the receiver:*

GRACIE: Hello, operator? If you're going to have any phone
    calls for me today, will you put them through for me now
    because I'm working near the telephone? Thank you.

So convincing is Gracie Allen on "The Burns and Allen
Show" that nearly everyone believes this is the way she was
in private life. But there was another Gracie Allen. The real
one. And she was also an incredible person.

7

GRACIE

ACCORDING TO

THE WORLD

Gracie was a lady.
—EVERYONE WHO KNEW HER

Often people who met Gracie Allen would learn to their utter amazement that she was as intelligent as a "normal" person. Psychology students at the University of Southern California even voted her "Hollywood's Most Intelligent Actress."

George is the first to insist that Gracie was an actress, not a comedienne. "In the 'Burns and Allen' shows we didn't have any comedians. They were all actors and actresses. . . . Gracie was a fine actress who played the part of that off-center girl."

The key to Gracie's great acting ability was her own method, not found in any textbook. "I really don't act," Gracie would often explain. "I just live what George and I are doing. . . . It has to make some sort of sense to me or it won't ring true. . . . No matter what the script says there's no audience and no footlights and no camera for me. There's no make-believe. It's for real."

In fact, Gracie was so frightened of the audience that she never looked at them. She always played as if she were in a room with four walls, not three. Once when she and George were in the middle of a live scene, she noticed the camera for the first time—and stopped dead in her tracks. She recovered quickly and went on with her dialogue, and no one noticed anything amiss. Immediately after the show she pulled Ralph Levy aside. "What's that little red light on the camera?" He explained to her that that was the camera taking the live picture; she'd been playing in front of it for a year and a half. "Turn it off—I never want to see it again," she said. "It scares me."

So real was each situation to Gracie, that she never said a line the same way twice. As George told a *TV Guide* reporter (November 6, 1954): "It's remarkable. Watch an actor the first time in rehearsal. If he picks up a glass with his left hand, that's the way he'll do it every time. Gracie will change from performance to performance. She says it keeps her from getting in a rut, yet you're never aware of her hands."

She was extremely gifted when it came to using her hands. Ralph Levy recalled: "In one show where she was putting a hem in a handkerchief, we had to have the prop men standing by with twenty handkerchiefs half-done, because when she finished rehearsing the scene, they could not undo that handkerchief. It was completely and perfectly hemmed. Her job was not to read lines and be funny—her job was to hem a handkerchief. This was one of the great aspects of a fine actress. 'I'm here to fix George's handkerchief and, incidentally, I'm speaking.' Her sense of concentration was unbelievable."

Gracie seemed to confirm this analysis. "It makes me furious," she once disclosed to *The New York Times*, "to see an actor go through the motion of writing an address on a piece of paper. They scribble it off in a second and you know they couldn't have written anything. Now I would actually write down a real address." Watch closely in a scene calling for Gracie to write down something, and you'll see that she really does this.

All of this is even more remarkable when you realize that
"The Burns and Allen Show" scripts never contained detailed
direction—just major stage movements such as "Gracie
crosses to the couch" or "Gracie serves coffee." All interpre-
tation was left to her.

Waiting for her entrance cue could make Gracie extremely tense. When this happened, one of the show's stage-
hands, Frank Osborne (now Director of Production Services
for NBC) would assist her. She'd wait off-camera with Frank's
huge hands encircling her neck, palms down, not actually
touching her, yet restraining her. At the right moment he
simply parted his hands, and she walked onstage. "If George
had forgotten the cue word," says Ralph Levy, "I think Gracie would have walked off the set, gone to the car, and gone
home. That is the way she concentrated. . . . [She had] a
fantastic ability to listen to the other actors; that, of course,
is the great art of acting—*reacting.*"

Her tension is easily understandable. The main burden of
performance was on Gracie. She was in nearly every scene,
and had an enormous amount of unnatural dialogue to learn.

GRACIE: . . . I think there's so much good in the worst of us,
    and so many of the worst of us get the best of us, that
    the rest of us aren't even worth talking about.

Try memorizing that and see how long it takes you! And
consider the following run, with only a few key words from
George (and no cue cards):

GEORGE: So you were in [the dentist's] office . . .
GRACIE: Oh, yes, and was their office crowded. Some were old,
    and some were young and there were short ones and tall
    ones and men and women. You know why they were
    there?
GEORGE: They had trouble with their teeth?
GRACIE: George, were you there?
GEORGE: This reminds me of the act in vaudeville.

GRACIE: Yes, well, anyway, I was sitting next to this nice old man with a bald head. He was terribly nervous, so the nurse said, "Will you stop worrying? Before the doctor pulls out the rest of your teeth, he'll give you gas." So I said, "Well! The dentist has a lot of nerve giving people gas. How would he like it if the service stations started pulling teeth?"

GEORGE: The man appreciated that?

GRACIE: Oh, he did. He said he was sixty years old and he had never lost a tooth until Dr. Clyde started pulling them—and I said, "You'd better keep an eye on that nurse. Somebody's pulling out your hair, too." He was very brave. You know it wasn't even his turn and he ran into the dentist's office. . . . Then I moved over to this woman who was scared to death to have her tooth pulled. So I told her about my Uncle Harvey. Somebody told him instead of going to the dentist, if he tied a string to his tooth and then the other end to the doorknob . . .

GEORGE: If somebody opened the door it would come out.

GRACIE: And it did! Before somebody stopped him, his tooth had pulled out five doorknobs.

GEORGE: After the story I bet the woman felt better.

GRACIE: You know, she was just as brave as the man with the bald head. . . .

Despite these runs of dialogue, Gracie was a pro and never blew her lines on TV.

Nobody else could read dialogue written for Gracie. This was discovered during the radio days when the very able comedienne Joan Davis substituted for her, and the lines fell flat. It was Gracie's delivery that made the words come alive.

Perhaps the greatest tributes to Gracie as both actress and person were from those who worked closest with her. George, as one might expect, had the highest praise for his wife's professionalism. In his 1955 autobiography, *I Love Her, That's Why*, he said, "On the set she gives absolutely no trouble and makes no demands. She arrives on time, does the job, jokes with the crew, and in general behaves less like a star than any actress I ever knew, particularly as when she shuts the dressing room door and goes home, she's through. The day's work is done and there is no further discussion about it. She figures there's no time for temperament when you're on every week."

Others involved with the making of the show at that time had similar high praise. Jane Vogt, the show's wardrobe mistress, considered Gracie "outstanding in every way." In an interview coinciding with the one hundredth show (November 1953), she remarked, "Gracie is something special because of her consideration for others. I've been with Gracie since she started in TV and have never seen her out of temper or seen her fail to extend every courtesy to fellow players and the personnel on the sets. The first one hundred shows have been a breeze."

Bertha French, the hairstylist, was also interviewed around that same time. She had worked for Lucille Ball, Spring Byington, and June Havoc and said that Gracie was the only star who left her hairdo entirely up to her. (She noted one idiosyncrasy: "Even though Gracie has tiny ears, closely set to her head, the lobes must be covered.") "She's a wonderful person," said Bertha, "always at ease. You can be yourself. She expects no coddling or babying and never comes to the studio wearing a grouch. She actually comes in at 6:30 in the morning *singing*. Gracie has the utmost confidence in the people who surround her and therefore allows them to do their respective jobs."

Gene Roemer, who was Gracie's makeup man, was also quoted: "Gracie is the most complete pro with whom I've ever worked. She knows nothing about upstaging. . . . She's solely concerned with giving a perfect performance. Gracie is cute, kind, and most considerate." Gracie, in turn, had such confidence in Gene that she usually went to sleep in the makeup chair.

Her consideration for others was pointed out by nearly everyone. In one scene, for instance, the bedroom was roped off until shooting would begin. Gracie was already in the set, and when George arrived, he called for a prop man to remove the rope. Gracie turned to him and ordered, "George, get under the rope like I did." And Gracie was so engrossed in her part that, after the scene, which called for her to sit on the bed, she automatically straightened the spread, as if she were in her own home.

So intense was her concentration on her work and on memorizing that often impossible dialogue that Gracie silently suffered from shattering migraine headaches. If she was lucky, she'd be able to go to bed for a couple of days, but rarely did her schedule allow such luxury. To compensate, she had their home decorated in subdued shades of green, pink, and brown, which she found the most soothing.

Perhaps because she knew suffering, she had an extremely sympathetic and understanding nature. Jack Benny's wife, Mary Livingston, told columnist Louella Parsons in 1958, "If I have the least problem bothering me, Gracie is the friend I seek for advice. She just seems to know instinctively the sane and right thing to do."

Gracie had many close friends, and when she could get the time she indulged herself in one of her passions—gin rummy. She'd discovered it back in their radio days, when she and several of the writers' wives would play cards from coast to coast. They would become so engrossed in the game, they even had their dinner brought into their private train compartment.

Strictly an indoor type, she never swam in her own pool. Once when her children were little she did a couple of laps across the pool to prove to them that Mommy could indeed swim, and then never went in again. She hated the sun, and confessed, "The only real fun I can think of in the daytime is shopping—real shopping or window shopping. All the salesgirls in Beverly Hills know me." She adored fine clothes and was frequently on the Ten Best Dressed Women list. Of course, being a celebrity made it difficult for her to be in public places. Paul Henning's wife, Ruth, talked about these shop-

ping excursions: "Gracie didn't like to go out by herself because she was recognized everywhere and mobbed, so I often
went with her. After she had signed a certain number of
autographs, it was my job to go up and say, 'Miss Allen, you
have an appointment, you just *have* to leave now.' And she
would say to the crowd, 'What can I do? She's making me
leave!' "

Gracie was very petite—she weighed 103 pounds and
wore a Cinderella-like 4½ shoe. One of her big thrills as a
young mother was when her daughter Sandra was tall
enough to fit into her clothes. Unfortunately, this only lasted
for about a year. By the time Sandy was ten, she left Gracie's
wardrobe in her wake as she soared in height.

When not buying for herself, Gracie enjoyed getting
things for her family, friends, and the cast and crew. She also
did all her Christmas shopping herself, and she always acknowledged the gifts she received with personally handwrit-
ten thank-you notes.

Another favorite pastime was listening to radio soap operas. She loved her soaps! Once George came home all excited
about their show being renewed for another season. "Gracie,
I've got great news for you!" he shouted. "Please, not now.
Ma Perkins is in trouble." George claims he had to sit there
until Ma Perkins got out of trouble before he could tell her
they had been signed for another year.

One thing she did *not* do at home—true to her onstage
character—was cook. Not much of a problem in the successful Burns household, which had a full-time cook. Gracie even
admitted she needed a cookbook to find out how to make
coffee. On cook's night off, they ate out. Her character once
joked about this in the show:

SALESMAN: Oh, it's warm in here. What are you cooking?
GRACIE: Nothing. I leave the oven on all day so the gas com-
    pany won't know we eat out a lot.

The real Gracie was charming and witty, but her sense of
humor wasn't at all like her television alter ego's. Ralph Levy

remembers the only "Gracie Allenism" he ever saw her do. He was having a dinner party at his home in the Hollywood Hills. "I lived up off Mulholland, on Woodrow Wilson Drive, and it was a little complicated to find it. I was setting up tables on the patio outside, and about twelve noon Gracie drove right up the driveway in her little convertible. I said to myself, 'My God, I hope she didn't think this was lunch.' I went over to her, and she said, 'Never mind.' I didn't know what she was talking about, so I asked her if she'd gotten the time mixed up. 'No, I just wanted to know exactly how to get here so tonight I'd be smarter than George!' "

The Burnses attended many parties, and Gracie adored them. Her enthusiasm for George's old jokes at these affairs was unbounded—even for the off-color ones. If she was shocked by George's language with his buddies, she never scolded him in public, but merely said, "Oh, George!"

She was always the perfect lady, a quality affirmed by everyone who knew her. When asked to describe her, inevitably the first words people utter are "Gracie was a lady."

8

THE

QUINTESSENTIAL

STRAIGHT MAN

To this day [George] retains his capacity for excitement, living the business 24 hours a day and loving every minute.
—TV Guide *(December 25, 1953)*

If Gracie and her dizziness were the centerpieces of "The George Burns and Gracie Allen Show," it was George who gave the program its sense of balance and kept her balloon from leaving earth too frequently. His key role was among the most difficult ever seen in television. He was not only the weekly actor in a play—he was also the narrator, the observer, and the offstage kibbitzer.

George was the calm in the eye of Hurricane Gracie. Seldom did we see him rattled by her latest scheme. She might have just bought thousands of dollars' worth of unwanted goods, invited a robber to tea, or planned yet another surprise party. Through it all was George—a rock, eagerly sharing his reactions with us.

There were two topics we associated most with George —his age and his singing.

Remarkable as it may seem, George Burns was doing age jokes even back in the fifties! He was only fifty-four when the show began, so it does seem a bit strange. Was this really considered "old"? Yet some of the best humor came from jokes about his age:

> I can't understand why I flunked American history. When I was a kid there was so little of it.

> Tennis is a young man's game. Until you're twenty-five, you can play singles. From twenty-five to thirty-five, you should play doubles. I won't tell you exactly how old I am, but when I played, there were twenty-eight men on the court—just on my side of the net.

> I remember the first time I voted. How could I forget it? It was the first time anybody voted. It was raining that day, and on my way to the polls I saw a kid standing in the rain flying a kite with a key on it.

Back then, George was very secretive about his age:

> Well, it's my birthday again. I wonder how old I am? I'll give you a hint. I wear a size-sixteen collar and black shoes, which makes me about the average age for a man of my years. . . . [Take] the Vanderlips . . . he says, "Lucille, I wonder what sign George was born under" and she says, "I think it said 'Lincoln for President.' "

Not even Gracie could resist chiding George about his age:

DECORATOR: This is a beautiful lamp.
GRACIE: My husband bought that.
DECORATOR: Early American.
GRACIE: Oh, yes, he's one of the earliest!

One final age joke:

> It looks like if I like it or not, I'm going to end up on a
> vegetable diet. . . . They say if you eat this stuff you can
> live to be 120. I'd rather eat steak every day and go at
> 119.

Over the years George took a lot of ribbing about his
singing. Steve Allen, in his book *Funny People*, describes
George's unique vocalizations:

> About his only concession to entertainment *shtick* at all
> is the singing of the obscure songs he recalls from the
> 1920s or even earlier times, and the odd thing is they are
> not funny songs; they are simply obscure. But he makes
> them seem funny. He sings them much too fast, in a
> nonvoice. Three seconds later we recall not a line of the
> song, nor even—in most cases—the title. But he holds
> our attention nonetheless. George is one of the master
> attention-getters in the history of entertainment.

Some of the songs on George's private hit parade had the
most intriguing titles: "Tiger Girl," "In The Heart of a
Cherry," "I'll Be Waiting for You Bill When You Come Back
from San Juan Hill," and the ever popular "I'm Tying the
Leaves So They Won't Fall Down, So Daddy Won't Go
Away."

Charming as these ditties sound, it would seem no one on
"The Burns and Allen Show" could stand to hear George sing
them—with the exception of Gracie. Both on and off screen,
she adored George's singing and called him "Sugarthroat."
Some of the compliments she paid him are classics:

> Oh, dear, when you sing, it sounds like a songbird has
> built a nest in your throat.

GEORGE: Maybe I'm getting too old to sing.
GRACIE: Why, that's ridiculous. Good things improve with age. Your voice is like rare old wine. It's like a ripe old cheese.

Others, however, were not quite as enthralled with his voice. Harry Morton once said, "It sounds like a disposal with a spoon caught in it." Blanche wasn't a fan either, and asked:

Why is it every time he sings, our canary lays at the bottom of his cage and puts his feet over his ears?

Harry Von Zell opined:

I know George is a great music lover, because a poet once said that every man kills the thing he loves, and I've heard what George does to a song.

George, however, never seemed to catch on. For example, after a party, he commented:

At twelve-thirty I said I was going to sing a few songs, and all the guests formed a circle around the piano. By the time I broke through I was too tired to sing.

George remained undaunted:

After all these years I guess you wonder why I keep on singing. It's just that I love beautiful music, and where else can I get it whenever I want it?

In real life, too, George loved to sing and entertain at parties. Ruth Henning recalled that no matter how many times Gracie had heard each song, she would always get excited whenever George was about to sing. "Oh, Nattie," she'd plead, "sing 'Down in the Garden Where the Red Rose Grows'!" and George was only too happy to do so. Once at a party, while Gracie and Bill Goodwin were engrossed in a

conversation, George was off singing in the powder room.
"What's that?" Bill asked. "Where's that coming from?" Gra-
cie replied, "From the bathroom." Whereupon Bill quipped,
"Get me a plunger and I'll fix it!"

However questionable George's singing ability may have
been, it's hard to deny that when it came to playing straight
man, no one could match him. He was the best in the business.
In an early episode he joked:

> Being a straight man I repeat everything I hear. The
> auctioneer put up a snuff box and said, "This is a genuine
> snuff box. Do I hear fifty?" And I said, "Fifty?" He said,
> "Sold to the man with the bewildered look on his face."

As comic performer/actor in "Burns and Allen," George
was a master. Fred de Cordova, one of the show's later directors, said in a recent interview in *Emmy* magazine, "George
is an enormously efficient writer and performer. And little—
he is such a little performer. By little, I mean all the takes are
small, all the gestures are small. He minimizes the gestures,
and, oddly enough, it amplifies the joke."

Perhaps the gesture most associated with George is his
constant puffing away on his trusty cigar. He first began
using this prop at the age of fourteen, to make him seem older
on the vaudeville stage. Since that time, he has never appeared before an audience without a freshly lit cigar. "I would
be lost without that cigar," George told a *TV Guide* reporter
(November 6, 1954). "It's many things to me—a prop, a
crutch, a straight man, a timing device. . . . It's also a good
smoke. . . . A comic's hands must become his straight man.
. . . In that time [while I puff the cigar] the audience hears,
digests, interprets, understands, and finally reacts to the
joke."

In an interview with Ellis Walker of the *Palo Alto Times*
(March 4, 1957), George admitted he relied on a long cigar to
time his jokes. "It's a handy timing device. If I get a laugh

with a joke, I just look at the cigar or twiddle it a little while I'm waiting for the laugh to die down. If I don't get a laugh, it's nice to have something to hang on to. When a joke calls for a delayed laugh, I exhale my smoke slowly. If the laugh never comes at all, I swallow."

George is noted as one of the neatest cigar smokers in the country. He attributes this to the camera angles. "The camera usually only shows me from the waist up during a monologue," he explained. "If it showed the floor, I'd lose the reputation. I'm standing up to my ankles in ashes."

So lost was George without his cigar in his left hand (his right hand is frequently in his pocket), that if he had to use any kind of hand prop instead, he'd fiddle with it as if it were a cigar.

This trademark also helped give George the confidence he needed to deliver those long, intricate monologues, every word of which had to be memorized. After they began doing the show on film, George could allow himself the luxury of forgetting a line now and then. On those infrequent occasions, he relied on Steve Ferry, the assistant prop man. Steve was also a "quick study"—someone with a nearly photographic mind who learned lines after one or two readings. Steve would memorize all of George's dialogue and prompt him when necessary. One time George forgot a line in his monologue and looked confidently at Ferry, but Steve unfortunately had dried up. George stuttered, stammered, and yelled, "Steve, how dare you forget the line that I forgot!"

On the day of shooting, George was always the first cast member on the set. If his call was for 7:45 A.M., he could usually be found at 6:00 having breakfast with the janitor. During this "quiet hour" he would polish his monologue. Then he would get into Gene Roemer's makeup chair, where he'd study some more.

George's real personality began to emerge as he gained more confidence with each monologue delivery. In an article she wrote, Gracie commented: "[George] was always at ease and a riot entertaining his friends. If he could do on a stage what he does at a party . . ." Steve Allen agreed in *Funny People:* "As funny as George is on the stage, on television, and in films, he is even funnier in person. . . . George would amuse you even more if you had dinner with him or spent an evening in his company."

There was one person whom George always managed to crack up—his best friend, Jack Benny. George and Gracie spent much time in the company of Jack and Mary Benny. They were constantly having dinner together, going out together, shopping together, or just relaxing at home and talking to each other.

Jack thought his friend George Burns was the funniest man alive. If George entertained at parties, he was really performing for only one of the guests—Jack Benny. In his introduction to George's book *I Love Her, That's Why,* Jack wrote: "I love the guy. I have a reputation for being his easiest audience. . . . He'll flick cigar ashes on the lapel of my new $250 suit . . . and I'm gone again." Al Simon, who was the associate producer on "The Burns and Allen Show," commented on the effect George's jokes had on Benny. "Jack eventually would be on the floor, pounding it with his hands, and George would just keep going on the same theme. Then he'd look at Jack and say, "Jack, you're embarrassing all of us!"

Jack wasn't the only one amused, of course. Once George got started, he was unrelenting. Al once saw George do this at a table full of people, and Harry Von Zell had to leave because he was in pain from laughing so hard. Another time George had his entire office staff in stitches. During a routine meeting he kept tearing up little pieces of paper and sticking them on his eyelids, his nose, his ears, while continuing with the discussion as if this wasn't going on. He just went about the business of tearing paper and sticking it all over his face, totally ignoring the growing hysteria.

Al Simon stated, "Nobody today really is aware of people's reactions to George back then. Now he's a star, but then, he was really in the background—Gracie was the star—so when he'd start on one of these rolls, it wasn't expected."

According to those who worked closely with George, he was an extremely generous person. Ruth Henning recollected that George's generosity included frequently sharing his home and pool with her family. "We'd come over and spend the day. . . . There was usually a nice group around, including his brother Willy and his family. Our daughter learned to swim over there. Sometimes George might come out and swim a few lengths before he went to the Hillcrest Country Club."

Herb Browar, "Burns and Allen"'s production consultant, also had words of praise for George. Herb described him as a very regulated, well-organized man, both at home and at work. Herb suspects that this may be one of George's secrets to long life. He also noted that George never let problems get to him.

Perhaps the key to George's longevity is his love for what he is doing. Back in December 1953 he told *TV Guide* that he couldn't remember a time when he didn't want to be in show business. "The guy who has to take a couple days off every week to get away from his business has a business he ought to get away from permanently."

Nowhere was George's love of his work more evident than in "Burns and Allen," especially when he and Gracie were working together as a team. And it was their relationship, both on and off the screen, that made the show work so well.

9

JUST A LOVE

NEST

First of all you've got to have talent.
And then you've got to marry her
like I did.
—GEORGE BURNS,
IN AN EARLY INTERVIEW

Husband-and-wife teams are not that unusual in Hollywood, although it is rare that both spouses are not only well-matched professionally, but are as in love with each other as George Burns and Gracie Allen were. William Ewald, columnist for the *Oakland Tribune*, went so far as to say that the "mating of George Burns with Gracie Allen almost leads one to believe some marriages are made in heaven." In his column of March 11, 1958, he continued: "There's no other way to account for the beautiful sourgum, cigar face meeting up with Gracie. They're a fascinating team to watch in action. They mix like mud and a small boy. He rasps, she twitters, he galumphs, she flutters, he bounces, she floats out of reach on a cloud."

There can be no doubt that the *real* George and Gracie were deeply in love, and George and his writers played up this fact in their characters' relationship in "The Burns and

Allen Show." George himself realized how rare their happy
marriage was for Hollywood. In a monologue, he comments
on an article Gracie has written for *Woman's Home Companion*:

> The real reason I let Gracie write this article about our
> marriage is that we're one of the few Hollywood cou-
> ples they were sure would still be married by the time it
> came out.

Time and again, people will shake their heads as if
George is crazy, wondering why he puts up with this strange,
off-center wife of his:

> People say to me, "George, why don't you straighten
> Gracie out, reason with her." Reason with her? That's
> like walking into an antique shop and saying, "What's
> new?" Besides, I want Gracie just the way she is.

In many episodes, George is approached by someone determined to find out his secret reason for staying with Gracie.
George's answer is usually out before the question can be
asked:

> POLLSTER: I've asked your wife quite a few questions, and
> now I'd like to ask you one.
> GEORGE: The answer is we've been married for over twenty-
> five years and I happen to love her.

Even Harry Von Zell can't figure George out:

> VON ZELL: You know, George, I can't understand this. Now
> Gracie wants to buy a ranch. A couple of weeks ago she
> got you thrown in jail because she met a fellow on the
> train who wanted to kill his wife. Tomorrow, who knows.
> Say, George, would you mind if I ask you a personal
> question?
> GEORGE: Because I happen to love her.

If George is crazy for Gracie, she is just as nutty over him. Once she bragged to Blanche:

George has more sex appeal in his whole body than most men have in their little finger.

Her personal compliments would sound a bit left-handed if they came from anyone but Gracie:

GEORGE: Would you ever think that such a beautiful mink coat would come from such an unattractive little thing that looks like a weasel.
GRACIE: Oh George, you're just fishing—you know I think you're handsome.

George can be difficult sometimes, but Gracie has learned her way around him quite well. In one show, George wants to go to the new 3-D movie that's playing—he says how he loves it when they throw the ball at the audience, a revealing insight into George's character's playfulness. Gracie, however, has her heart set on going to the opera, and is confident that she can get George to reconsider:

VON ZELL: Then you think George will change his mind and go to the opera?
GRACIE: Oh, sure. George is very fair. He knows that marriage is a fifty-fifty proposition.
VON ZELL: Well, it should be.
GRACIE: George knows I never change my mind, so he always changes his to keep things even.

George is not averse to pulling his weight in their marriage, however, and once even offers to help fix dinner. George gets all the things ready—the salad bowl, the platters, the table. Then he tells Gracie to get the food. As soon as she opens the refrigerator she knows she has forgotten something. Unruffled, George calmly asks her, "Where would you like to eat?"

Like any husband, George occasionally ends up in the doghouse and has to bail himself out. When that happens, he more than likely decides to buy her a gift to pacify her. Using his monologue to think out loud, he'll usually start with something small, like flowers or candy . . . then progress to a much better item, like a wristwatch or maybe a mink coat. "Yeah, that's what I'll do," he'll say. "I'll get her some flowers!"

George is constantly taking it on the chin over the question of who has the talent in the family, and there seems to be general agreement among his neighbors and friends that he's married to it. The Mortons frequently have spats over the question of George's abilities:

HARRY: Blanche, let me tell you something about George Burns. You don't get to the top in show business unless you've got something. Jack Benny has got it. Eddie Cantor has got it. Jimmy Durante has got it.

BLANCHE: Yeah, they got it the hard way. George married it.

Yet George is always the first to admit that he does owe it all to Gracie:

I don't laugh at superstition. It's been a part of show business for years. For instance, Ed Wynn still wears the same pair of shoes he wore when he made his first theatrical appearance; he wouldn't walk on the stage without them. Georgie Jessel never walks on the stage without a rabbit's foot in his pocket. Danny Kaye carries a lucky coin. I'm superstitious too. I owe my success to it. I never walk on the stage without Gracie.

George has always given Gracie virtually all of the credit for the team's success. "What made us a good combination," says George, "was that Gracie had a very big talent on the stage and I had a talent offstage. . . . I was able to think of things, and Gracie was able to do them. That's what made us a good team." George always advised and directed Gracie, and even spoke for the team. He was thoroughly convinced

that she was the greater acting talent—the "star." Gracie
was always receptive to any input from George on her readings and timing. There was no professional jealousy—she
knew *he* was the genius.

Ralph Levy commented on the couple's working relationship: "George and Gracie never rehearsed together. I don't
think they ever read their lines together till they came to the
studio, and that way they never had any domestic spats over
what was funny or what they did or didn't like. On Saturday
and Sunday, a secretary from my office would go out to work
with George in the morning on his lines. Then they would have
lunch, the three of them. Then she would work with Gracie in
her boudoir in the afternoon on her lines. But when they met
onstage, they had never worked the lines together. That way
there was peace in the family at home, and it was very fresh
when they got onto the stage. It was important in keeping a
happy relationship as a team."

And a happy team they were. In his 1976 autobiography,
Living It Up, George confided, "You know, lots of times
people have asked me what Gracie and I did to make our
marriage work. It's simple—we didn't do anything. I think the
trouble with a lot of people is that they work too hard at
staying married. They make a business out of it. When you
work too hard at a business you get tired; and when you get
tired you get grouchy; and when you get grouchy you start
fighting; and when you start fighting you're out of business."
George has stated many times in interviews that he and Gracie never had a fight. "Gracie never cooked, so we couldn't
fight," he joked in a 1984 Phil Donahue interview.

One of the reasons that they were truly a "contented
couple" may be that they weren't spoiled by their enormous
success. Gracie never took off the twenty-dollar wedding ring
George had given her when they were first married. They
lived in the same thirteen-room house in Beverly Hills that
they had bought during World War II. Also, they never took
each other for granted. In a magazine article, Gracie wrote:

"I never say, 'Do this or that.' I ask him and thank him and he does the same. . . . The only problem about being married to George [is] he used to drive me out of my mind . . . with his ideas. He was everlastingly knocking on my dressing room door or waking me up in the night to say, 'I changed a line,' or, 'What do you think of this?' "

Although theirs was a mixed marriage, this never presented any problems. George gave Gracie a free hand in raising their two children, Ronnie and Sandy, as Catholics. "George never suggested my altering my faith, and if I wanted to go to church five times a day that would be all right with him—so long as I was at the studio on time for the show," she wrote.

And of course, as lovers will, they had their pet names for each other. George called Gracie "Googie" because one night Gracie couldn't sleep and she asked him to say something funny. "Now at two in the morning my repertoire is limited," George admitted, "so I just mumbled 'Googie, googie, googie.' Somehow this made Gracie laugh and somehow that became her name." She called him "Nat" or "Nattie" since that was his real name and the first one by which she knew him. However, on the set, she had to remember to call him "George" because if she yelled "Nat," more than likely the prop man, Nat Thurlow, would come running.

There couldn't have been a more romantic theme song chosen for the show than "The Love Nest," written by Otto Harbach and Louis A. Hirsch in their 1920 musical comedy, *Mary*. The now familiar music was first selected for George and Gracie's radio program, and later millions of television viewers grew to associate the opening strains of this tune with "The George Burns and Gracie Allen Show." It's a pity the words were never heard on the program, as they so beautifully describe the loving relationship that George and Gracie shared:

Just a love nest, cozy and warm,
Like a dove rest down on a farm,
A veranda with some sort of clinging vine,

Then a kitchen where some rambler roses twine,
Then a small room, tea set of blue
Best of all room, dream room for two,
Better than a palace with a gilded dome,
Is a love nest you can call home.

10

BLANCHE AND HARRY

AND HARRY AND

HARRY

BLANCHE: *Just look at these dresses. Harry, would you like me in jersey?*
HARRY: *I certainly would. If you'll go there, I'll gladly pay your fare.*

George and Gracie's home at 312 Maple Drive may be a love nest, but right next door—at 314 Maple—there's a veritable hornet's nest. For that is the home of Blanche and Harry Morton, the Burnses' neighbors and good friends.

By way of comparison to another popular television program of that era, Blanche Morton is to Gracie Allen what Ethel Mertz is to Lucy Ricardo on "I Love Lucy"—best friend, confidante, and coconspirator when it's "the girls" versus "the boys." Indeed, many episodes derive their story lines from just that simple sort of conflict: Gracie and Blanche want to (a) buy new dresses, (b) take a trip, (c) buy fur coats, (d) decorate their houses, or (e) do all of the above; and George and Harry won't let 'em.

Blanche can always be counted on to lend her unending support to her closest friend. She adores Gracie, although

she's not that fond of George and doesn't think he deserves
Gracie. She will rush to her friend's defense with endless
tolerance for her daffiness, calling her "honey" as one would
a dear sister. She never scolds and seldom tries to straighten
Gracie out, although she is not beyond an occasional but fruit-
less attempt. She begins valiantly: "No, honey, that's not
what he meant. He meant . . . uh . . . yeah, how about that!"
and usually just drops it with a shoulder shrug and a smile.
Her patience is almost infinite:

BLANCHE: I just got a phone call from Lucille Vanderlip and
    she told me Margie Bates got a beautiful diamond brace-
    let from her husband.
GRACIE: I can't believe it.
BLANCHE: Why not?
GRACIE: If Lucille's husband gave another woman a diamond
    bracelet, you'd think she'd be the last one to mention it.
BLANCHE: Er . . . Gracie . . . you misunderstood me.

Fortunately, Blanche has a terrific sense of humor, with
a memorable laugh, resembling a cross between a machine
gun and a woodpecker.

But it was her memorable *voice* that got Bea Benaderet
her start in show business. She was known as one of radio's
most versatile actresses before she went on to the "Burns and
Allen" TV show.

Bea was born in New York City on April 4, 1906 (the same
year as Gracie Allen), the only child of a Turkish/Sephardic-
Jewish father and an Irish mother. Her father was a tobacco-
nist, and when Bea was five, the family moved to San Francisco, where he established a chain of tobacco stores in that
city and in Oakland.

She entered show business at the age of six, playing a
violet in a San Francisco flower pageant. She was twelve
when the station manager of KGO discovered her singing in
a children's production of an operetta. While still in high
school at St. Rose Academy, she joined the staff of radio

station KFRC, where she acted, sang, wrote, produced, and sometimes even announced. After graduation, she attended the Reginald Travis School of Acting in San Francisco, and acted in little theater and stock companies.

By 1935 she was heard regularly on "The Blue Monday Jamboree" from San Francisco on CBS radio. In 1936 she migrated to Hollywood, where she first achieved fame as Gertrude Gearshift, the Brooklyn telephone operator on "The Jack Benny Show." Bea discovered she had a knack for dialects and characterizations, which soon made her much sought after. Some of the voices she created were Mother Foster on "A Date With Judy," Mrs. Carstairs on "Fibber McGee and Molly," Eve Goodwin on "The Great Gildersleeve," Iris Atterbury on "My Favorite Husband," Amber Lipscott on "My Friend Irma," and Gloria the Maid on "Ozzie and Harriet."

In August, 1938 she married announcer/film actor Jim Bannon. They had a son, Jack, and a daughter, Maggie. Today Jack Bannon is a successful television actor in Hollywood. He recalled a story about his mother just prior to the birth of his sister, Maggie: "In 1947, right before my sister was born, my mother got out of a taxicab and fell down and broke her pelvis. . . . The trauma of that caused her naturally black hair to start going very gray, very fast." Her husband suggested that she dye her hair blonde, and she wore it that way from then on.

One of Bea's early roles was the character of Blanche Morton on the "Burns and Allen" radio show, and it was only natural that she continue in this part in the TV version. She once joked, "When TV began, I think there was some doubt as to whether I could walk or not."

Then there was the question of the proper spelling of her name in the show's credits. In them, you will see "Benadaret." However, the correct spelling is with only one a—Benaderet. Why the error in the credits? On the first show, her name was printed that way, and Bea decided to retain that spelling for good luck. (And whoever made up those cards for the end credits once had trouble spelling her first name too—there were five or six episodes where she was named after the insect: Bee. Someone finally noticed it and made the correction.)

The other half of the Morton family is Blanche's husband, Harry. Or rather *husbands*. In all, there were four Harrys in the series, three in the first year alone.

Harry Morton the First was played by Hal March. He was the handsomest of the Harrys but, unfortunately, he didn't last more than the first seven live shows. In the middle of Live Show #8, George says:

> That's my neighbor Harry Morton calling, excuse me. Oh, by the way, Hal March, who has always played Harry Morton, has gone to New York to do his own show with his partner, Bob Sweeney. Gracie and I want to wish them the very best of luck. So tonight Harry Morton is played by John Brown.

Hal did on occasion return to "The Burns and Allen Show" in guest roles—among these, ironically, Harry Morton's real-estate partner, Casey. Bob Sweeney also guested from time to time as Phillips the Gardener and in various other roles. But Hal did find his niche shortly. He became the well-known host of the most popular quiz show of the 1950s —"The $64,000 Question."

Harry Morton the Second, John Brown, lasted a bit longer— ten live shows. He was a British-born American citizen who had played an estimated fifteen thousand radio roles, the most famous of which was Digger O'Dell on "The Life of Riley." There are conflicting reports as to why he left "The Burns and Allen Show." One source suggested that his name appeared on a "verboten" list, and, in fact, two and a half years after his departure from "Burns and Allen," John Brown was summoned before the infamous Senator Joseph McCarthy's inquisition, where he refused to be coerced into testifying.

Enter Fred Clark, the third (but not the last) Harry Morton. Fred is introduced during Live Show #18, again by George:

GEORGE: By the way, there's going to be a change in our cast. John Brown, who has been playing the part of Harry Morton, can't be with us anymore because of other commitments, so we've brought in another fine actor to do Mr. Morton. I know you'll enjoy him. You've seen him on the stage and on the screen. He's a wonderful performer. I'd like you to meet him right now—Fred Clark. *(They shake hands.)* Fred, I want to welcome you to the neighborhood. We're very happy to have you with us.
FRED: Thank you, George. I'm happy to be here. By the way, I haven't met my wife yet.
GEORGE: Blanche Morton. *(Bea walks on.)* Bea, I'd like you to meet . . .
BEA: Fred Clark!
FRED: Bea . . . Bea Benaderet! *(Bea and Fred embrace.)*
GEORGE: Oh, you know one another.
BEA: Sure.
GEORGE: Well, from now on you two will be husband and wife.
FRED: Then we'd better cut this out.

With the installation of Fred Clark as Harry Morton, a characterization could finally be locked down. We come to know this Harry as a rather indolent man who dabbles in real estate, but seldom is seen actually working in his office. There's a running joke that he is stuck with swampland that he's continually trying to unload:

HARRY: You know those four acres I sold last month?
BLANCHE: You mean he doesn't like swamps?
HARRY: Imagine an ingrate like that having the nerve to sue me after I saved his life.
BLANCHE: When did you save his life?
HARRY: After he bought it he insisted on seeing it. He sunk in up to his waist and I had to pull him out.

One of the idiosyncrasies of *this* Harry Morton is his voracious appetite. We usually see him seated at the Mortons' kitchen table, indulging in his favorite hobby—eating. (Amazingly, he stays at a normal weight.) Many of the show's gags center on Harry and his food binges:

VON ZELL: Hi. Oh, I'm sorry. I always seem to come in when Harry's eating.

BLANCHE: You know, if you came in at four o'clock in the morning you could still say that.

George frequently pokes fun at Harry's eating:

I've seen that guy eat a whole turkey. I saw him eat a steak big enough for three people. Another time he finished six lamb chops by himself. That's at my house. I have no idea what he eats at home. Do you know that Blanche told me she has to pack a lunch for him to eat on the way to the dining room?

I spoke to him about it once and he resented it. He said, "A man's got to eat to live." I said, "Like a horse?" He said, "Well, not a whole one, but I'll split one with you."

But George can be generous with his neighbor, too. Once he planned a birthday surprise party for him:

Tonight at the party, I'll fix him a nice big chocolate birthday cake. He loves chocolate. Last year Blanche fixed him one for his birthday and he ate it so fast, we had to pry his mouth open to blow out the candles.

Blanche is mildly indulgent of Harry's eating habits. Blanche is also mildly indulgent of Harry. One characteristic of Harry Morton remains unchanged throughout the entire "Burns and Allen" series: No matter how many times Blanche has a "new" husband, the basic concept of Harry and Blanche Morton is an ongoing battle of the spouses. It is established that they have been married for about eight years when the series begins, although *how* they met is never quite clear. Here's one example:

BLANCHE: That's right, we did meet at a masquerade.
HARRY: Sure, and what a romantic night that was.
BLANCHE: I'll say. We fell madly in love.
HARRY: Then we took off our masks.

There's a bit of the Mortons in all marriages, and their mild put-down humor keeps audiences coming back for more. They love each other—they just have a peculiar way of showing it.

Fred Clark's bare dome was a familiar weekly sight in seventy-four episodes of "The Burns and Allen Show," but he hadn't always played comedy. The talented performer, born in 1914, began his film career as a serious dramatic actor. A Stanford University graduate with a B.A. in psychology, Fred was taking a premed course when, in his senior year, he appeared in school theatricals and decided to turn actor. He won a two-year scholarship to the American Academy of Dramatic Arts in New York, and was on the Eastern stage for several years before coming to Hollywood. One of his first pictures was Universal's *Ride the Pink Horse* with Robert Montgomery in 1947, in which he played the "heavy." Among his best-known films are *A Place in the Sun, Sunset Boulevard,* and *Auntie Mame.*

It was primarily his background in film that landed Fred the part of the third Harry Morton. According to Ralph Levy, "Fred Clark was the perfect example of a working actor. He never got better or worse. I never saw him rehearse a line. Between scenes he read paperbacks. . . . He was ready; he knew his lines perfectly." Herb Browar added that Fred "never associated with anyone on the set. He'd go into a corner between scenes, sit in his chair, and read." His wife, singer Benay Venuta, was doing a show in New York, and he'd fly there to be with her on weekends. His loneliness for her no doubt was one reason he left the show after two years.

11

THE MILK

FROM

CONTENTED COWS

GRACIE: *This Carnation Evaporated Milk is wonderful. But you know, Blanche, there's one thing that puzzles me. How do they get milk from carnations?*

On "The Burns and Allen Show," Carnation Milk was as much a character as the other members of the cast, and the familiar can was on permanent display in the kitchen. If Gracie served tea, she never failed to mention that she always used Carnation Evaporated Milk. In fact, any guest on the show was liable to get a minicommercial while in the Burns home. Not even the tax assessor was exempt from this one. While he appraised the furniture, Gracie served coffee, and there on the tray was C.E.M. The tax man looked at Gracie and queried, "You serve Carnation Evaporated Milk on a silver platter?" To which she enthusiastically responded, "Yes. Also on cereal and strawberries. You can serve it on anything!"

Carnation went out of its way to promote a down-home folksy feeling about the company. Every other week we were greeted with tranquil scenes of cows placidly munching in vast pastures. We learned that their milk products contained vitamin D—the "sunshine vitamin"—and we were subjected to the intimate details of Carnation's cattle as well. "Carnation Homestead Daisy Madcap," for example, was the world's champion producer of butterfat, having produced more butterfat in one year than seven average cows—enough to make more than seventeen hundred pounds of table butter! Another evening we were told that her offspring, "Carnation Tip Top," won first prize for yearling bulls at the Pacific International Livestock Exposition, and his blue ribbon was proudly displayed on the show.

As if this weren't enough, regular commercial breaks were worked into each show as part of that week's story. This made them much less painful to watch and often as amusing as the rest of the show. The Irwin, Wasey Agency had created an effective selling tool that was envied by all the other advertising agencies and never successfully copied.

It was not uncommon for actors to double as pitchmen, but "The Burns and Allen Show" continued to break the rules by making *their* announcer a full-time member of the show's cast.

This enviable task went to Bill Goodwin, a native of San Francisco, who had started his radio career in Sacramento. After becoming a staff announcer, he moved to Hollywood and quickly caught on as an M.C. and straight man. He worked with Bob Hope and Edgar Bergen, and ultimately joined Burns and Allen in 1934 during their radio heyday. In addition to doing the voice-over announcement opening and closing the TV show, Goodwin portrayed the announcer on George and Gracie's "other" television show. This dual role allowed him to spend a lot of time in the Burns home. We always knew that when Bill came on the screen with that offbeat excitable delivery of his, a commercial was not far behind. He *loved* talking about Carnation! What we never knew was how he would work it into the plot.

For example, by now we all knew Carnation Milk was the milk from contented cows. In one episode, Gracie was trying

to paint and asked Bill to pose for her. He wanted to oblige
our heroine, but he had to get right over to the Carnation Milk
plant. There was an emergency, and the board of directors
had called him. It seems that out of all those contented cows,
they found one that wasn't. Her name was Ruth, and she was
upset because she didn't know what was happening to all that
wonderful milk she was giving. He then went on to tell us
what did happen to it. George, who had been listening to all
of this, thought Bill was just making up a story to get out of
posing for Gracie. After George left the room, Bill confided
to Gracie that he did make up one thing. The cow's real name
was Claudette, but he didn't think George would believe him.

These clever anecdotes were not the work of the "Burns
and Allen" writers, but of one man in particular, Charley
Lowe, the advertising agency's rep for Carnation. He sup-
plied the commercial material for the show. The rapport between the agency and program was such that Charley became
a close and trusted friend of the Burnses, and in later years
often made valuable suggestions for the series in general.

Carnation also took advantage of the show's popularity
to offer promotional items such as a new ninety-six-page Carnation cookbook, *personally* autographed by Gracie.

After fifteen years of doing the "Burns and Allen" radio
shows, and the first twenty-five episodes of the television
series, Bill Goodwin left the show. A new announcer/actor
was needed, and George brought in Harry Von Zell. He was
introduced in that twenty-fifth show, arriving one afternoon
at the Burns home with Bill. The two began a routine about
baby formulas made with Carnation Milk. Halfway through,
Von Zell took over, and Goodwin couldn't get a word in edge-
wise. Nothing could stop Von Zell and his pitch. At the end of
the number, Bill grinned at Harry, "Okay, Von Zell. You stole
my commercial, but I'll get even. I'll steal your girl."

In the next episode, George interrupted a scene between
Blanche, Harry Morton, and Harry Von Zell with "Hold it!"
whereupon everyone froze in their tracks and remained mo-
tionless while George turned to the camera.

I'm sorry to stop the show, but I want to tell you about Bill Goodwin. Bill has gone to New York to star in his own television show, and we all want to wish him every success and happiness. We've gotten Harry Von Zell to take Bill's place. He's a wonderful performer and I know you're going to love him. All right—continue!

George stepped back out of the picture, and everyone continued with the scene they had been doing as if nothing out of the ordinary had occurred.

Harry discussed his new role in a 1952 interview: "I didn't want anything to happen to Bill Goodwin, but this was a show I very much wanted to be on. When he went east to do television, I was hoping I'd be his replacement."

Harry Von Zell was born in 1906 (the same year as Gracie and Bea) on a farm near Crawfordsville, Indiana. Athletically inclined, he played football until an injury put a halt to that career possibility. He then took a more sedate job as an assistant payroll clerk for the Union Pacific Railroad. Still determined to be in sports, he tried boxing after college at the University of Southern California. He fought five painful bouts, and quit to pursue his other boyhood dream—acting. "When I was a kid, I always used to run to the vaudeville theaters and stay until somebody came and got me."

His show business career began in 1927 as an announcer on KMIC radio in Inglewood, California. His first big break came in 1929, when he auditioned for Paul Whiteman, who liked Von Zell's good-natured delivery and chose him out of 250 other applicants to do the commercials on his show. Von Zell went with Whiteman to New York in 1930 and for the next six years was a staff announcer for CBS. He became the announcer for "The March of Time," and also handled the New York end of Admiral Byrd's broadcasts from the South Pole.

As he once said, "The reason I became an announcer was in those days [he] was the only guy in the studio who received a regular salary. I did everything, sang, did characters, announced, sold spots—if actors had been able to get regular salaries, I probably never would have become an announcer." But he did, and lucky for us. It was Harry Von Zell who was responsible for that wonderful blooper, "Ladies and gentlemen—the President of the United States, Hoobert Heever!"

His metamorphosis from full-time announcer to actor/ sometime announcer occurred while working with Fred Allen, Phil Baker, and Eddie Cantor. In 1944 Von Zell returned to California and began working with Dinah Shore, Joan Davis, and Burns and Allen. When Fred Allen came west to do a picture, Von Zell was cast in it—the first of more than thirty films he was to do.

It was in the "Burns and Allen" television show, though, that Von Zell first hit his full stride as a character comedian. His personality lent itself to the low-key, never-far-from-trouble, always-trying-to-get-a-raise-and-not-get-fired character we all came to know. He constantly ran ineffectual interference between the Burnses and the Mortons, and inadvertently became Gracie's cohort in most of her schemes. Gracie had an amazing ability to concoct a complicated premise, involve an innocent Harry, and unknowingly leave him holding the bag. Often Von Zell himself would suggest a plan of action to Gracie, and she would run with it, forcing the inevitable confrontation between Von Zell and George. George would let poor Harry squirm just long enough before letting him off the hook.

Von Zell summed up his relationship with Gracie in the following exchange with Blanche. She's just told him her husband won't come home if Gracie is visiting:

BLANCHE: He still hasn't gotten over what happened two weeks ago. He went fishing and found out his rubber boots had the toes cut off.

VON ZELL: Gracie?

BLANCHE: Yes, she figured if water came in over the top, it would run out of the bottom.

VON ZELL: Well, when you've got Gracie for a friend, you really need one.

It wasn't too much later that the writers decided to let Harry be one-up on George. In a show where Gracie tries to help an illegal immigrant stay in the country, she almost gets George deported. George has been helping her out by pretending to be Spanish, complete with poncho and guitar. Von Zell tries to get George to stop singing, frantically looking back and forth between George and an immigration official. George is oblivious to the trouble he is in until the official starts to take him away:

GEORGE: What does this mean?
VON ZELL: He's an immigration official. He thinks you sneaked into the country.
GEORGE: Why didn't you stop me?
VON ZELL: If I'd known when you sneaked in, I would have.

Von Zell's deadpan delivery is perfect.

After each story was resolved, it was Harry's voice that announced: "And now, here are Carnation's own contented couple, George and Gracie. . . ."

Most of the time the closing routine was a couplet of dialogue summing up the episode we'd just seen, but these few minutes were also used by George and Gracie to announce the "stay tuned for" promos. The 1950–51 season was followed by Robert Q. Lewis's "The Show Goes On." Also, because "Burns and Allen" aired every other week, it was important for the network to keep viewers tuned during those off weeks. George would often remind us that:

Gracie and I will be back again in two weeks. Next week don't forget to look in on Garry Moore. It's a swell show.

In their second year, "Burns and Allen" alternated with Peter Lind Hayes and Mary Healy in "Star of the Family," which elicited similar pleas from George.

This was also a time to do public-service plugs. George
and Gracie asked us all to "Be a Big Brother," and "Buy
bonds." We had forgotten during the previous half hour of
silliness that we were in the middle of the Korean War, and
it always came as a surprise in those closing moments to see
Gracie turn to the camera and, in a very serious tone, implore:

> Ladies and gentlemen, I know you want to help our
> Armed Forces, and you can. Donate your share of blood
> for the wounded. Contact your local chapter of the
> American Red Cross. It's urgent.

"The George Burns and Gracie Allen Show" was only the
third CBS television series to emanate from Hollywood. ("The
Ed Wynn Show" and "The Alan Young Show" were the first
two.) It was a very prestigious beginning and proof that Hollywood was capable of being more than a home for the movies. Yet, all through 1951, the "trades" were running daily
articles trying to convince producers that television could be
done better on film in Hollywood than live from New York.

In spite of all the positive press "Burns and Allen" received on their live shows, the advantages of film beckoned
because of its quality and the potential for reruns. Once
again, George saw very clearly the next step he should take,
and on the last live show (September 25, 1952) he informed us:

> Thank you very much. Gracie and I will be back again two
> weeks from tonight. And from then on, every week for
> our present sponsor, the Carnation Company, and for our
> new sponsor, the B. F. Goodrich Company. . . .

12

THE UBIQUITOUS

GEORGE

*I had just two offices during the radio
show with Gracie; now I have eleven.*
—GEORGE BURNS,
1952 INTERVIEW

Financially, the future lay in film, not in kinescopes. The quality of kines was such that they could not be reused. Also, film meant reruns, and reruns meant residuals. Alas, film also meant a higher production cost per episode. "The Burns and Allen Show" had always been a CBS production. If they wanted to change over to film, someone would have to be responsible for the additional cost. George assumed that responsibility and formed his own company. His new offices would be on the General Service Studios lot at 1040 North Las Palmas Avenue in Hollywood. In choosing a name for his production company, he remembered that his brother Willy lived on McCadden Place in Hollywood. "McCadden" had a nice ring to it, and so McCadden Productions was born.

Their first decision was to do the filmed show without a live audience. An audience required shooting the show straight through, in continuity. The most efficient method of filming was to arrange the lights and shoot all the scenes that take place in one set together, then move to the next set and do those. Also, this allowed them the luxury of stopping and redoing a scene if someone flubbed a line. All in all, an easier schedule for everyone—except Gracie. Her dialogue was structured in such a way that shooting out of sequence would make it all the more difficult to remember.

Even though shooting the show out of sequence saved some time, filming with one camera would take several days. Each scene would have to be shot a minimum of three different times to get the necessary camera angles—the master, or "full set" shot, George and Gracie's close-ups, and the other cast's close-ups. The solution seemed to be to film with three cameras placed strategically on the stage, all running simultaneously.

Al Simon, the first associate producer on "I Love Lucy," was one of the masterminds behind the three-camera film system. In the summer of 1952, he and "Lucy" 's stage manager, Herb Browar, went to General Service to do "I Married Joan" for NBC. The show's star, Joan Davis, didn't want to work in front of an audience, so Simon and Browar devised a multiple-camera system for her show. George learned of these young innovators and immediately hired them to put his show on film.

George had to invest quite a bit of his own money to get started, and Al and Herb were responsible for the spending of that money. Although George and Gracie had done motion pictures, George had never gotten involved with the production end. Now he would not only be concerned with his regular acting and writing duties, he would also be responsible for the executive producer chores, and he would be footing all the bills himself.

It was here that those who had worked with George before noticed a marked personality change—the penny-pinching began. The license fee for each show was approximately $35,000. The Carnation Company and the B. F. Goodrich Company, as alternating sponsors, provided this fee to cover salaries for George and Gracie, the director, writers, guest stars, extras, and crew, as well as sets, wardrobe— everything. Anything that went over that amount came out of George's pocket.

Herb Browar remembered those early days of McCadden: "George was very budget conscious. It didn't take him long at all to understand the picture business—how it ran, what cost money, what didn't cost money."

Ralph Levy remembered those days, too. "I would get calls, any time of day. He'd call and say, 'I understand that if we have our reading at three-thirty instead of at three o'clock, we don't have to pay overtime.' Or things like, 'Ralph, I understand that you could have gotten such-and-such an actress for less money if you hadn't called her in on Monday.'"

George was everywhere. If the writers came in with a scene that required a new set, he would work with them to find a way to use an existing one. When a new set had to be built, the carpenters were subject to George's constant scrutiny. On one occasion, after watching for a few minutes, he returned to his office and immediately placed a call to Ralph. Ralph recalled, he was having lunch at the Brown Derby when George phoned. These budget-related calls had been coming continuously, day and night, and this one was the straw that broke Ralph's back. "Ralph," George asked, "why are you using three-inch nails to build a set when you only need two-inch nails?"

No one should have been surprised to learn that George was quick to grasp the importance of the dollar in making a television show. He was already showing his potential as a producer in the early live shows:

GEORGE: The fellow who played the part of the insurance adjuster is a movie actor, Charles Lane. He's very expensive. He wanted a thousand dollars to do that bit but said he'd do it for a hundred dollars if I'd give him a close-up.

If you don't mind, it will only take a few seconds. Come
on out, Mr. Lane. Okay, boys, move in. *(The camera
moves in for a close-up, the actor smiles; camera moves
back over to George.)* That's it, Mr. Lane. *(To audience)*
I just saved nine hundred dollars and it helps. We're only
on every other week.

And it wasn't even his money!

George was instrumental in developing the concept of
preproduction meetings. At these he and his staff would go
over upcoming scripts and estimate the costs involved. He
realized the sooner the scripts were finished, the more time
they would have for double-checking production expenses,
building new sets, arranging for special wardrobe—whatever
might be needed. McCadden soon became known as one of the
most efficient production companies in Hollywood. Herb Browar said, "It was the smoothest, most efficient show I ever
worked on, from concept to completion. And it all stemmed
from George and 'no nonsense.' "

In his monologues, we were regularly reminded that now
George was also the producer of his show:

GEORGE: In ten minutes I'm sure Gracie and Blanche will have
    another scheme. But ten minutes of television time costs
    a lot of money. It might even cost more than a week in
    Palm Springs. I think I'll save that dough.

And with that, he moved the clock ahead ten minutes. . . .

Being a producer meant more than just watching the budget;
it meant watching everything. And that meant little time to
mince words. His staff quickly learned that one of the ways
George gained respect for someone was to get into an argument with him—and win. Ralph Levy is a perfect example, as
he had his share of run-ins with George.

Ralph, who produced and directed both "Burns and
Allen" and "The Jack Benny Show," compared the two differ-

ent personalities involved. Benny, if he had a bone to pick with
Ralph, would get petulant and just not speak to him. All his
messages would be relayed through his secretary: "Mr.
Benny would like this . . . or that. . . ." If Ralph had to give
him instructions over the P A system from the director's
booth, Benny would take the direction, but not reply. George,
on the other hand, would blow up over something, but ten
minutes later it was forgotten.

Joe Depew, the assistant director, once said, "George
does get fired up. Never over big things like the breakdown
of equipment or a delay in finishing a big set. He recognizes
that by the law of averages, equipment must break down,
scenery can't always be there on time, and these kinds of
delays he accepts philosophically. However, it's the minor
things which cause him to storm up an explosion—a missing
prop, a misplaced cigar, a page extracted from his script without his knowledge. Then beware his wrath, and keep out of
his path. But he calms down just as quickly. George thinks so
far ahead of everyone else connected with the show that he
has everything 'set' in his mind as to how the show should go
—angles for the cameras, movement of the performers, han-
dling of props, and when people, not being aware of his ad-
vanced thinking, do something contrary to his plans, he belts
out a bellow. But when he realizes, which is immediately, that
this has happened, he is the first to laugh at himself."

Herb Browar summed it up when he stated: "George was
a professional and strictly business, not one to kick back. If
he felt like saying something, he would really tell you off.
What happened was you were a little in awe of him, and he
was from the old school—a lot of yelling. He was very force-
ful. You became a little timid, but after you got to know him
and you had your one argument, you became part of the
family and he would have respect for you. It was a matter of
proving yourself to him."

And, typical of George, just when you thought you had
him pegged, he'd turn around and surprise you. Joe Thompson, the property master, recalled, "Occasionally something

would go wrong. Once in a kitchen scene I covered a plate of meat with a napkin. I thought they were finished with the prop. It turned out the cameras picked up the plate and the entire scene had to be replayed." Everyone held their breath expecting a blowup, and instead George agreeably grinned at his crew and remarked, 'We will be sanitary at any cost.'

George had a terrific rapport with his staff. Anyone could make a suggestion, even the janitor, and George would listen. He gave everyone a chance to get involved. Recently, George recalled when he first developed this practice. "It doesn't hurt to listen—you get it for free. I learned this a thousand years ago." It seems that once after playing in a theater in Far Rockaway, New York, George was returning home by train when a fellow passenger said to him, "I saw your show last night and liked it very much. But the joke you do about the positions, instead of *saying* 'position' all the time, you should say, 'How do you like this?' and *assume* a funny position."

"I asked him what he did for a living and he said, 'I'm in the bakery business.'

"I took his advice," Burns laughed, "and you know, the joke worked much better—no question about it. I learned to listen."

He elaborated further on this attitude: "On our set, everyone is encouraged to speak up. Sometimes you know the errand boy will whisper to the cameraman and the cameraman will whisper to the director and so on. At my age, if they don't sound off direct, I might be dead before the whisper gets to me. Anyway, I'll always listen, I can be so wrong. . . ."

George not only listened to his staff and crew, he listened to his audience. The accusation that the television audience has the mind of an average twelve-year-old never sat well with him. He firmly believed that the surest way to lose an audience was to talk down to them. Sooner or later people would turn away from a program that didn't respect their intelligence. He was more aware than most that "everybody who owns a television set owns a theater. Everybody is his own manager. . . . The first thing an actor learns is to get along with the manager. He does well when he doesn't forget it."

In spite of all the crises that the "Burns and Allen" company survived, Ralph Levy fondly remembered those times. " 'The Burns and Allen Show' and Jack Benny's show were essentially one-man operations. Nowadays, there are literally dozens of people grouped around TV shows, and to get a comedy idea past them, you have to run a gauntlet. In those days we were enjoying our work. I don't go walking on sets anymore to visit people the way we used to do. It's not fun anymore. One guy's there saying, 'You're going overtime.' Another guy's saying, 'You're over budget.' Everybody's tensed up and nervous. Oh sure, we had plenty of our own crises, but they were usually constructive ones, based on doing the best possible show we were capable of."

13

TAKE ONE

*Television's got one thing for me that
no other form ever had. It's this:
You're always guessing. That's the
exciting thing. Whether you're right
or wrong, every week you have a new
chance to guess.*
—GEORGE BURNS,
TV Guide *(December 25, 1964)*

At General Service Studios, new sets had been built on Stage 6 under the direction of Frank Durlauf. On the left side of the sound stage was the Mortons' house; in the middle stood the front entrances to the Burnses' and Mortons' homes, and the Burnses' living room and kitchen. The right side was occupied by a little patio with the pool (tank), a diving board, and the swinging gate that separated the Burnses' and Mortons' backyards.

Changes had been made in the televised look of the sets: a step down from the vestibule was added to the living room; the backyard was no longer by the kitchen; double French doors added to the living room opened onto a patio, and Blanche's kitchen window now faced Gracie's large kitchen window. All the appliances in Gracie's kitchen worked: the stove could cook—even if Gracie couldn't—and water could be turned on in the sink. The *audience* accepted these changes without question, but not Gracie. Several encounters with her new kitchen door left her very puzzled:

GRACIE: Oh, this new Dutch door—it's always coming apart in the middle. . . . You know, the Dutch must be awfully short people.

The live shows were still being done every other week. Starting in June, the cast began alternating locations—one week doing the live show at CBS, the next rehearsing and filming the new shows at General Service Studios.

Ralph Levy also began double duty. No stranger to the multiple-camera technique, he had directed the very first "three-motion-picture-camera" television show, starring Edgar Bergen, back in 1949.

The script was ready for that first filmed show, and the premise was a typical "Burns and Allen" story:

Jane, the wardrobe woman (played by Elvia Allman), tells Gracie she's just won a trip for two to Hawaii. Gracie isn't aware that Jane is married and doesn't think she should go alone, so she attempts to find Jane a husband before the trip. When Harry Von Zell balks at the suggestion of matrimony, Gracie contacts a marriage broker (played by Hal March) who arrives with photos of prospective mates. While Gracie waits for the groom, Jane's husband comes by, ready to leave on their trip. Gracie jumps to an erroneous conclusion. She approves of the broker's selection, but thinks he's a little too familiar with Jane for a first date. Jane explains this *is* her husband. Gracie is delighted she found someone so quickly and sends them on their way while throwing rice at the "newlyweds."

After two years of reporting on the live shows, the press was anxious to see this new filmed effort. George and Gracie had suffered in the ratings by being off the listings every other week, and Hal Humphrey's column in the *Los Angeles Mirror* alerted viewers that:

[All] that will be changed beginning tomorrow night [October 9, 1952] when "The Burns and Allen Show" tees off with a weekly series on film, and I can highly recommend this one—the first of their filmed shows.

Nothing has changed as far as George and Gracie are concerned. Gracie reminds me of "Harvey" the rabbit —she's not quite real but very charming and very nice. George continues to get laughs by repeating Gracie's upside down lines.

In this initial film, you'll see Gracie doing her version of a hula while George sings an off-key accompaniment. It's all part of his effort to make Harry Von Zell see the virtues of a honeymoon in Hawaii with a woman he doesn't want to marry. It's also some of the best comedy you will see on your screen this season.

The Mortons (Bea Benaderet and Fred Clark) still do a bang-up job of it, and producer/director Ralph Levy has taken to this as easy as a duck wading in water.

This first film show almost never got off the ground. Phil Tannura had signed on as cinematographer. (He knew his trade well, having started as a photographer with the signal corps when the Marine troops went to Russia in World War II.) On Wednesday, June 25, at 8:30 A.M., everyone was gathered on the set. Filming was to begin at 9:00—but where was Phil? By 8:45 he still hadn't arrived. At 8:55 a frantic Herb Browar called the main gate, thinking maybe Phil was lost. The studio guard told him that yes, a Phil Tannura had been by earlier but hadn't been cleared. Phil had figured there'd been a change in plans and just gone home. With all the final preparations they'd been making for this first filmed show, somebody had forgotten to leave the cameraman a pass. A fast phone call brought Phil quickly back, and this time the guard willingly let him on the lot.

In a *TV Guide* story, George recounted his personal problems with those early film shows: "Gracie'd as soon toss off a line and stare at the backdrop. She's a natural for film.

With me, it's different. I've had to get used to delivering those monologues to a camera. It's surprising how little personality a camera has, and the loudest noise in the world to me is that silence that falls when the director shouts, 'Quiet!' "

Apparently, whatever early hesitation George had about playing to a camera instead of an audience worked for him. In *The Saturday Review*, Gilbert Seldes wrote about all the other comics (Jack Benny, Bob Hope, etc.) who had tried monologues and were never entirely successful at it, but said of George's performance: "The slight uncertainty works well for George in a way that it falls in with his relation of his character to Gracie's—the air of total failure to understand her and total indulgence and faith in her."

In October 1952 everyone left CBS and moved onto the General Service lot, where George still has his office today. The sets were moved from Stage 6 to Stage 1, which for the next six years would be the permanent home of "Burns and Allen." Visitors today can see a brass plaque dedicating Stage 1 as "The George Burns Stage."

The routine for doing a weekly film show was quickly established.

MONDAY. George would meet with his writers at eight in the morning and work until they had a story line. They tried to stay two to three scripts ahead of each show's filming. Sometimes they could come up with a story quickly; other times it would take all day. But they didn't leave the room until a story was laid out.

While George wrote, Gracie was busy having wardrobe fittings that took up to four hours to complete. She would take a nap in the afternoon to rest for the work still ahead of her —after dinner she had to study her script for another three hours before calling it a day.

TUESDAY. Rehearsal Day. George and Gracie would arrive at the studio at 9:00 A.M. to work with the cast, director, and

cameramen. They would block out the action and camera
moves for the next day's shooting. This was a long day since
the script would be rehearsed in continuity, line for line, movement for movement.

Tuesday and Wednesday were days for pampering themselves at lunch. George always ate at Davey Jones' Locker,
a seafood restaurant on Santa Monica Boulevard near the
studio. He enjoyed his one-martini lunch even then, and this
was the closest place to the studio he could have one. George
and any cast or crew who wanted to join him would all descend
on Davey. George always ordered the same thing: scrambled
eggs and salami, toast, and coffee. Each morning on these two
days, Davey would have to go to a special deli down the street
to get George his salami. He didn't mind, and George had his
favorite lunch.

WEDNESDAY. The Big Day. Filming took twelve hours, usually
wrapping the last shot around seven at night. Each scene
would be rehearsed, then filmed. It was assembly-line filming.
When they finished all the scenes in one set, everyone would
move over to the next one and start the whole rehearse-shoot
routine again.

Between setups, George would either talk with the director or study his next scene. Firmly attached to the arm of his
off-set chair was an ashtray for the ever present cigar. Gracie
had a little pouch attached to hers that held a pair of shell-
rimmed glasses and her comfy shoes. The high heels she wore
on the show were very tiring to be in all day, so between
scenes she would slip them off while she studied her lines.

Gracie said her biggest thrill was folding back a page of
her script when that bit of dialogue or business was finished.
She had a lot of thrills on filming day, because out of that
forty-page script, at least thirty pages were hers.

THURSDAY. George would be cloistered with the writers again.
They would bring in the pages they'd been working on from
that Monday story meeting. At noon they'd all break for
lunch, but no luxury this time. They would deliberately head

for a coffee shop with the worst food in town, and be back in the office by 12:30, where they'd work until about 4:00.

Gracie had it a little easier. Thursday was her day off. But it was the only day of the week she had for personal business. She told a reporter once, "If I should need a doctor on Monday, I would have to wait until Thursday." She smiled after she said it, but, looking at the rest of her week, it's hard to believe she was kidding.

FRIDAY. George would work with the writers again, this time starting at 9:00 and working until 4:00. No interruptions, not even any phone calls disturbed this session.

Gracie was back with wardrobe again, selecting the outfits she would wear on next week's show.

SATURDAY. Weekends were still workdays for George. In the morning, he would put together all the material he and the writers had been working on. Then he would indulge himself in the afternoon by heading for Hillcrest Country Club to sit with friends in the television and movie business, discussing whatever problems they might be having with their work and offering each other advice. Saturday night, the mimeographed script would be delivered to the house, and George would comb through the fifty-odd pages looking for cuts to bring it down to shooting length.

SUNDAY. Another busy day, starting with the arrival of a secretary to take the script notes. At 10:00 A.M. the director would come over to discuss the script and make any final decisions regarding the upcoming show. Gracie would attend these meetings because 90 percent of the discussions involved her character.

Sunday night George would sit back and watch TV. It was the only time he had to see what everyone else was doing. While George checked out the competition, Gracie would start studying her lines again. She once said, "Sometimes I throw the script across the room, but I always have to pick it up and study it. If I sit down to write a letter, I think, 'I should be

working on my lines.' '' When she was through for the evening, she would join George, and they'd watch TV together.

This weekly schedule remained basically the same for the
next six years. Fred de Cordova, a later director on "Burns
and Allen," summed it up: "We'd rehearse a day, shoot a day,
and then write three days, discuss, and do it all again. We did
as many as thirty-nine shows a season that way."

The first filmed episode premiered October 9, 1952. "The
Burns and Allen Show" must have been doing something
right, because it was a success—but working the kinks out of
a new process always has its problems, and "Burns and
Allen" had its fair share.

All men may have been created equal, but the same can't
be said for film. Phil Tannura had always been partial to using
one particular brand. A couple of weeks into filming, the camera suddenly jammed—just stopped dead in its tracks. One
reel had just been completed and one thousand feet of unex-
posed film were inside that camera. Nothing Phil tried could
get it started, and the only alternative was to open the casing,
which would expose the film. With no other choice, Phil
opened the side of the camera, and, to his horror, what looked
like a rat's nest spilled out.

Apparently the film he'd been using was just a hair's
width wider than the gate, and as the film had been rolling it
was shearing off this minute fraction of an inch, filling the
casing with fine, hairlike strands of film. Everything they'd
shot that morning would have to be redone. George nearly
fainted. Time was money—George's money! He wisely insisted they not use that film anymore.

Herb Browar ran across the street to Eastman, only to
discover he would have to pay cash to buy a day's worth of
film. Herb patted his pockets. Not enough. He was welcome
to set up an account, but Herb didn't have ten thousand dollars on him for the deposit, either. Ever resourceful, he ran
back to the studio and poked his head into Stage 5, where
"Ozzie and Harriet" was shooting. Luckily they had film to

spare, and he was able to borrow enough until he could set up an account at Eastman.

George was extremely budget conscious, continually looking for ways to give the show a rich look without it costing too much money. Changes of sets were one way to achieve the effect, but what about the cost? Then he discovered the L set.

An L set is just what it sounds like. Two walls, set at right angles to each other, that could be photographed from several different angles to give the illusion of a complete room. Herb Browar was constantly raiding the construction dock, looking for old set walls—something with a door, something with a window. Additionally, to help save on cost, if a window was called for, they would hang a Venetian blind on it, close the louvers, and eliminate the need for a backdrop.

Don Wells, the superintendent of construction, quickly got wise to Herb. The construction department needed some means of keeping track of the adjustments Herb made to the walls. Together they came up with a purchase order system, giving each element of a new set its own number. The other shows on the lot soon adopted this procedure. But even the best laid plans often have a loophole, and "The Burns and Allen Show" accidentally managed to fall through one.

One sunny afternoon, Herb was summoned to the construction dock by a furious Don Wells. It seems that "Ozzie and Harriet" was also using this new system, and somehow had come up with a number that was the same as a "Burns and Allen" set number. Both sets had been built, but only one bill was sent out—to "Ozzie and Harriet." Because there weren't any sketches of either show's set, when all the receipts came in, there was no way to match the expenses with the proper show, and "Burns and Allen" got a free set. From that day on, Wells hung a huge sign over his desk: YOU CAN'T BUILD A SET WITHOUT A DRAWING!!

As important as the sets were, George felt, "The sets were secondary—it was always the story, it was Gracie . . . if they're looking at the sets, then something's wrong."

14

WRITTEN BY . . .

GEORGE: *I've got to get to Palm Springs. My writers are waiting for me. They've been down there for a week and so far all they've written is my name on the bottom of all the restaurant checks. They need me. I'm the only one who can type.*

Ask any television writer, and the answer is always the same: comedy is the hardest kind of writing there is. Contrary to the image we might have of people sitting around being funny, anyone who might happen to open the door to a comedy writing session would discover a group of deadly serious men and women—some pacing, some sitting with heads in hands, others staring blankly into space. Occasionally a "What if . . . ?" will punctuate the silence, followed by more deep thought, random attempts to see if the proposed idea will go anywhere, usually terminating with a, "No, that won't work . . . ," and it's back to square one. When a concept for a story, or a great line finally does emerge from the vacuum, *then* the laughter can be heard all the way to the parking lot.

The "Burns and Allen" writers had a very special task set before them. Although at times the story lines seemed almost too simple, creating the chaos that would come with

Gracie's involvement took painstaking care. For instance, in one episode Gracie is on a train, returning from a visit to her mother in San Francisco. Her fellow passengers have taken unfair advantage of Gracie's naïveté, and one man tells her he is going to murder his wife. Gracie believes him, and when she gets home, she immediately tells Blanche. Blanche tells Harry, and Harry tells Gracie to call the police and report it. That should take care of the problem, but not with Gracie at the helm. She picks up the phone and calls the Beverly Hills police department. Now listen carefully:

GRACIE: A man is going to murder his wife.
DETECTIVE: Are you sure of that?
GRACIE: Yes, he told me. . . .
DETECTIVE: Wait, let me write this down. *(As he gets a piece of paper, Gracie continues.)*
GRACIE: . . . And a friend of mine advised me to call the police.
DETECTIVE: Now, give me this man's name and address. . . .
GRACIE: That's Harry Morton, 314 Maple Drive.

And the chase is on. Gracie merely gives the detective the answer to the last statement she made. To further compound matters, Blanche is temporarily missing. Harry tries to explain that she went shopping, but to the police Harry looks very, very guilty.

Often plot complications arise out of everybody's trying to help everybody else—without the others' knowledge. If Gracie thinks Blanche and Harry are having trouble, she concocts some story to help. If George and Gracie are having problems, Blanche might ask Harry to intervene by backing up Gracie's story. Inevitably, just before the helpful friend arrives to corroborate the "lie," the other party will have figured out the truth. Hearing the new "truth" only starts the snowball rolling again.

Although never actually stated as such, there are several rules of thumb that were kept in mind when writing for Gracie:

RULE 1. The Gracie character doesn't think she's dumb. She thinks she's smart. Every line written for her keeps that in mind.

This "Gracie law" provided us with unique dialogue that, out of anyone else's mouth, just wouldn't have worked. Here, Gracie is going to help Emily Vanderlip with her homework:

EMILY: I wish Geometry were as easy as Spanish.
GRACIE: Maybe I can help you. Say something to me in Geometry.
EMILY: Something in Geometry?
GRACIE: Yes, go ahead.
EMILY: All right. Pi r square.
GRACIE: Is that what they teach you in school these days? Pie are square?
EMILY: Yes.
GRACIE: Pie are round. *(Picks up cookies.)* Cookies are round. Crackers are square.

RULE 2. When you write for Gracie, keep her consistent. She can be doing *anything*, but she'll always react in the same manner.

Her literal translation of any subject gave the writers a wealth of material. But it took very careful writing to make the setup just right for Gracie's misinterpretation:

BLANCHE: I have to stop at Sears and Roebuck. We don't have a garbage disposal.
GRACIE: Isn't that a long way to take your garbage every day?

Or . . .

APPLIANCE MAN: You'll really like this range, Mrs. Burns. For instance, you put in a roast, you set the oven control, then you go out all day. When you come home at night, the roast is done.

GRACIE: Haven't you got one where I don't have to go out?

Often, George makes use of Gracie's literalness in his monologues. In one, he tells why the butler and maid quit:

> Gracie found out she was going to have to pay them portal to portal, so much an hour from the time they left home. She spoke to the butler and found out he left home when he was twelve years old. She thought eight thousand dollars was too much to pay for one meal.

RULE 3. If it is a logical premise, Gracie pursues it illogically. If it is an illogical premise, she pursues it logically.

This last rule is the one that makes Gracie's character so special. Clever writing, plus Gracie's own special attention to detail with her wonderful concentration, gives us some sensational moments.

One episode opens with Harry Morton looking over the Dutch doors into Gracie's kitchen. She is at the stove pouring boiling water into jars, quickly sealing them, and then running to put them in the freezer. Without speaking a word of dialogue, she does this not once, not twice, but three times, while Harry looks on with a deadpan expression. Watching, we are fascinated. We *have* to know what she's doing. Finally, Harry asks:

HARRY: Gracie, isn't that boiling water you're putting in the refrigerator?

GRACIE: Yes, I'm freezing it.

HARRY: You're freezing it?

GRACIE: Um hmm, and then whenever I want boiling water, all I have to do is defrost it.

With runs such as these, we can always count on a payoff. We are just never sure how the writers will handle it. In this particular episode, it is quietly and subtly played back several times throughout the show. Once, while showing a chef around her kitchen, she points out the stove, the oven, the sink, and the refrigerator—in case he needs any boiling water. And later, when Blanche is in bed with a cold, Gracie brings her a hot-water bottle. When her friend gratefully takes it, removes the towels, and plops the bag on her tummy under the covers, the expression of shock at the ice-cold hot-water bottle says more than any dialogue could express.

Other payoffs might play back as they do in the "Spanish Lesson" episode. In watching that show, we too have an enlightening lesson:

Gracie wants to learn Spanish. The teacher arrives and Gracie tells him she doesn't know how to speak any Spanish, but asks if he'd like to sit down. She gestures broadly toward the sofa. The teacher sits and says, *"Gracias."* Aha! You can almost see the little bulb lighting up inside Gracie's head— she's learned a new word already. Anxious to try it out, she asks him to stand up so she can ask him to sit down in Spanish. She again gestures "sit down" and says, *"Gracias."* He starts to correct her, then thinks better of it, and sits. The concept is now locked in. *Gracias* means "sit."

This new word becomes increasingly frustrating for Gracie. She has offered him some coffee, but each time she tries to bring in the tray, he says *"Gracias."* She's now halfway to the kitchen and has to run back into the living room and sit. The same thing happens when she tries to get a pencil and paper to write the word down.

This type of visual and verbal humor could be enough in most comedy shows, but not "Burns and Allen." In this case, Gracie has told Blanche about her new word, *gracias.* It means "sit." Blanche doesn't think that sounds right, and goes to Harry for confirmation. Harry is busy working on tax forms at the kitchen table and doesn't want to be bothered. Blanche knows he took Spanish in school, and hovers over him, imploring him to answer just one question: "What does *gracias* mean?" Exasperated, Harry looks up from his work and says simply, "Sit down." Blanche digests this information and wanders off muttering, "Gee, Gracie was right."

Another unwritten rule is that Gracie usually has her own train of thought—and nobody else is aboard.

JANE: We had some friends watching your show at our apartment. You never heard such laughing.
GRACIE: I don't know what they were laughing at. You have a lovely apartment.
JANE: I mean they thought your show was funny.
GRACIE: Oh. Then why were they laughing at your apartment?

In one episode Blanche has bought a fur stole and asks Gracie to hide it from Harry. Through a series of mix-ups, Gracie discovers the fur is missing and tries to report it to the police. Detective Sawyer (a recurring character played by Jim Flavin) learns that Gracie is on her way and quickly hides, leaving the bewildered captain to discover why his top detective has disappeared. He soon learns:

GRACIE: My neighbor, Blanche Morton, left her fur stole in my house. I was keeping it for her, and it's gone.
CAPTAIN: Oh, you want to report a stolen fur?
GRACIE: Yes.
CAPTAIN: I see. Just where was this fur stole?
GRACIE: Excuse me, you don't mean where was this fur stole? You mean, where was this fur stolen?
CAPTAIN: Didn't you just tell me this fur was a stole?
GRACIE: Sure it was, but I don't know who a-stole it . . . I bet you know some wonderful recipes for spaghetti.

Clever dialogue like this was second only to the writers' creativity when it came to whole situations centering on Gracie's literalness. Take the following scenario:

Gracie is fixing stewed chicken for dinner. In keeping with her character, throughout the story she keeps running to the back porch where she gives sips of bourbon to a chicken. We later learn that the chicken has gotten loose, staggered across the street, attacked the Vanderlips' cat, then swaggered back to Gracie's porch for another little nip.

Some lines Gracie refused. You won't hear any mouse jokes on "The Burns and Allen Show," nor did Gracie ever make a joke or reference to any physical affliction. "I'd never talk about a man who limps," she declared in a *New York Times* interview.

Although she didn't get actively involved in the story conferences, she would occasionally change a line "to fit her mouth" as she called it. In that same interview she confided, "And when I do, George says I've picked on the best line in the whole show." George admitted that after he slept on her suggested revisions and took them back to the writers, they usually agreed that Gracie was right.

The writers often made reference to themselves in George's monologues. It is interesting to note that they frequently put themselves down, but in such a way the audience knew not to believe a word of it.

My writers think up the plots for these television shows in the elevator on the way up to my office. But unfortunately, my office is on the second floor. I'll either have to get better writers or move to a higher floor.

Can you follow this plot? You see, Harry thinks Blanche is nuts, Blanche thinks Harry is nuts, and I think they're both nuts. To get an authentic feeling into the show, I had my writers go and talk to a psychiatrist. He spoke to them a few hours and I may be allowed to visit them next Thursday.

Just who were these anonymous writers we kept hearing about?

The senior writer on the "Burns and Allen" team was Paul Henning. Originally from Independence, Missouri, Paul was the youngest of eleven children—and "ten of us grew up," he said with a smile. He eventually moved to Los Angeles to pursue his career, and when the Second World War broke out, Henning was in L.A.'s Cedars of Lebanon Hospital with a very serious illness. He spent three months in the hospital, and when he finally was able to go home, he discovered that all the other writers in Hollywood had been drafted.

Paul started writing for George and Gracie in 1942 on their radio show, and it was he who usually came up with the concept for each episode. He remembered fondly the letter to his mother about his new job: "I now write for George Burns!" and she wrote back and said, "Who writes for Gracie? She's got all the funny stuff."

Paul Henning was in on those first meetings that transformed the radio show into a television hit. He refers to his ten-year association with Burns and Allen as "happy, prosperous years. In the ten years I was with [George], I never asked for a raise. I didn't have to. Each year, he'd give me a much more generous raise than I would ever ask for." He stayed with "Burns and Allen" until 1952 and later said, "The only reason I left was because I had a chance to produce." He later went on to create and produce McCadden's "The Bob Cummings Show," plus other popular TV shows, including "The Beverly Hillbillies" and "Petticoat Junction."

Sid Dorfman is another writer who was involved in the transition from radio to television. Sid has been described as being "kind of quiet," and he and Harvey Helm were largely responsible for the crazy things Gracie would say. Sid continued through two years of live shows and the first year of filmed episodes before leaving to try his hand at other projects. He went on to become a staff writer on "M*A*S*H" and produced "Good Times" for Norman Lear and CBS.

Harvey Helm started writing for George Burns by selling him jokes when George was in vaudeville. He worked with George on his radio show, and through all eight seasons of the

"Burns and Allen" television show. George said of Harvey, "[He] was more than a writer, he was a personal friend." Harvey subscribed to a variety of magazines with such comedy-inspiring titles as *Popular Mechanics* and *The Poultry Journal.* He would sit for hours at his typewriter, a cigarette dangling from his lips, staring at the pictures, hoping for something to spark that wild imagination of his.

Willy Burns was George's younger brother and had worked with him since vaudeville. His first job with George and Gracie was mostly as a secretary, filing and cross-filing jokes. If George needed a hunting joke, for example, Willy would look through the "hunting" file and find something appropriate. Then George could rewrite it to fit his immediate needs. Willy had a good business head and planned to go into the insurance business. When George and Gracie started making real money, they went to the only person they could trust for advice. Willy became not only their business manager, but a writer for their show as well.

Willy's talent was less with the typewriter than as a "pitcher." His forte was tossing out great ideas; when all the writers sat around looking for funny situations or runs of dialogue, Willy would really shine.

George repeatedly said that Willy had one other function he was sure his brother didn't enjoy. Whenever George got mad at one of the other writers, he would take it out on Willy. George couldn't risk having one of his writers misinterpret his actions and quit, and he knew that Willy understood his quick-flare/quick-calm temper and would ride out the storm. In an interview, George once stated, "My brother Willy hasn't got an easy life. If the rating is down, it's Willy's fault. If it's up, I'm wearing a red tie."

After Paul Henning left "The Burns and Allen Show," two young writers joined the staff—Jesse Goldstein and Nate Monaster. Jesse and Nate were only on staff for one year before going their separate ways. Nate went on to write for "December Bride" and "Bachelor Father" in the 1950s, and "Andy Griffith" and "Get Smart" in the sixties, as well as several features and many episodes of hit series in the seventies. Jesse, a former high school teacher, stuck with the classic radio and TV comedians, writing for such stars as Milton Berle, Judy Canova, and Jack Carson.

In the 1953 season Nate and Jesse were replaced by Keith Fowler. Keith had been Paul Henning's partner on the "Burns and Allen" radio show. And a more mismatched pair couldn't be imagined. Paul loved movies and kids; Keith and his wife had no children, seven cats and saw maybe four movies a year. Keith collected books and odd facts. "A Master of Useless Information" is how he once referred to himself. "I can name, for instance, the names of the first two American soldiers killed in World War I." Keith was a welcome addition to the staff, and after Sid Dorfman left, Keith Fowler, Harvey Helm, Willy Burns, and a new addition, Norman Paul, made up the writing staff for the balance of the series' run.

Everyone who worked with Norman Paul always said the same thing: "He was a very good writer." He was that rare combination of a good storyteller/constructionist, and a good joke writer. This talent isn't come by easily. In Norman's case, it meant his mind was usually 100 percent on his work, and not on trivialities like whether or not his socks matched, if his suit had ever been pressed, or what to do with a necktie—if he even owned one. He was even unfazed the day his car caught on fire.

Norman's convertible was a rolling wastebasket. Somewhere, hidden under piles of old scripts, newspapers, odd bits of clothing and take-out food containers, there really was a backseat. Couple this with Norman's chain-smoking and you have a disaster waiting to happen. It did, right on Santa Monica Boulevard. Norman apparently flipped a cigarette out the window and it blew back into the rear seat. The paper went up in flames as Norman drove on, vaguely aware that something must be wrong by the frantic attempts of pedestrians and other drivers to flag him down. Checking his rearview mirror he saw the problem, shrugged it off, and kept on driving—right up to a new-car dealer, where he promptly turned in his now useless car for a new one, threw some scripts into the backseat, and drove off.

This diverse combination of personalities and talent was the backbone of "The Burns and Allen Show." And at the heart of this group was George himself. His philosophy was, "Good writers will give you what you want, but if you don't know what you want, they can't give you anything."

Fortunately, George always knew exactly what he wanted.

15

FADE IN

GEORGE: *I could clear this situation up in a minute, but my writers would kill me.*

As you drove onto the General Service Studios lot, the "Burns and Allen" offices were just to the left of the main building. Upon entering that complex, you would walk down a long hallway to a door that opened into a tiny outer office with a little alcove, a desk, and two more doors. One door led to a small office, the other to George's main office, through which you would reach the room that was home to the writers.

The furnishings in George's office were sparse—a long couch, one large desk, a bookshelf, and several side chairs. Above the couch, pinned to the knotty-pine paneling, were photos of each of the "Burns and Allen" sets. It was in this room that the stories for each episode were conceived and the dialogue honed to perfection.

Sid Dorfman and Harvey Helm were always the first to arrive. Harvey liked to get up at 5:00 A.M., which also happened to be Sid's favorite time of day to write. They would get together, and by 8:00 A.M. they had their day's writing completed, just in time to present it to George.

At precisely 8:00 every morning, George would enter to begin his workday. He and brother Willy shared the oversized desk, and whoever came in first would check the in basket. Opposite the desk was Norman Paul, occupying the couch—all of it. He could write only in a prone position, so the couch was reserved for him. Tommy Clapp, the writers' secretary, would sit at a typewriter, his fingers flying over the keys, never missing a word as the writers spoke. George would alternate between sitting in a side chair and walking through some of the routines.

It was all very informal, and to break the tension of plotting the stories, the writers would take an occasional joke break. As George once told a *TV Guide* reporter, "Sometimes I get up and sing them a song. It's not like a job."

One day the entire staff interrupted their day's work to compose a letter to George's old friend Jack Benny. Jack was working in London and had sent George a telegram asking, "What's new?" George and the writers sent a long, detailed letter about everything that was new—the shoe repair shop on Santa Monica Boulevard had moved across the street; his neighbor had bought a new car; they'd changed the menu at the corner deli—pages and pages of "news," but absolutely nothing about Gracie and George.

Eventually, however, they would settle down to business. Time was precious, and there could be no frantic, last-minute writing. Scripts had to be written well in advance because of all the convoluted, brain-twisting lines Gracie had to learn.

Many of the plots were recurring ones. Within any given season we could count on the writers' giving us at least one episode containing a surprise party; a Gracie-dents-the-car story; a girls-versus-boys story; and other running themes. George became the center of so many surprise parties, he began to turn sour on them. In one monologue he groused:

I'm crazy about surprise parties. A lot of people come that you don't know and they mix with a lot more that you wish you didn't. They're happy and gay and eat your food and burn holes in the rugs and break the furniture, tear down the drapes, and when the party ends if the house is still standing, that's my surprise.

A number of episodes found George being hauled off to jail because of Gracie's mix-ups. She was very understanding, and even sent him a calendar with every other day blacked out. Her explanation: "So the months'll go by faster."

The writers would often put Gracie in a situation where she would have unknown plans for George. Eventually, Gracie would get caught doing something she was trying to hide from him, and she wouldn't have a lie ready. Instead, she would agree with whatever information George volunteered. For example, in one episode it was established early on that George *hated* cultural events. Gracie is talking to a man selling box seats to the ballet. When George says, "What is he, an undertaker?" Gracie quickly agrees. (Now the writers have set us up for the laughs to follow.) When he tries to sell George a box that "holds four people," poor bewildered George has no idea what's going on.

Much later in the series, the writers did manage to give George some relief from Gracie's scheming by gifting him with a "magic TV set." But early in the series, George is not *always* aware of what is happening. When he is, he clues in the audience:

Oh, the Mortons. Watch me have some fun with them.

Sometimes he recaps a plot for us and we are amazed to find that he knows so much about what has been going on (it also helps keep things clear for us):

Well, let's see how far the plot is now. Blanche thinks that Harry got me out of the house. Harry thinks that I'm

a mind reader because I know about the insurance man.
I think he's a jerk for getting mixed up in this. Gracie
thinks—no, that's going a bit too far. Anyway, we're
ready for our next development. And here he comes now.
Ladies and gentlemen, the insurance man.

Having George speak to the audience was one of the
writers' tricks that made "Burns and Allen" so special, and
the writers were unabashed in their mischievous use of this
technique. They treated the audience as if we were in on the
real lives of George, Gracie, and the others, not home in our
living rooms watching characters on a TV show. As George
frequently jokes, "You know, if you saw a plot like this on
television, you'd never believe it. But here it is happening in
real life." On one occasion, in the middle of a scene, George
turns to the audience and says, "Don't touch that dial. The
plot is still unsolved," and goes right on with his conversation
with the other characters. Another time George asks his audience, "You've been watching the show. Will you phone me if
there's something cooking that I don't know about?" and
later in the show he reminds us, "Look, I think something is
going on. I'm still waiting for your phone call, and this time
you can reverse the charges." And at the end of the episode,
he announces, "A ten-cent phone call could have saved me a
fortune. I'm mad at you!"

Following agreement on a general idea for a program, the
writers would break up into teams, some working on Gracie's
dialogue, the rest on other parts of the script. As the writers
read through the dialogue they'd written, each line was carefully polished, but never overworked. In the December 25,
1953, issue of *TV Guide*, George explained, "That first impression is the same impression I hope the audience is going
to get. If I mull a joke over and over and twist it and change
it and otherwise try to elaborate on it, it soon loses its fresh-
ness, and I've completely forgotten what it sounded like in the
first place."

Al Simon gave most of the credit for the successful writ-

George Burns and Gracie Allen on their porch, where at the end of each show George bids his wife, "Say good night, Gracie!" (Courtesy USC)

(*OPPOSITE*) *Gracie Allen at age twelve poses in the Spanish costume she wore at dancing school.* (*Courtesy USC*)

(*BELOW*) *George and Gracie, in one of their radio guest appearances on rival network NBC (their own show was on CBS).* (*Courtesy USC*)

(FAR LEFT) *George and Gracie plant a grapefruit tree in front of their first house in Beverly Hills, 1934. George still lives in that house today.* (Courtesy USC)

(LEFT) *A 1940 publicity gimmick saw Gracie running for president. Here she poses with her mascot(s), selected because of the slogan, "It's in the Bag!"* (Courtesy USC)

(BELOW, LEFT) *An early posed publicity still. The autograph reads, "Best Wishes, Sincerely, Gracie Allen—George Burns."* (Courtesy USC)

(BELOW) *The television show's first director, Ralph Levy, goes over a script page with Gracie and George.* (Courtesy Ralph Levy)

Bea Benaderet in "glamour" publicity shot during her days as a radio performer. (Photo by Ben Polin; courtesy Jack Bannon)

Bea Benaderet as Blanche Morton on the "Burns and Allen" TV series. (Photo by Gabor Rona; courtesy Jack Bannon)

Hal March—the original Harry Morton—takes time out with director Ralph Levy. (Courtesy Ralph Levy)

George discusses a problem with neighbor Harry Morton, this time played by John Brown. Note the number 312 over the Burnses' door. Although the set is an early one, their address remained consistent throughout the entire series. (Courtesy USC)

Harry Morton (John Brown) and George try to keep a secret from their wives. (Courtesy USC)

(*LEFT*) *Fred Clark, Harry Morton the Third. This Harry had a voracious appetite, as shown here sneaking hidden food while supposedly dieting. (Courtesy USC)*

(*RIGHT, TOP*) *Blanche shows off a new watch to George in this early live show. Note the block wall portion of the set used to depict the exterior of the Mortons' house. (Courtesy USC)*

(*RIGHT, BOTTOM*) *George and Harry Morton (Fred Clark) dressed for an evening on the town, much to George's obvious dismay. (Courtesy USC)*

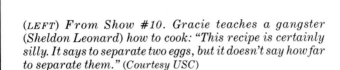

(LEFT) From Show #10. Gracie teaches a gangster (Sheldon Leonard) how to cook: "This recipe is certainly silly. It says to separate two eggs, but it doesn't say how far to separate them." (Courtesy USC)

(BELOW) Director Ralph Levy positions Gracie, as George and actor Jim Flavin (Detective Sawyer) await their cues. (Courtesy Ralph Levy)

(*TOP*) *From Show #17. Harry Morton, George, and Harry Von Zell are in jail, thanks to a mix-up caused by Gracie. Detective Sawyer (Jim Flavin) looks on. (Courtesy USC)*

(*BOTTOM*) *From Show #17. Harry Morton and George share a cell in the Beverly Hills jail. This scenario was used so frequently that the jail became a semipermanent set. (Courtesy USC)*

(ABOVE) *From Show #19. Gracie rules the kitchen, as George and special guest star Mayor Fletcher Bowron of Los Angeles get a lesson in dishwashing. (Courtesy USC)*

(BELOW) *From Show #28. Gracie and Blanche proudly show off their new fur stoles to their reluctant husbands. (Courtesy USC)*

(TOP) *George, Ralph Levy, Gracie, and Jack Benny go o[...]
was George's best friend and a frequent guest star. (Cou[...]*

(BOTTOM) *In the Mortons' living-room set, Ralph Levy e[...]
Bea and Gracie, as the script girl takes notes. (Courtesy[...]*

On set with George and Gracie as they share a laugh in their "living room." (*Courtesy USC*)

Cast and crew take a moment to read a review. Left to right, standing:
Phil Tannura (cameraman), George, Nat Thurlow (original prop man),
Ralph Levy. Seated: Gracie, Harry Von Zell. (Courtesy Ralph Levy)

ing to George's talents. "A lot of people who write comedy don't understand comedy. George is a master." One reason for this may be that George realized it all started with pencil and paper—that writing was the most important thing on the show and without good writing, nothing else mattered. And George had an uncanny knack for recognizing what would play and what wouldn't. It is not uncommon in comedy writing for the dialogue to get bogged down, and a producer to cry, "Send for the writers to add lines." George knew better. He'd send for a scalpel and *cut* lines that were getting in the way of the progress of a scene.

In television today, if somebody on the set doesn't like a line, it can be rewritten on the spot to suit the director or an actor. But once George put his okay on a script, there was no changing it.

"We do our show easily," George said. "We don't try to get all the laughs. There's very little pressure. Most performers work hard and fast. When you watch their show, you eat fast. When you eat fast, you get indigestion and don't watch the show again."

What were some of the ingredients that made "The Burns and Allen Show" so timeless that it still holds up beautifully today? One of the hard-and-fast rules was that the gags could not be topical, primarily because the shows were written months in advance of airing. You will rarely find any political humor. About the closest "Burns and Allen" ever comes to this is the following little bit of chauvinistic humor (although no one thought so at the time):

GEORGE: You know, I hear women say "You've got to be clever because it's a man's world. They run everything." That's not true. There's no law that says a woman can't be President—unless she happens to be a Republican.

Nor are there many references to the fifties era. Most stories center on the universal aspects of daily life that are still a part of the world in the 1980s—maintaining the house-

hold, buying clothes, entertaining friends, etc. Of course, the
show undeniably has the *look* of the 1950s—Gracie's tightly
curled hairdos and long, full skirts attest to that. And it was
only natural that, as a product of its time, the show would see
Gracie as a kitchen-bound housewife in those pre–women's-lib
days, dependent upon her husband for an allowance, fearful
of facing George if she put yet another dent in the car's
fender:

VON ZELL: Gracie, why are you washing clean dishes?
GRACIE: I haven't any dirty ones. I've been too upset to eat.
VON ZELL: You *are* upset.
GRACIE: Yes, but upset or not, a woman has to do her
    housework.

And observe this remark by George:

> How do you like Gracie trying to hide that dented fender
> from me? Wives and husbands shouldn't have secrets
> from each other . . . unless they have a television show
> and it helps the plot.

Occasionally there's some reference to current prices
that will have you longing for the bygone days of the fifties,
as in this question of Harry Morton's:

> Blanche, what's the use of owning a lovely twenty-five-
> thousand-dollar home if we have to go somewhere else to
> fight?

Or the time Blanche is on the phone with the grocer and
asks the store to send the bill for last week's order. She nearly
faints when she learns the charges:

> Oh, by the way, how much is it? Eighty-four dollars? Are
> you sure? Oh, that's right, Mr. Morton ate out a couple
> of nights.

The laugh comes because not only is eighty-four dollars an outrageous amount to spend for one's weekly groceries, but it is actually *less* than Blanche is accustomed to spending, given hubby Harry's monstrous appetite.

The writers were inadvertently prophetic from time to time. Over the years they predicted—and pooh-poohed—many things we take for granted today, all unheard-of at the time. For example, owning your own telephone:

Gracie opens an envelope:
GRACIE: Another phone bill?
GEORGE: Well, sure, we get one every month. I've been paying it for fifteen years.
GRACIE: Well, when is it going to be ours?
GEORGE: Look, Gracie, it's never going to be ours. You don't buy the phone! . . .

Frozen yogurt:
Perhaps one of Harvey Helm's unusual magazines was the inspiration for this scheme of Harry Morton's. Harry has been talking about John Waldo Atterbury, the famous chemist who invented a process for freezing meats and vegetables so they could be sold in packages:

HARRY: Soon a new product will be made available to the public—frozen yogurt.
BLANCHE *(Sarcastically):* Oh, we must give a cocktail party for him.
HARRY: He doesn't drink.
BLANCHE: Harry, he couldn't have invented frozen yogurt when he was sober.

The invention of smog devices:
Harry Von Zell tries to entice George into financing his latest scheme. From a $7500 investment in a gizmo you attach to the exhaust pipes of cars, George and Harry project that

they will make millions selling the devices for one dollar each
to 14 million car owners. The purpose of these gadgets? To do
away with smog. Outrageous!

The hardest task before the writers each week was coming up
with clever dialogue for Gracie. There were several areas that
were always available to them, and these could be counted on
to turn up at least once during any given episode. For instance, there was Gracie and the phone:

BLANCHE: I want to change my clothes and go down to the
     telephone company. We have to put a longer cord on our
     telephone.
GRACIE: Oh, you don't have to do that. We have an extra-long
     · cord on our phone.
BLANCHE: How can that help me, honey?
GRACIE: Well, you phone me and when I answer, you keep
     pulling on your end until it's the right length.

Gracie and electricity:

GEORGE: What's that?
GRACIE: Electric cords. I had them shortened. This one's for
     the iron, this one's for the floor lamp.
GEORGE: Why did you shorten them?
GRACIE: To save electricity.

Gracie and cooking:
     Gracie is preparing dinner and has two roasts in the oven,
a big one and a little one. Why? Because she knows that's the
secret to cooking a perfect roast. At a dinner party, she announces to her guests: "The little roast is burning, the big
one's ready. Let's eat."
     Another common Gracie-ism was her use of mixed meta-
phors:

GEORGE: Gracie, I can straighten this whole thing out in no
     time.

GRACIE: It's too late—you've buttered your bread, now sleep in it.

GRACIE: It was my first experience in politics, but I took to it like a cat takes to water.
GEORGE: Gracie, you mean a duck.
GRACIE: That doesn't make sense, "Like a cat takes to a duck."

Often the writers would resort to using vaudeville humor—the kind of jokes usually followed by a drummer thumping out "B-dump-bump!"

DOCTOR: Did your parents enjoy good health?
GRACIE: Oh yes, they loved it.

GRACIE: The night before last, George came home from the office feeling terrible.
BLANCHE: Probably flu.
GRACIE: No, he drove the car.

B-dump-bump.

Over the eight-year run of the show, the writers developed a number of running gags—variations on certain jokes that the audience might possibly recall having heard in other episodes, but that were said each time in a slightly different manner. The "Big Roast/Little Roast" joke, for instance, had a "Big Cake/Little Cake" version that worked equally as well:

HARRY MORTON: Two cakes, huh?
GRACIE: Yes, but I'll only be able to eat one.
HARRY: What do you mean?
GRACIE: Well, every time I bake a cake I leave it in five minutes too long and it burns.
HARRY: So?
GRACIE: So, today I put in one cake, and I put in another five minutes later. When the first one starts to burn, I'll know the second one's finished.

There was a running joke about Gracie's system for reading:

GRACIE: Blanche, you know I read a book twice as fast as anybody else. First I read the beginning, and then I read the ending, and then I start in the middle and read toward whichever end I like best.

A variation on this gag was a description of how Gracie serves a meal, as related in one of George's monologues:

Gracie brought in a shrimp cocktail and dessert and asked us all to taste them. Then she said, "Now I'll bring in the meat and you can start with that and eat toward whichever end of the meal you like best."

Another running gag concerned Gracie's concept of the U.S. mail:

GRACIE: Harry, would you mail this letter for me? It's to my mother.
VON ZELL: I'd be glad to. Uh, Gracie, there's no stamp on it.
GRACIE: It's all right. There's nothing inside.
VON ZELL: You're sending your mother an empty envelope?
GRACIE: I wanted to cheer her up. You know, no news is good news.

GEORGE: *(weighing letter in his hand):* This letter feels kind of heavy. I'd better put another three-cent stamp on it.
GRACIE: What for? It'll only make it heavier.

(Remember the days when a letter cost only three cents?)

The toothpick joke mentioned in the Preface to this book was so popular that it appeared regularly. In an early episode when the mayor of Los Angeles comes to dinner, he eats an hors d'oeuvre, holds up the toothpick, and says to Gracie,

"This is delicious! What is it?" Looking right at him, she replies, "It's a toothpick." This is used in so many episodes that we congratulate ourselves on correctly anticipating the punch line even before Gracie has a chance to deliver it. The writers subtly alter the gag each time, but we still roar over her remark:

George has just eaten an hors d'oeuvre and is holding the empty toothpick:
GEORGE: Nobody's eating anything. I can't understand it. This is delicious.
GRACIE: Well, if you think that toothpick was delicious, you should have eaten what was on it.

Another type of running gag concerned long lists of women, with Gracie always having the last word:

GRACIE: You can't give up, Blanche. Women don't do that. Look at Betsy Ross, Martha Washington—they didn't give up. Look at Nina Jones.
BLANCHE: Nina Jones?
GRACIE: I never heard of her either because she gave up.

There were lots of runs about Gracie either being in line for something, or in the midst of a large group of people. While she talks to them, the line rapidly gets shorter as one by one the people leave. She's suddenly at the front of the line and asks innocently where everyone has gone. They tell her, "There's a crazy lady in line," and Gracie is relieved that they told her—she doesn't want to run into that lady either!

One of the most anticipated routines was Gracie's famous hat closet. Whenever men who were unfamiliar with Gracie visited the Burns home, they would leave in such a confused hurry that they'd go off without their hats, and Gracie would dutifully label the forgotten hat and place it in a closet that could put Bloomingdale's headgear department to shame. This closet was established very early—we get our first look at it in filmed Show #7—and later we learn that there have been some famous visitors to the Burns household, as we glimpse a general's hat neatly labeled "Eisenhower." The writers easily set us up for the laughs that came with this closet—all we had to do was watch a man take off his hat in Gracie's living room, and we knew that sooner or later we'd be treated to a peek inside that wonderful closet.

Finally, the most famous running gags of all were the Uncle Harvey and other "relative" jokes. Most of these were basically vaudeville routines like the ones George and Gracie did when they first began working together, and the writers would use these runs both during the course of the show and in the closing routines. We learn about this "uncle" of Gracie's very early in the series; in fact, Live Show #9 contains a rare physical description of him. He's a "tall red-headed fellow with a scar on his nose. He got it when he mistook a rabid dog for a glass of beer and tried to blow off the foam." You could tell that there was some sort of family connection with this man who seemed so Gracie-like. Most of our knowledge of him comes from George/Gracie runs like the following:

GRACIE: Uncle Harvey never needed a watch. He always told time by his wallet.

GEORGE: Uncle Harvey told time by his wallet?

GRACIE: Yes. Every night he'd go down to the corner bar and keep looking in his wallet and when it was empty he'd say, "Well, it's time to go home."

GRACIE: Uncle Harvey loves crowds. Crowds and ice cream. That's what he loves. Now, once Uncle Harvey was walking along Main Street eating ice cream. He had two ice cream cones in each hand and suddenly his belt broke.

GEORGE: That must have been terrible.

GRACIE: It was. After he finished eating the ice cream, he had to walk back two miles and get his pants.

Another area the writers had to address themselves to was the commercials. Beginning in 1952, the commercials were filmed separately by McCadden, rather than integrated into the program. It had always been the job of the advertising agency to supply the copy for these ads, and that policy continued, with Charley Lowe in charge. However, from time to time the writers were called upon to create some lead-ins for the commercials—all of which, unfortunately, have been cut from the syndicated version of the show now being aired. One early lead-in came just after George's monologue:

GEORGE: Well, the plot is getting thick again. I think I'll take a little walk until this trouble blows over.

VON ZELL: I'll walk with you, George.

GEORGE: Why, Harry? You in trouble too?

VON ZELL: No. Everybody walks today. People don't ride all the time. You think they spend too much time in cars to be on their feet? You ought to see some of the millions of shoe soles and heels coming out of the big B. F. Goodrich plant in Clarksville, Tennessee. . . .

. . . and on into the commercial.

In another show George is in the middle of his monologue when he looks out the window and says:

GEORGE: I don't believe my eyes. It's snowing in California! *(Cut to Harry Von Zell, in front of the curtain, throwing confetti in the air.)*

VON ZELL: No, George. This is only confetti. I'm just trying to get in the right mood. Selling mud-snow tires from Southern California isn't easy. But snow is a real problem to a lot of motorists. . . .

. . . and the commercial would roll. It was "Burns and Allen" that, on alternate weeks, gave us that wonderful visual image in their B. F. Goodrich commercials of the tire rolling over the board of nails, punctured beyond belief, yet amazingly never going flat, as Harry Von Zell implored, "Think twice—you'll switch to Life Savers."

Not even the show's final moments were exempt from unusual touches by the "Burns and Allen" writing team. Normally, each story was neatly resolved before the closing commercial and final George-and-Grace routine. This was standard. However, there were times when these creative men couldn't resist having some fun with this seemingly routine area. One week in his closing dialogue George suddenly announces, "This show has no ending," and goes on to describe how sometimes his writers can't think of any way to end the show. As he speaks, the camera does a slow fade, the picture irises out to a tiny dot, then disappears into black. But the writers were not content to let this get by the audience. A few weeks later, they did it again:

MRS. QUIGLEY: Mr. Quigley and I always enjoy your television show. But I was crazy about the one you did a couple of months ago when you said you had no finish and the screen closed in around you. Was that your writers' idea?
GEORGE: No, that was the network's idea. You see, when the sponsor is ready to show the product and if you're not off the screen, there's nothing the network can do about it. If they've got to push you off, they push you off.
MR. VANDERLIP: I don't believe that.
GEORGE: You don't? *(Looks at watch; begins walking.)* I know what I'm talking about.

At this point, a widening black band begins moving across the screen as George walks off, ad-libbing. The black area backs him completely off the screen, but he pushes back the "black" as if it were a curtain, and he winks at the audience. Then the screen goes black. (And if you watch Gracie in the background of this scene, you'll note she's completely oblivious to the "show" they're doing—she's busily serving coffee!)

In the show's endings, George often makes reference to the fact that this *is* a show we're watching. In Show #74, a marriage counselor is needed to help the Mortons with an imagined problem, but he doesn't arrive until the very last scene. George proclaims:

GEORGE: I'm sorry, doctor, our time is up, but if you stay right here and don't move you can talk to Arthur Godfrey.

(Godfrey's show was on right after "Burns and Allen.")

In another show, everyone has been waiting for a plumber to show up. Finally, at the end of the show, they are leaving to go to dinner when the plumber arrives. George catches him at the door and informs him, "You're too late, the show's over."

The show's closing routines—George and Gracie together, in front of the curtain or on the front porch of their house—were an opportunity for them to plug products, do public-service announcements, or promote some personal venture such as an article written about or by George and/or Gracie. Generally the writers tried to work in some humor, as in this plug for the magazine article written by Gracie:

GEORGE: Gracie, I read the article you wrote for *Woman's Home Companion.* It's wonderful.
GRACIE: Thank you. It's one of the best magazines in the country.
GEORGE: I know. Anyway, it's on the newsstand now. I bought three of them.
GRACIE: George, why buy three? One newsstand is enough.
GEORGE: Say good night.
GRACIE: Good night . . . and don't forget to read my article.

Sometimes the public-service announcements were written in connection with the sponsor, B. F. Goodrich, and were part of a campaign to promote driver safety. Suddenly George and Gracie would turn serious, as they sermonized:

GEORGE: Folks, remember what the National Safety Commission says: Whether you're a driver or a pedestrian, a
moment of carelessness can change your life or take it
from you. Accidents don't always happen to the other
fellow.

GRACIE: Be careful. The life you save may be your own.

GEORGE: That's right. Say good night.

GRACIE: Good night.

Not the sort of thing comedy writers thrive on. Fortunately,
that little bit of business over, the "Love Nest" theme music
would cheerily chime in, Harry Von Zell would announce the
evening's guest cast, and we'd all bid farewell to George and
Gracie until next week.

FADE TO BLACK

16

BUSINESS

AS USUAL

GEORGE: *You ever notice the long words Harry uses? An ordinary man could take one of Harry's words, break it into pieces, and have enough for a whole day's conversation.*

During the summer of 1953, with a full season of filmed shows comfortably under their belts, several changes were made in the staff of "Burns and Allen."

Ralph Levy, who had originated the look of the series with George, had to bow out. In 1952, when the network saw how well "Burns and Allen" was received, they convinced Jack Benny that he too should go on television. And once again, they called Ralph Levy. Benny's show was to be done live, every other week, from Hollywood. For the past year, Ralph simultaneously had been doing both "Burns and Allen" and "The Jack Benny Show"—a show and a half a week; although, as Levy put it, "I was young and I managed to survive." But it had taken its toll, and in 1953, Ralph told a disappointed George that he was going to have to give up one or the other. Ralph had always preferred live television over film—the thrill of opening night that was missing from filming on a soundstage.

Ralph would be missed by all who had worked so closely with him over the past three years. Bea Benaderet's son, Jack Bannon, said, "He was wonderful to watch. He knew what he was doing. Most people kind of mumble and fake it, but Ralph knew what he wanted. People responded and worked well for him because they felt comfortable with him." The production staff had similar words of praise. Herb Browar, whose responsibility it was to see that Ralph's vision was made a reality (even though that often required altering the vision to fit the technical availability), said of Levy, "Ralph was such a bright guy. Always way ahead of you. Once he had faith in you, he never bothered you. Whatever you wanted, he'd shoot it that way." Levy himself, in looking back over his career, summed up his experience with "Burns and Allen": "It was a great thrill working with those people."

Ralph went on to continue breaking new ground in television history. He produced and directed "Salute to Rodgers & Hammerstein"—the first entertainment show to be telecast simultaneously on all three networks; he won a directorial Emmy for "Shower of Stars"; in addition to the "I Love Lucy" pilot, he directed the pilots for "The Beverly Hillbillies," "Green Acres," "Life with Luigi," and "The Groucho Marx Show." He was the producer/director for NBC's "The Bob Newhart Show" in the 1960s, and directed two seasons of "Petticoat Junction," as well as several motion pictures. In the 1970s, Levy moved to Europe, continuing to produce and direct all over the world, before returning to the United States to make his home in Santa Fe, New Mexico. Not content to retire, Levy is still active in theater in his home state, and lectures frequently at the College of Santa Fe.

In television as well as the Broadway stage, "The show must go on," and the search for a new producer/director began. The man selected, Fred de Cordova, had a strong theatrical background. He was a stage manager on Broadway for *Ziegfeld Follies* (1935), and directed the popular *Hell-*

zapoppin' as well as other successful plays. In 1945 he moved to Hollywood and for the next seven years directed close to twenty motion pictures including *Desert Hawk* with Rock Hudson and Ronald Reagan's *Bedtime for Bonzo*.

Meanwhile, Fred Clark had been offered a part in *The Teahouse of the August Moon* on Broadway. He missed his wife and New York, and with everyone's blessings left the "Burns and Allen" family.

The next (and final) "Harry Morton," Larry Keating, came to television after having made thirty-six big-budget motion pictures. Born in St. Paul, Minnesota, in 1899, Keating's early schooling took him from Oregon and San Francisco to Sydney, Australia—where he saw his uncle Tommy Burns, onetime world heavyweight boxing champion, lose his title to Jack Johnson. In 1917, Keating joined the Oregon Cavalry, and at the end of World War I, he shipped aboard a freighter as a seaman in order to see the world.

Keating's father pioneered theaters in the St. Paul area, and when Larry returned to the United States, his talent as an actor was quickly established. He toured with various stock companies and in 1920 landed on Broadway, where he worked until 1934. He then abruptly changed careers and went into radio as an announcer. In 1949, a studio scout visited ABC's "This Is Your FBI," and, ignoring the rest of the show's cast, singled out Keating for a movie screen test, resulting in his roles in such well-known films as *When Worlds Collide, A Lion Is in the Streets*, and *Come Fill the Cup*, with James Cagney.

Changing actors in the middle of a series is always a problem for the other regular cast. Sponsors and network executives become nervous and wonder if it wouldn't be better to have new "neighbors," rather than replacing just the husband or wife. Fortunately, Bea Benaderet didn't have to worry. George never took those concerns any more seriously than did most viewers. His philosophy of always being honest

with his audience had paid off in the past. He would simply
say, "We've got a new Harry Morton," and that would take
care of it.

And that's more or less how it happened. On that first
telecast of the fourth season, viewers were not aware of anything different about "Burns and Allen." Blanche and Harry
had had a fight, and Blanche was waiting for him to come
home. About seven minutes into the show, Blanche heard
Harry coming. She grabbed a heavy catalogue and held it
over her head, ready to clobber Harry with it as he walked in
the door. At this moment, George stepped out from the side
of the stage and said: "Stop the camera!"

Blanche froze her position, catalogue poised, while
George continued:

Ladies and gentlemen, I have a very important announcement to make. For the past two and a half years, the part
of Blanche's husband, Harry Morton, was played by Fred
Clark. But this year Fred went to New York City to
appear in a Broadway show, so we had to get a new
Harry Morton. Incidentally, this is Blanche's fourth husband on the show. So if you single girls want a little tip,
get into television. We've got a fine actor to play Harry
Morton now, and I'd like you to meet him. Ladies and
gentlemen, it gives me great pleasure to introduce Larry
Keating.

Applause greeted Larry's entrance. George and Larry
stood to the side and took care of the social amenities while
Blanche remained in the background, catalogue still raised
over her head. George then decided it would be nice to introduce Larry to his new wife, and called for Bea to come over.
She lowered the catalogue and stepped over to George and
Larry:

GEORGE: Larry, this is Mrs. Morton, Bea Benaderet. Bea, this
is Larry Keating, your new husband.

BLANCHE: Hello, Larry, I know we'll have a wonderful time working together. I've enjoyed you so much in all those movies you've made.

LARRY: Thank you, Bea. And I've enjoyed your work in the "Burns and Allen" TV series from the very beginning. You've been simply great.

GEORGE: Look, you'd better break this up, if you're going to be nice to each other, nobody will ever believe you're married. Okay, start the show!

George stepped offstage, Bea walked back to her original position and raised the catalogue, Larry walked in through the kitchen door, said, "Hello, dear," and she promptly bopped him on the head with the catalogue. It was business as usual on "Burns and Allen."

The introduction to Larry Keating took place when Gracie was off camera, and yet all through the balance of the show she treated him as though he'd been Blanche's husband for years. It wasn't until the closing routine that Gracie mentioned something seemed amiss:

GRACIE: You know, George, I've been confused all day.

GEORGE: I don't believe it.

GRACIE: There's something entirely different about Harry Morton this week. I finally figured out what it is. He never wore brown shoes before.

GEORGE: Say good night. . . .

The previous Harry Mortons had all been in real estate. With Fred Clark they added his incredible appetite. Larry Keating called for an entirely different type of Harry Morton. No longer in real estate, Morton would now be a C.P.A., and Blanche's term of affection would become, "My human adding machine." He always wore three-piece suits, and often brought his work home at night to do at the kitchen table. In times of trouble, Harry reached for the bottle of blackberry cordial made by his father in 1938. Harry's was the only

stomach that could handle it. Whereas Fred's Harry would
eat anything that didn't get up and run away, Larry's Harry
was a health-food addict, preferring mushroom sandwiches
on gluten bread and papaya juice. This was added to make him
even more eccentric in an era when yogurt was decidedly
unfashionable. We, as viewers, noticed very subtle changes in
the Morton home. The bookcases in the dining room had always been filled with little ceramic knickknacks; now they
were loaded with books and trophies. One small loving cup in
particular was George's favorite, and every chance he could,
he used it as an ashtray.

Harry Hugh Morton, Jr., had spent his entire life trying
to live up to the image of what his Bostonian father thought
he should be. Thus Harry Morton was overly status conscious, which in addition to giving the character added depth,
provided a completely new arena for the writers in which
to use George Burns and Gracie Allen as neighbors. New
challenges for the writers also came with the concept that
Harry Morton, as played by Keating, was now an ambula-
tory thesaurus. While on a plane bound for Paris, Harry
turns to George to ask the simple question, "Look what
our wives have gotten us into now. What next?" Instead,
it comes out:

HARRY: George, we have cherished our wives with an abiding
    constancy and lavished upon them all the worldly goods
    at our command. Do they repay our openhanded bounty
    and staunch devotion with a commensurate esteem? No.
    Instead they concoct Machiavellian schemes to hoodwink
    and defraud us, proving again that the guile and deceit
    of womankind is a perpetual menace to the unwary male.
    How far can they go?
GEORGE: That I don't know about them. But we've traveled a
    hundred miles since you started that last sentence.

Harry and Blanche's marriage gains some new zip with
the addition of Larry Keating. They still fight:

BLANCHE: Oh, I wish I was a man! I'd knock some of that pompousness out of you.
HARRY: Yes, it's too bad you're not a man. We might have been good friends.

Blanche still gets in her digs to Harry. When he accuses her of seeing another man, Blanche retorts with:

Since the day I married you thirteen years ago, there's *never* been a man in my life!

Even Harry's critiques of Gracie to Blanche take on added dimension coming from Keating's characterization:

Your dear friend's brain is like the eye of a hurricane. It is a vacuum, yet wherever it goes, havoc is wreaked.

Larry Keating described the transition from dramatic actor to comedian as "tough going" (*TV Guide*, November 6, 1953): "Switching suddenly to farce comedy is like facing up to a southpaw boxer. Takes you a little time to get the hang of it. [At first] I was reacting normally to George's lines—and when you react normally to a farcical situation you look ridiculous. You have to exaggerate to make it believable. Screwy, isn't it?"

If new directors and new cast members weren't enough to keep George busy, his plans for the expansion of McCadden were. By the following spring, McCadden was filming the commercials that were used on "Burns and Allen," and Paul Henning's idea for a series starring Bob Cummings was in production, with Paul as producer.

"The Bob Cummings Show" first aired on January 2, 1955, and would remain a hit series for the next five years, as well as garnering two Emmys for Ann B. Davis as Shultzy in the Supporting Actress category.

Because McCadden was coproducer with Cummings's

Laurmac Productions, George took an active interest in all the
writing, casting, and directing. "The Bob Cummings Show"
was shot the same way as "Burns and Allen"—all in one day,
but with only two cameras. On rehearsal day George made it
a point to dash over to Stage 6 for their run-throughs, always
fine-tuning the dialogue and direction. At least once a day he
would stop in and meet with the writers to offer what advice
he could for their scripts.

Although Jack Benny's show was still being done live,
Benny did about six specials, directed by Ralph Levy, that
were put on film. McCadden had the facilities, and knowing
the longtime friendship between Benny and Burns, CBS
asked George if they could use McCadden's complex. Only
one of these specials was never able to be rerun. In it, George
reprised his old vaudeville act of "Goldie, Fields, and Glide"
with Benny and Bing Crosby playing Goldie and Fields, complete with white carnations, striped ties, and straw hats. Unfortunately, Crosby had asked for the same amount of money
in rerun residuals that he was initially paid to do the show. At
that time such a request was unheard of, and consequently
after the first airing it was never seen again.

McCadden continued to grow, with CBS wanting to use
their facilities to produce "Life with Father," starring Leon
Ames. However, the General Service lot was filled up. "Burns
and Allen" were on Stage 1, Volcano Productions had Stages
2 and 3, Ann Sothern's "Private Secretary" and "The Lone
Ranger" shared Stage 4, "Ozzie and Harriet" was on Stage
5, and Bob Cummings was on Stage 6. Where were they going
to put "Life with Father"? There was an unused "tank" (for
filming water sequences) that the construction department
had taken over as a scene dock to house extra sets, walls, and
backdrops. These lost out to the need for the additional stage,
and seven and a half weeks later Stage 7 proudly stood where
the tank had been. Filming was under way on this latest
McCadden production.

17

ASSORTED NUTS

AND BOLTS

If one guy doesn't do his job and pull up the curtain, nobody *goes on! Everybody's job is important—each person is part and parcel of a show.*
—GEORGE BURNS, 1984

Viewers of most television shows are aware of the cast and sometimes of the writing and directing, but George Burns knew it took more than great actors and writers to produce a good product. As often as he gave credit to his writers in his monologues, he also made sure that others on his staff got fair mention.

In Show #55, Gracie has been called for jury duty. Since George can't afford to be without Gracie for a whole month, he and Harry Von Zell try to figure out which staff member they can send in her place. Harry had made sure to ask George for that month's check in advance before offering any suggestions.

VON ZELL: . . . You can't spare Freddie de Cordova, the director. He's very important. You can't spare Joe, his assis-

tant. Can't get along without Phil Tannura, the cameraman. You'd have no show. You can't spare any of the
stage crew. We need them. Couldn't spare the makeup
man. You can't spare me. . . . *(George looks up at him.)*
You're paying me in advance. I don't know how to say
this, but actually, George, there's only one person we can
get along without.
GEORGE: Who's that?
VON ZELL: Sign the check first.
GEORGE: You said it fine.

When not referred to directly, the staff's names were
often used as character names in the scripts. This was more
than just fun for everyone—it was a necessity to use "safe"
names in case someone in the audience with the same name
was offended or embarrassed by the actions of a character
with his name. During the run of "Burns and Allen," we met
"Ruth Henning" (Paul's wife) of the Beverly Hills Uplift Society; "Herbert Browar," a personality consultant; "Little
Charley Lowe," a young boy; "Dick Fisher," a production
manager (Dick Fisher was the name of George's real production manager); "Bob Sweeney" of the "McCadden Finance
Company"; "Al Simon," another production manager; and An-
thony C. Montenaro, the set decorator, became "Tony Montenaro," Uncle Harvey's neighbor. Even phone numbers were
used cautiously. In the early episodes, George and Gracie's
home phone number, CRestview 5-4221, was actually a rotary
number of Saks's Beverly Hills switchboard, and later the
number was changed to CR4-5199 (which now belongs to First
Interstate Bank).

Joe Depew, the assistant director, was with "Burns and
Allen" from the first episode right through to the last. He
started his career in film as an actor before moving behind
the camera. Once the director had made his creative decisions on how the show would be shot, it was Joe's job to
make sure everyone on the crew knew what those shots

would be and when each actor would be working. On the anniversary of the one hundredth show, Depew said he was eagerly looking forward to the next four hundred. He wanted to be there every Wednesday at 9:00 A.M. to say, "Quiet . . . and roll 'em!"

There is a history of strong loyalty among the "Burns and Allen" staff, and Nat Thurlow was a perfect example. Al Simon and Herb Browar first met Nat on "I Love Lucy," where he was the property master. When Herb and Al began work on "Burns and Allen," they brought Nat with them. In the early years of doing the series, Nat's eyesight began to fail. Although he was still able to see objects, he could no longer read clearly. He offered to quit, but the unanimous response was no. They knew that in order for Nat to be eligible for his full pension, he would have to continue working. He was made assistant prop man, and Joe Thompson was brought in as property master.

Joe was in charge of all props used on the show. These are anything the actor actually touches. If a cup and saucer, for example, are visible on a shelf, but never handled, they are considered "set dressing," but if one of the actors is drinking from a cup, then it becomes a prop.

In 1923, when the General Service lot was called The Hollywood Studio, Thompson was an assistant director. He worked with Cecil B. DeMille for close to twenty years before moving on to work with comedians like Jack Benny and Burns and Allen. Back in the early days of vaudeville, Thompson's sister was a cashier at the Orpheum Theater and his brother was an usher. Each night they would come home praising the team of Burns and Allen, but it would be the mid-1950s before Joe finally got to work with them.

George frequently used his monologues to fill us in on the details of production, and in one of those he made sure we noticed the props. In this particular episode, Blanche, Von Zell, and Harry Morton have prepared a steak for George, whom they think is about to commit suicide. While tearfully discussing George's fate, they all pick at the steak. After the scene, George steps out:

> How do you like that acting? It wasn't easy to stage that. One wanted the steak rare, one medium, and one well done. So we compromised. That steak they were eating was a piece of bread covered with gravy. That's why the crying was so real.

Al Simon and Herb Browar first met each other in Riverside, California, where they were both enlisted in the Air Force. They not only remained good friends, but continued to work together throughout their careers. These two men saw to it that anytime someone on the staff or crew was ill, everyone else was alerted. They always arranged for flowers to be sent, and whenever possible Herb and Al would take time to visit those who were hospitalized. When Jimmy Lloyd, a grip (lighting man) for the show, retired, Al and Herb, knowing how he had always wanted to paint, bought him a thousand dollars' worth of artist's supplies.

Bertha (Bert) French, Gracie's hairstylist, was another person who, as a young girl, used to watch George and Gracie at the Palace; she would think to herself that someday she'd like to do Gracie's hair. She had a natural talent for styling, and left high school at fifteen to go to New York and pursue her dream. Seventeen years later she moved to Los Angeles, where she was responsible for the tresses of such famous actresses of the era as Lucille Ball, June Havoc, Spring Byington, Eve Arden, and Joan Davis. Her lifelong goal was finally realized when she signed on for the first filmed "Burns and Allen" show.

Gene Roemer, George and Gracie's makeup man, had an extensive motion-picture background. Before coming to television, he had been the makeup artist for Marilyn Monroe, Zsa Zsa Gabor, Barbara Stanwyck, Irene Dunne, and

Rosalind Russell. No wonder Gracie always looked so beautiful.

The staff of "The Burns and Allen Show" were constantly looking for ways to show their appreciation to George and Gracie. One of the first things Herb and Al decided to do was give Gracie a bungalow of her own to use as a dressing room and place to rest when she wasn't needed on the stage. At first, the only dressing room they had for Gracie was a trailer, as there were only a couple of available bungalows on the lot and those were reserved for guest stars. As soon as one became available, Herb grabbed it, and had the art department decorate it, using pastel colors and wallpaper with tiny rosebuds. Gracie knew nothing about it until the day they surprised her by handing her the key.

But as often happens with good intentions, there was one little flaw. The bungalow was quite a distance from the stage, so whenever Gracie needed to use the rest room, she had a long hike to get to her new dressing room. When it rained, the streets would flood, so someone always had a car standing by. Rod Amateau, who was directing "The Bob Cummings Show" and was also a close friend of the family, realized something had to be done. He talked it over with George, who went to Herb to find out if some kind of bathroom could be built on the set.

Stage 1 backed up to the editing rooms, and Herb discovered that he could run plumbing lines from the rest rooms in the editing building to the wall that separated the two structures. The stage wall was only three feet thick, but it was enough to build a small guest bathroom. He went to Jimmy Nassar, who with his brother George ran General Service Studios, and told him what he wanted to do. Jimmy agreed, and the studio paid for Herb to build the room right in the wall of the soundstage. Said Herb, "It was the narrowest bathroom you ever saw." While they were at it, they converted the nearest editing room into a private dressing room for George, so he too had a place of his own by the stage.

On the other side of that stage wall you'd usually find Stan
Frazen and Larry Heath, the editors. Frazen was supervising
editor, and he cut the picture, while Larry worked primarily
with the sound. By the second year, Larry was cutting picture
as well as supervising the sound editing.

Although George and Gracie did not want to film their
show in front of a live audience, they did want the natural
sounds of laughter to be on the track. Every other Thursday,
George would take two edited episodes with him to RCA
Sound Studios on Orange Avenue in Hollywood, where two
hundred lucky viewers were invited to come to a preview
screening of two "Burns and Allen" shows. It was at these
screenings that the actual laughter of the people watching the
shows for the first time was recorded and added to the sound
track of the show.

For anyone else, the job of cutting a show to allow for
laughter that was to come much later might have been a
tough job. Fortunately for Stan and Larry, George knew instinctively the size, quality, and length of every laugh the
preview audience would give.

There is an old adage that "comedy timing can't be
taught." Whoever said that never watched George Burns on
a film stage. Robert Easton, an actor who had the recurring
role of Brian McAfee on "The Burns and Allen Show" in the
later years, offered an inside look at George's uncanny knack
for timing. "George would say to me, 'Bob, when Gracie says
that line, I want you to count one—two—three; I want you to
look at me and count one—two; then look back at Gracie and
count one—two—three—four; *then* you say your line.' If you
did it exactly as he told you, he was right every time.

"When the audience watched the finished film, Gracie
would say her line, I'd do what George said—the 'take' to her,
the 'take' to him, back to her—and the laugh would build and
build and crest and then start to come down just at the magic
moment as if we were doing it onstage. My character on
screen would come in exactly at the fraction of a second that
was right."

At the preview screenings, George, Gracie, and often other members of the cast would be there. George and Gracie would do one of their old vaudeville routines and then say, "Now we're going to sit down and enjoy the show with you." The audience loved it, and would laugh that much harder.

George's first entrance on film was always greeted with show-stopping applause. Whenever Gracie was in the thick of a plot and about to get in deeper, the audience would go "Uh-oh . . ." and "Oh, no!" All of these comments were left on the sound track, adding to the illusion that the show was filmed in front of an audience.

Deciding how to record the laughter was difficult. Six hidden microphones would pick up the sounds of the audience. Unfortunately, they also picked up the dialogue coming from the speakers—creating an echo effect on the sound track. In addition, if the editors had to go back in and cut the show after the laughter had been recorded, they couldn't—because they could hear the rerecorded dialogue on the laugh track. Some shows, like "Private Secretary" and "Ozzie and Harriet," had the audience put on headphones to hear the dialogue clearly without the mikes picking it up, but it also meant that they couldn't hear each other's laughter. Consequently, their laughs always sounded slightly self-conscious. Stan and Larry were able to solve the problem of the echo by simply adjusting a few sprocket holes in the track, but that couldn't help if they had to recut. Therefore, it was imperative that the shows be timed perfectly.

In the mid-fifties, there was a lot of talk about canned laughter on television shows. There were three ways to get laughter on a sound track: (1) you filmed in front of an audi-- ence; (2) you played the finished show for an audience and recorded their laughter separately, and (3) there was the little black box. Out of this device one could get anything from a titter to a maniacal cackle of prerecorded laughter. A more sophisticated version of this box is used today to "sweeten" shows—that is, add laughs where there were none on the sound track. Networks today invariably insist on these laughs being in every half-hour comedy, but back in the fifties, they seemed to think there was something spooky about laughs coming from a box, and one network even banned its use. George was very honest with his laugh track, and in many interviews commented: "If at these previews we're unlucky and a joke lays an egg, we cut in a chuckle—about what the joke is worth. In other words, we allow it to lay an egg, but not a complete egg." He and the director would work together to make sure there was coverage and legitimate business going on wherever there was a line that should get a laugh. One camera was always on the person making the joke, the second on the person reacting. If Gracie had the joke, she might also be carrying a vase of flowers. After her line, she could take the vase, walk across the set and place it on a table. The other camera would stay on George's reaction to her line. If no laugh came on George's reaction, after the screening the editors would use the piece of film that showed Gracie setting the flowers down. This would fill the hole where laughter might have been, and because there was nothing funny about setting down flowers, no one missed a laugh.

Friday morning, around 7:30, Stan and Larry would run the two shows for George and take out anything that didn't play well. It was here they would decide to sweeten the track if needed. George gave the editors notes only twice on each show—once after the preview and once again after it had aired. He was always striving to make the shows tighter and the laughs time out perfectly. These sessions benefited the editors in their work, and George in his as well.

There seemed to be an unwritten law in the 1950s that housewives, as portrayed on television, always had to be wearing lovely dresses complete with high heels and pearls, even when preparing breakfast or vacuuming the rugs. Donna Reed on "The Donna Reed Show," Jane Wyatt on "Father Knows Best," and Harriet Nelson on "Ozzie and Harriet" are perfect examples of this *Stepford Wives* mentality.

Gracie Allen was no exception, although the real Gracie made it a practice to dress this way in her off-camera life too. Her personal philosophy about her appearance was, "I have nice clothes and I always wear my best, every minute." In fact, in 1955 she was named the best-dressed woman in California by the West Coast designers. It is interesting to note that she was never seen in anything but three-quarter length sleeves, because as a baby she pulled a pot of boiling liquid off the stove, severely burning and scarring her arm and shoulder.

Gracie's reputation for dressing well started in vaudeville. Usually female performers had to wear the same costumes week in and week out. The wear and tear from frequent cleanings (or lack of them) was often visible to the audience. But Gracie's clothes were always impeccable. Her clothes became an asset to the act and were talked about as much as her performance.

In the eight years of "The Burns and Allen Show" she never wore the same outfit twice. In the forty episodes a year, she sometimes wore as many as three different dresses in each show. Both she and Bea Benaderet would do their own shopping for wardrobe, but as much as Gracie loved to shop, Bea hated it. One interviewer said of Bea, "[She was] a traitor to her own sex."

Don Loper designed Gracie's gowns in the early shows, and later De De Johnson of California and Marjorie Michaels received alternating credit for her gowns. Oddly enough, with all these beautiful dresses, what most women watched for each week were the wonderfully feminine aprons Gracie would wear. In fact, her sister Hazel Boyd was once stopped on a San Francisco street by a stranger who told her, "I just love your sister's program. It's wonderful, but what I really like are the aprons she wears. Some of us have formed an apron club. We meet and make aprons like hers." Gracie's reaction: "We pay thousands of dollars for gags, and what do they like? My aprons!" Actually, Gracie had a soft spot for those aprons. They were a constant reminder of her grandmother, Gracie said, who "had the most beautiful ones I've ever seen. In the morning she wore a great long one, at night she wore tucked ones, but the beauties were the organdy and crocheted ones she wore for tea when ladies came."

Since Gracie had to wear so many different outfits in the course of a season, she was forever having wardrobe fittings. All her clothes had to be customized because she was so tiny she couldn't fit into clothes off the rack.

Jane Vogt, the Wardrobe Mistress, was the woman with whom Gracie probably spent most of her waking hours. Jane's droll sense of humor was evident when someone once asked her to tell her age. "[I'm] as old as my tongue and a little older than my teeth. . . . A woman who'll tell her age will tell anything!" And she didn't, either.

Jane had a busy schedule each week. In addition to being responsible for Gracie's clothes, she oversaw the rest of the cast's as well. At the Monday production meeting it was decided what type of outfit Gracie would wear. Then Jane would contact the other members of the cast to make sure they didn't plan on wearing the same colors or patterns. Tuesday she started at 9:00 A.M., checking in the wardrobe ordered for that week's show and going over all the other clothes to be used. Tuesday was also the day she sewed Gracie's wonderful aprons. Wednesday, filming day, began at 6:00 A.M., with Jane making all the last-minute wardrobe checks. At the end of the day, she gathered everything that hadn't been used so it could be returned. Thursday the returns were made and Jane did her bookkeeping. She kept a log of every outfit worn on the show—right down to the accessories. Friday was her day off, while Gracie went shopping for the next week's show.

Christmastime at McCadden was always fun, especially as the company grew, and more and more people joined the staff. Presents were chosen by drawing a name from a hat, with a predetermined price limit on all gifts. Each year, Santa would make a grand entrance on the soundstage where the Christmas party was held. Herb Browar was the man behind the white whiskers—a tradition begun when he did a favor for Al Simon by showing up dressed as Santa for Al's four-year-old son, David. (David Simon, incidentally, grew up to be the man who was director of planning for the 1984 Olympics under Peter Ueberroth.)

Making a unique entrance each year became quite a challenge for Herb. One year Herb borrowed the mock-up of the Krider-Reisner bi-plane used in the "Bob Cummings Show," climbed in the cockpit wearing his Santa gear and carrying his sack of presents, and had a studio guard pound on the large soundstage door. When the huge steel door was rolled up, to everyone's delight, in coasted Santa with goggles and flowing scarf.

Gracie always did her own Christmas shopping, carefully choosing each gift, usually something for the home. There was always a personal touch to her presents. George, too, would pick out the gifts for those closest to him, although, like the Lone Ranger, before you could thank him, he'd disappeared. He loved to give, but was embarrassed by thank you's.

Color was coming to television and only one network, NBC, had it. Periodically, their rainbow-colored peacock would show up on the screen to proudly announce that the following program would be broadcast in "compatible color."

Because television sets had such small screens, CBS and ABC both felt people would rather go to a movie to see color pictures than watch them at home, and so they stuck with black and white. Conversely, even though the film studios had the technology, the motion-picture exhibitors feared that if money were put into producing color television shows, people would *stop* going to the movies. George Burns, with his innate knowledge of human nature, summed up the situation in simple terms. "Even if people have a cook, it doesn't mean they won't go to a restaurant once in a while."

That may have eased the minds of the movie studios, but it didn't offer any answer to the television networks. Audi-

ences that could afford the new color sets began turning away
from their favorite programs to watch NBC shows because
they were broadcast in color. And, when audiences turn away,
sponsors get worried.

Both CBS and ABC saw the writing on the wall, but ABC
held back, while CBS took action. If CBS was to survive, it
would have to make the transition to color, and in 1954 it
allocated funds for certain of its programs to do a trial color
episode. "Burns and Allen" was one of the shows chosen.

The script was typical "Burns and Allen": George has
invited the press to the house to watch their fifth season
opener, and he is busy instructing Gracie on the proper things
to say. Gracie, wanting to help, invites a group of strangers
to come over and watch the show, too.

The filming went very smoothly, thanks to the help of a
color expert sent over by the network to assist the production
crew. Not until the editors went to work the following day did
they realize something drastically wrong had happened to the
sound during shooting. All of the dialogue was garbled,
sounding as if someone had put his thumb on a record while
it was playing, and the speakers were under water. Nothing
like this had ever happened before, and because this was a
one-time-only special show, there was no way they could re-
shoot. The cost of this one episode was double what a normal
episode cost, and everyone feared what would happen when
George learned of the problem. The editors told him there
would be no film to look at on Friday because "the lab had
screwed up." No one ever questioned this explanation. Labs
have been the excuse for every mistake imaginable in the
history of filmmaking.

The first order of business was to discover what had
caused the problem. It was traced to the young man who
recorded all the dialogue. On his sound box there were two
switches for the motor—one marked "constant" and the other
marked "variable." It was his first day on the job, and he
accidentally hit the switch for the variable motor while recording. Normally, this speed is used strictly for recording "wild

(PRECEDING PAGE) Gracie cleans Ralph Levy's glasses with her latest apron. According to Ralph, "Every five minutes she would take off my glasses and clean them." (Courtesy Ralph Levy)

(BELOW, LEFT) George and Ralph Levy take a break on set. Their instant dislike of each other upon meeting soon gave way to mutual respect and friendship. (Courtesy Ralph Levy)

(OPPOSITE) Larry Keating, better known as the fourth (and final) Harry Morton. (Courtesy USC)

(BELOW, CENTER) Harry Morton (Larry Keating) and his wife, Blanche (Bea Benaderet). This Harry was an accountant, and at times he seemed more married to his job than to his wife. (Courtesy Jack Bannon)

(BELOW, RIGHT) Harry and Blanche (Larry and Bea). He was actually the most affectionate of Blanche's four husbands, even going so far as to give her an occasional kiss. (Courtesy USC)

*Harry Von Zell and George, ready for yet another costume party, take a
break from the day's shooting. (Courtesy USC)*

Advertising agency rep Charles Lowe drops off some of the sponsor's products. Charley (husband of actress Carol Channing) was responsible for the Carnation commercials. (Courtesy USC)

(ABOVE) *Gracie readies another hat for her famous closet. Harry Von Zell and George watch bemusedly, while the Mortons seem on the verge of hysteria. (Courtesy USC)*

(RIGHT) *Taking time out from a writing session, George and brother Willy Burns (in dark glasses) relax a moment with director Ralph Levy and Gracie. (Courtesy Ralph Levy)*

(*OPPOSITE, TOP*) *An intensive writing session at the McCadden offices. Left to right: Tommy Clapp (the writers' secretary), George, and Harvey Helm. (Courtesy USC)*

(*OPPOSITE, BOTTOM*) *Writers Norman Paul (left) and Keith Fowler (right) and George enjoy laughing at their latest joke. Note the set photos above. (Courtesy USC)*

(*BELOW*) *George breaks up as he hears a new joke from one of his writers. Although he sat in on every writing session, he never took screen credit as a writer. (Courtesy USC)*

(*LEFT*) *Harry Von Zell, announcer-cum-actor, set for a day at the beach.* (*Courtesy USC*)

(*BELOW*) *Harry Von Zell with executives from B. F. Goodrich, the alternate sponsor, going over the latest commercial script.* (*Courtesy USC*)

(*FAR BELOW*) *A rare scene in the Burnses' bedroom. Note the complete bathroom set.* (*Courtesy USC*)

Harry Morton (Larry Keating) wows Gracie with his pugilist's physique.
(Courtesy USC)

(BELOW) *Blanche, Harry, and Harry Von Zell watch as Gracie makes a final makeup check before they take a trip together.* (*Courtesy Jack Bannon*)

(FAR BELOW) *Harry Ackerman, then CBS Television vice-president in charge of programming, presents Burns and Allen with silver film cans, holding prints of their one hundredth filmed show.* (*Courtesy USC*)

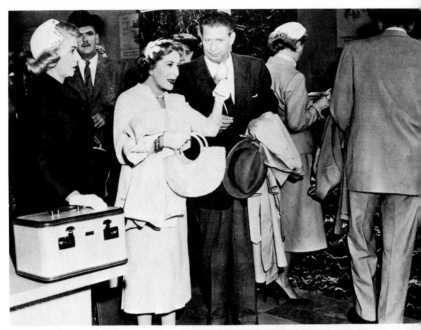

(*LEFT, TOP*) *George Burns, on the "den" set, studying scripts for his "television show"—the one we never see.* (*Courtesy USC*)

(*LEFT, BOTTOM*) *George Burns the pitchman. McCadden did a series of commercials for the Colgate Company.* (*Courtesy USC*)

(*OPPOSITE*) *"Goldie, Fields, and Glide." On "The Jack Benny Show," Jack (left) is joined by George Burns and Bing Crosby (right) in a reprise of George's vaudeville days at the Palace. A copy of this photo can be seen in the set of George's "den."* (*Courtesy Herb Browar*)

(ABOVE) *Ralph Levy, who left "Burns and Allen" to do "The Jack Benny Show," checks the marks for the "Goldie, Fields, and Glide" act with Jack, Bing, and George. (Courtesy Ralph Levy)*

(BELOW) *Gracie's many handmade aprons were very popular with the ladies of the audience. Here, in an early show, Ralph Levy directs the Burnses in a kitchen scene. (Courtesy Ralph Levy)*

lines"—that dialogue spoken off camera to be cut into the show later, or to dub over an existing line of dialogue during editing. Consequently, all the dialogue during filming was recorded at the wrong speed.

RCA owned up to the responsibility. It was their sound man who goofed, and it was now their obligation to fix it. Larry Heath remembers it was a gentleman named McDaglish, a sound mixer on RCA's dubbing stage, who saved the day. While McDaglish put every word of dialogue on a loop of tape, Larry put every sequence of film frames that made up a word on another loop. Using a variable-speed motor, they painstakingly matched every frame of picture with the sound, one syllable at a time. It took them the entire weekend. On Monday morning, George watched perfect "dailies" and was none the wiser. In fact, it wasn't until years later that he found out what had happened during the filming of that show.

The October 4, 1954, *TV Guide* had one of its infrequent boxes with the word "COLOR" written beside the CBS heading at 8:00 P.M. When the reviews came out the following day, the fact that it was broadcast in color had no effect on the critics. They gave their customary praise, based solely on the show itself.

> This was one of the hot-shot shows with a crack story that didn't let up on the laffs and knew where it was going every minute of the way. A chance observation by neighbor-pal, Bea Benaderet, causes Gracie to put a flock of strangers on the invitation list. With this motley crowd . . . there began to unfold in rapid vignettes some of the weirdest capers in comedy. . . . It was also the largest cast collection in the show's history and was undoubtedly so booked to afford a mixture of color values (but the program is being appraised here solely as a black-and-whiter).

The press continued to lavish praise on "The Burns and Allen Show," and constantly kept the public alerted to further

goings-on at McCadden. In June 1956, *Daily Variety* as well
as the *Los Angeles Times* and *The New York Times* carried
stories about McCadden's success. Al Simon and Maurice
Morton (business affairs) were given V.P. stripes, and five
series would be going before the cameras next season:
"Burns and Allen," "Bob Cummings," "The People's Choice"
(starring Jackie Cooper), "Impact," and "Courage" (the last
two both developed by Al Simon)—180 new half-hour episodes, each budgeted at $35,000, giving a production outlay
of $6.3 million.

This figure did not include the more than five hundred
commercials that McCadden also produced. Carnation was
still their number-one sponsor, with McCadden filming all the
commercials used on "Burns and Allen," as well as foreign-
language spots and even four Carnation commercials in color
to be used on ABC's "Mickey Mouse Club." Friskies Dog
Food, B. F. Goodrich, Colgate-Palmolive, R. J. Reynolds, and
Procter & Gamble were among the other advertisers working
with McCadden. When asked about the diversification of in-
terests, George Burns replied that he felt it was a sounder
enterprise than dramatic or comedy shows. "A cake of soap
or a piece of steel wool can't blow a line."

As for the sudden rush of new shows, George Eells, in a
Look magazine story, recounted the strategy behind George
Burns's partnership in "The People's Choice": producer Irving Brecher was hoping to persuade Burns to invest in the
show. He began his selling pitch, "This fellow comes through
the woods, and it is Jackie Cooper. And he is followed by a dog
who says . . ." George interrupted, "The *dog* says?" Brecher
told him he'd heard right. George then turned to Maurice
Morton and said, "Give him the money. That's good enough
for me." Burns wasn't acting rashly—he knew he could gamble on Jackie Cooper's popularity, the novelty of
the concept, and Brecher's competence as a producer. "The
People's Choice" (with Cleo, the talking dog) first aired in
October 1955, maintained high ratings, and had a healthy
three-year run.

The Al Simon/McCadden effort, "Impact" (an anthology series to star different actors each week), suffered a rockier start. First announced in *Variety* in January 1956, "Impact" would go through three title changes ("Impasse," "Crisis," and finally "Panic") and fourteen months of postponements before premiering March 5, 1957. "Panic" lasted only one season—but it started a format of using a "hook" or a "teaser" at the top of the show before the opening credits, a technique still being used today.

Besides commercials and new series, McCadden was lining up pilots for the next season, including "The Marie Wilson Show," "The Delightful Imposter," and "Experiment." George supervised all of these new shows, and still found time to make some drastic changes in "The Burns and Allen Show."

18

THERE'LL BE
SOME CHANGES
MADE

The whole family is nuts.
—RONNIE BURNS,
TV Radio Preview (*September 1957*),
WHEN ASKED IF GRACIE WAS
AS FUNNY OFF CAMERA AS ON

In 1955 George Burns decided that he and Gracie should become parents. This idea was conceived in George's fertile brain, from which, like Zeus giving birth to Athena, the "child" sprang forth fully grown. And two episodes into the season they were the proud mom and dad of a bouncing twenty-year-old boy named Ronnie Burns. (Coincidentally, their twenty-year-old son, Ronnie Burns, played this new character.)

At the same time, another innovation occurred in the show's format. It was decided that "Burns and Allen" would be set entirely in New York City. According to director Fred de Cordova, "The decision to move the show locale to New York was made by Mr. Burns . . . [who] thought a new area of humor could be opened to the show by having George and Gracie live in a hotel. They could use bellhops, elevator people, night clerks, et cetera. The only problem was to figure out why Bea and Larry [Blanche and Harry Morton] would be in New York. They worked on it for a long time before they came up with the reason."

Show #157, "The Burnses and Mortons Go to New York," first aired on October 3, 1955. The entire show takes place on a train bound from the West Coast to New York City, and the whole cast is along for the ride. In George's opening monologue he tells the curious audience about the move:

> If you're wondering about this trip, Harry Morton is going to New York because he's got a big accounting job that'll keep him there for months. Gracie's going because she wants to be near Blanche. I'm going because of the food. Not that the food isn't good in Beverly Hills too, but if I don't do our TV show where Gracie is, there is no food.

As they chug across the country, we glimpse periodic stock shots of a speeding train. Occasionally there's a freeze-frame—the train stops, the picture dissolves, and George steps into the entryway to deliver his monologues.

The main plot, of course, is the move to New York and the reasons for it. Also, there is a side story: a famous atomic scientist is aboard, and Von Zell tries to get Gracie and this man together for a publicity photo. But the idea backfires, and Von Zell and George end up wining and dining a traveling salesman, while Gracie indulges herself in her passion for gin rummy, with none other than the famous scientist. At the end of the show George comments on the frequent special effects:

> All right—you knew who the professor was all the time and I didn't. But how many fellows do you know who can stop a train to tell a joke?

But this was not quite the ending of the show. Another new format change, one that would last for the remaining run

of the series, had been made only eight episodes earlier, in
May, with the addition of what became known as the "Afterpiece." Those lovely vaudeville routines between George and
Gracie, in which she tells us the latest in the life of Uncle
Harvey or another equally weird relative, were now done as
an entirely separate segment instead of being buried in the
middle of the show. And, rather than standing on the back
porch, George and Gracie appeared hand in hand in front of
a curtain. George introduced the very first Afterpiece by saying:

> Thank you very much. You've been so nice tonight, Gra-
> cie and I are coming back to entertain you with one of our
> stage routines. Of course, it isn't easy to get Gracie
> started on one of those routines. I'll probably have to say,
> "Well, Gracie, what happened?" And then it'll be hard to
> get her to stop.

One week after the train show, the Burnses and Mortons
were settled into their New York apartments at the St. Moritz
Hotel, when they got a surprise—George and Gracie's son,
Ronnie, arrived. The audience was equally surprised; until
now, there had been no mention of any Burns children, at
least in the lives of the characters they played. Where has
Ronnie been for the past twenty years? Alas, we never learn.

Ronnie has just arrived from California and surprises
George and Gracie. George's reaction, naturally, is to do a
monologue:

> That's my son. Yeah, that really is our son. This is a
> pleasant surprise. You know Gracie and I have a son
> and a daughter. My daughter, Sandy, is happily married
> and has a lovely little girl, and Ronnie was at the
> Pasadena Playhouse studying to be an actor. I wonder
> what he's doing in New York. I'd better go in and see
> him. I'm so anxious to see him I won't even tell my last
> joke.

We learn later in the show that Ronnie is in New York to study at the famous "Actor's Academy." He wants to be a serious dramatic actor and is embarrassed by the fact that his parents do comedy. He eventually is proud of them, but for a long time he thinks comedy is beneath him.

It seems only natural that Ronnie would turn up on "Burns and Allen"; it would have been hard not to have had some of that environment rub off, since both Ronnie and Sandy knew nothing *but* show business from the day they were brought into the Burns household.

Both children had been adopted as infants from an Evanston, Illinois, agency called The Cradle. Sandra Jean arrived first, born July 28, 1934. A year later they added Ronald John to the family, shortly after his birth on July 9, 1935. George and Gracie were living in New York at the time, and Gracie told the press she selected the name Ronald John Burns "because I want him to have a Park Avenue name."

Sandy was a healthy, rapidly growing child, while Ronnie was a delicate, sickly infant who had to be bathed in oil and wrapped in cotton. By the time he reached seven, however, he began a growth spurt that didn't let up until, as an adult, he attained the height of six-foot-one.

Both Ronnie and Sandy graduated from Chadwick High School in Palos Verdes, near the blue Pacific, and it was here that Ronnie began his lifelong interest in the sea. His teen years were filled with the water sports he loved—swimming, diving, surfing, and sailing—and his room at home reflected this passion, with its blue and green lights, which he had acquired from a ship, as well as seashells and trophies from the South Seas and Hawaii.

Sandy attended UCLA and Santa Monica City College and held summer jobs such as receptionist, secretary, and switchboard operator—all parts she later played on "Burns and Allen." During her first year in college she married Young Wilhoite, and they later had four daughters.

Both Sandy and her brother had quite a bit of experience

with the series. Their earliest appearance was in Show #13
(filmed), which opens with them both seated in their living
room, about to watch Mom and Dad's TV show. Neither of
them has any dialogue. Later, Sandy began getting small
parts with one or two lines, but preferred doing voice-overs,
rather than being seen on camera. Her earliest speaking role
was in Show #75, in which she plays a receptionist named
"Miss Wilhoite" (accidentally credited at the end by Harry
Von Zell as "Sandra Burns as Miss *Jones.*") In the show's tag,
she's introduced on the porch by George and Gracie, and she
stands there towering over them, smiling shyly.

Sandy had been a shy, solemn-faced child who seldom
smiled. George cured her of this by promising her a poodle if
she smiled every day for a year. She got the poodle, and began
a lifelong love of animals. At one time she had ambitions that
included everything from breeding poodles, to wanting to be
a nurse, to raising children. She satisfied these by raising
dogs, bearing children, and nursing them all through their
respective types of illnesses. She continued working on
"Burns and Allen," making about thirty appearances altogether. Sandy later divorced and remarried twice (including
a brief marriage to "Burns and Allen" director Rod Amateau). Today she is single again, a grandmother who still
pursues her love of children by teaching school in San Diego.

Ronnie, on the other hand, had early ambitions to follow in his
parents' footsteps and enter the business, with acting his
prime interest. In 1953, at the age of eighteen, he enrolled at
the University of Southern California to study law (at
George's suggestion). A few months later the young man
changed his mind. An excellent artist, he toyed with the idea
of becoming an architect or oil painter. Then he settled down
to study cinematography at USC, working for George at
McCadden Productions as a film cutter during the summer.
He also dabbled in acting, and in 1954 Ronnie appeared in a
short subject for Columbia, entitled *Hollywood Fathers.* In it,
he plays checkers with George.

Ronnie had made several appearances on "Burns and Allen" prior to playing the part of himself, although his early dialogue was usually limited to a line or two. In Show #109 (October 18, 1954) he played "Jim the Groom" and had one line, and like his sister in an earlier show, Mom and Dad introduced him to the audience at the end of the program.

Soon Ronnie began to entertain thoughts of becoming a producer, although he continued to work at polishing his acting. In the summer of 1955 he enrolled at the Pasadena Playhouse, and landed the mature role of the tramp in *Picnic*. It was then that George began to take notice of Ronnie's abilities, but Ronnie was still uncertain as to his future. "Have you ever thought of an acting career?" asked George. "No," said his son. "Think about it," said George.

Soon after that, Ronnie began working full time on "Burns and Allen." "It was not an easy decision for me to make for two reasons," he told the *New York Herald Tribune* (January 27, 1957). "One was because I wanted to be a producer, not an actor, but secondly and probably more important, I was concerned with the personal element likely to be involved when working that closely with my mother and father. I think every guy likes to feel a certain amount of independence, and being the boss' son could present a problem. As things turned out, I couldn't have been more off base. . . . [Dad] assured me that although he and Mother were there to offer counsel, my success or failure was up to me. Though I knew acting was no simple task, I'll have to admit that I felt my new job as a performer wasn't going to be too demanding. After all, I was going to be playing myself, and who else, I thought, knows me as well as I do? Afterwards though, I realized that just walking to the door or chatting across the breakfast table wasn't quite as easy as it is at home. The folks knew then that Ronnie Burns was ready to learn how to play Ronnie Burns. From that day on, every day on the set was an education."

After his first show playing the part of Ronnie Burns, he rushed up to his father and asked, "How was I?" George answered, "The first time I played the Palace with Elsie Janis, my mother was sick. They had to carry her into the theater. After the show I asked her, 'Mama, how was I?' She gave me a hard look that had a little twinkle around the edges and said, 'Elsie was better.' " Ronnie was left to draw his own conclusion.

Actually, both George and Gracie were delighted with their son's performance, and a lot of the fans agreed. Encouraged by his strikingly handsome appearance and obvious teenage appeal, the McCadden publicity office queried viewers, "Would you like to join a Ronnie Burns Fan Club?" Some five thousand viewers wrote back and said, yes, where, and please hurry!

Ronnie's presence added a dimension of domesticity to "Burns and Allen," and, along with the format change involving the move to New York, viewers were now being treated to all sorts of innovations.

New sets for the New York move had to be built on the General Service lot. The Burnses and the Mortons had apartments at the St. Moritz Hotel. A New York skyline was now used for the opening logo of each program, and a similar vista could be seen from the Burnses' twenty-second-floor living room.

Another important set for that year was an ice cream parlor/sandwich shop called "Rumpelmayer's," located off the lobby of the hotel. George made great use of Rumpelmayer's, finding more and more ways of doing scenes there. Carpenters were constantly having to add on to this set, and soon there was a running gag around the studio, with workers elbowing each other and grinning, "They're adding onto Rumpelmayer's again!"

Sometimes, rather than stopping for a bite in Rumpelmayer's, the Burnses would order from room service, and in this way we got to know a new character, Peter the waiter. Peter really looked forward to his encounters with Gracie, as she always gave him some wonderful lines, which in turn made him a hit among the other waiters:

GRACIE: Something smells good.
PETER: It's Mr. Morton's ribs.
GRACIE: Really? George just puts cologne on his face.

And Peter would frantically scribble down her lines on his order pad, eagerly looking forward to telling Gracie's latest to the boys in the kitchen.

About this time, George Burns became the author of his first book, an autobiography entitled *I Love Her, That's Why*. To help with the hype, an entire show was given over to promoting the book. In it, the cast presented a musical version of George's tome, and he and McCadden sent out press releases ("written by" George) to practically every newspaper in the country:

> "The Burns and Allen Show," this night, Nov. 7, will do something off-beat. I've persuaded Mac Gordon, noted song writer, to make one of his rare TV appearances. Story has to do with a syndicate of New York producers making a musical version of my autobiography *I Love Her, That's Why*. The song, "I Love Her, That's Why" will have its world premiere on this telecast, sung by Gracie and me, although I'm no Mario Lanza. I've just changed my mind. I am. Hope you can catch it.

And this show wasn't the last we heard of the book. For the remainder of that season, George would work in its title at least once per show. He even managed to have Ronnie plug the book. In Show #165, George and Gracie are celebrating their anniversary, and at the end of the program, they don party hats and play with noisemakers. Ronnie turns to the camera, and although no one asks a question, he volunteers:

RONNIE: Why? I love them, that's why.

Another departure that season was the presentation of an entire vaudeville show (Show #184, "Night of Vaudeville," April 9, 1956). McCadden press releases touted it as "the most ambitious segment ever filmed by the couple for their network series." And indeed, perhaps it was. One of the major tasks connected with this show was the building of a special stage, which needed to be 25 feet across and would include a working curtain and false proscenium. Taking all this into account, Herb Browar wrote up an estimate of $1700 and placed it in George's in basket. Almost immediately, Herb was summoned to George's office. "It was right in the middle of a writing session," recalled Herb. "The writers were in the other room—Willy was there, Al [Simon] and George. I walked in; [it was] deathly silent, and George had my preproduction estimate in his hand. He said to me, 'What the hell do you mean, $1700 for a set? We don't need all that space!' " Herb insisted that they did, George continued to deny it. Finally, Herb yelled, "Do you know how much twenty-five feet is?!" and proceeded to pace it off. "That's twenty-five feet!" he exclaimed triumphantly. George just looked at him, knowing that Herb was right. Lowering his voice to a whisper, George said, "You'd better close the door—we're disturbing the writers."

This "Burns and Allen" episode was similar to the old Judy Garland–Mickey Rooney films of the 1940s, when the band needed uniforms and someone would shout, "Hey, kids, let's put on a show!" In this one, Ronnie's drama school is losing money and Gracie talks them into doing a variety show with vaudeville routines instead of their usual annual production of *Othello*. George directs and Gracie acts as mistress of ceremonies in this clever departure from their regular format.

One of the numbers is a parody of George and Gracie as vaudevillians, with Ronnie Burns playing the part of his father, and one of the drama students, Diane Jergens, playing Gracie. Just before she is to go on, the student decides that the role is beneath her—it's comedy, not the kind of high drama for which she's been training. In a rare departure from character, Gracie gives the young lady a pep talk, and in return we are treated to a special glimpse of Gracie Allen the talented actress. It is one of the finest moments of the entire "Burns and Allen" series:

> Did you hear the man say five minutes? Do you know what that means in the theater? It means if you're able to hear it you're going on. And if you don't, you're in the wrong business, because you have no courage. To be a dramatic actress, you've got to have courage. To be a dancer or a singer, you've got to have courage. When an audience is waiting for you, you don't disappoint them. Now get up! Now fix your lips! Now get out there and give a performance!

In another format innovation, there was a continuous flow of time from week to week, rather than each story being completely unrelated to any other. The following week's program, for example, picks up the morning after the vaudeville show, and continues the story with the successful previous evening's performance having gone to Ronnie's head. Several weeks later they used this technique with two shows involving a trip to Europe (Shows #188 and #189, airing May 7 and May 14, 1956). Another ambitious show with regard to set construction, this one called for creation of the interior of a transatlantic plane, customs offices, a kiosk, and a sidewalk café, as well as plenty of stock shots of airports, planes in flight, and Paris exteriors, to give it that on-location feeling (although they never left the stage at General Service Studios).

Most viewers might think this seems like a multitude of changes for any one season. Yet, at the end of the next season, George insisted to a reporter (*Star Free Press*, August 10, 1957), "It doesn't help a series to change the locale or bring in a new star. You can bring in new subject matter. We added Ronnie, our son, to the show and it opened up a new subject for stories—the problems of a twenty-year-old boy. Changes are gradual. We don't have guest stars and write a show around them. . . . Furthermore we don't wait until the end of a season to change anything. In the middle of a season, we went to Europe . . . the changes are gradual."

And more gradual changes were on the way.

19

MAGIC

GEORGE: *I'd better turn on my television set. . . . I want to catch up
with you people. I'd like to know
what's going on, too.*

Although the New York format had opened new doors for
characters and stories, George and the writers decided to
"move" everyone back to Los Angeles for the beginning of
the seventh season. Ronnie would now be attending the University of Southern California, which would allow for more of
a college atmosphere that had been lacking with Ronnie's
drama school in New York.

Fred de Cordova, who had produced and directed "Burns
and Allen" for the past three years, left at the end of the
"New York" season. He continued to direct motion pictures,
including *Frankie and Johnny*, starring Elvis Presley, as
well as producing and directing such television hits as "December Bride," "The Jack Benny Show" (six years), "The
Smothers Brothers Show" (1965), and "My Three Sons." In
1970 he became the producer of "The Tonight Show," where

he can still be found today. Six Emmy awards grace his book-shelves, along with eleven nomination certificates. Fred de Cordova and George Burns have retained their friendship began so long ago and still see each other whenever their schedules allow.

Once again, "The Burns and Allen Show" was faced with finding a new director. The man selected was Rod Amateau, who started his directing career in feature films, where he also did occasional stunt work. In fact, Rod was behind the ape mask in *Mighty Joe Young*. That film put a stop to his career as a stuntman when he developed a bacterial infection from the hot, rubberized suit and lost all of his body hair. (Fortunately, his hair grew back.) A short time later he made the changeover to television. He had directed seventy episodes of "The Bob Cummings Show," and George decided this was the person he wanted to produce and direct "Burns and Allen." Rod had pinch-hit for Fred de Cordova in January 1956, when Fred asked for a two-week leave of absence to direct *Blithe Spirit* for a CBS Spectacular. Rod was familiar with the cast, the format, and the crew, so it was an easy transition for everyone concerned.

Rod and George were made for each other. In an interview given immediately following his move to "Burns and Allen," Rod said that during the two years he directed "Bob Cummings," he and George "matched prejudices and found them identical." They both deplored comedy that required exaggerated physical action and anything that played down to an audience. Rod stated, "Our approach to comedy is the same. No one in 'Burns and Allen' is funny per se, they are actors in funny situations. Our program is a curious mixture of tremendous involvement in situations and, at the same time, a detachment in that George always makes it clear to the audience that he is working on sets in front of cameras with writers standing nearby." When asked his secret for knowing when something is right, Rod revealed that his only standard is his personal embarrassment. "This tells me better than anything else when something is wrong.

Whether it be a dress, a scene, a piece of business, or a page of dialogue."

Recently, Rod reflected on his experience working with George Burns. "[George] was more authoritative. Not in the pejorative way. He created a work atmosphere that was excellent. It wasn't communal. Yes, I was the captain, but he owned the yacht. It was no different on 'The Bob Cummings Show.' I never had a screaming match with George. I wouldn't presume to scream at him. I don't know a person I respect so deeply in terms of comedy. George's knowledge of comedy is encyclopedic. It's also instinctive."

A typical example of this natural talent occurred during the filming of an episode where Rod was trying to get Gracie to do a wide-eyed take, but when asked to open her eyes even wider, Gracie replied, "That's as wide as they go." George stepped over and told her to "play to the balcony, they'll look bigger." She did, and it worked. When Rod rushed over to thank George, George thoughtfully rolled his cigar between his fingers before answering Rod. "I wonder. Are we outsmarting ourselves?" His concern was that the take would hold up the plot. "Let's drop it," he said, and they did.

As in the previous season, the writers were faced with how to effect a coast-to-coast change of locale. The season opener had everyone preparing to return home, with Ronnie having gone ahead to enroll at USC. George and Gracie arrive sooner than Ronnie expects, and discover that he has more than a dozen "homeless" students staying at the house until they can find living quarters. George's house is not the only one that's been turned into a fraternity of sorts; the Mortons' home has an equal number of young ladies taking up temporary residence. After living for a year at the St. Moritz, George and Gracie end up spending their first night back home in a hotel.

About this time, Gracie Allen was beginning to show the effects of the nonstop work schedule she'd been on for the past thirty years, and the addition of more young people in the cast gave her the opportunity to sit out some scenes. The critics were undisturbed by the format change, but they were concerned about the low visibility of Gracie. *Variety* (October 3, 1956) began its review of the new season:

> The old order of comedy by this rollicking team of funsters has been little disturbed. If there was any noticeable change it was in the scarcity of Gracie's participation, and that's not good. On her droll note of distorted humor has long rested the success of the team's commercial longevity.

One of the most surrealistic devices ever conceived for a half-hour comedy show was George's magic television set. It allowed George to peek in on his friends and family without their knowledge. By so doing, he was able to either encourage the plot or hamper it, depending on his whim. It was an idea that would have done Rod Serling proud. Suddenly on the seventh episode of the seventh season, George turned on the television set in his den, and there was the show we at home were watching. George's face lit up, and he commented:

> Say, there's Gracie. This is the first time I've seen her on television. She looks cute. I'm going to watch her every week!

The use of the TV became integral in most of the subsequent plots. It wasn't uncommon for George to watch a screw-up in the making, turn to the camera, and apologize that although he could clear up the situation, it would leave the show fifteen minutes short. Then, just to make sure those fifteen minutes would be interesting, he would grin and contemplate what little bit of mischief he could throw in to confuse the issue at hand even further.

George loved his new "twenty-seven-inch keyhole," as he once referred to it. None of the other characters knew about it, and whenever George heard someone coming, he would merely change the channel to a Western, and no one was ever the wiser. Even Ronnie's love life was not a secret from his father. For example, one day when Ronnie asked his father for advice before dating a pretty foreign exchange student, George gave him a French phrase to say if he wanted the girl to give him a kiss. Confidently, Ronnie left for his date. George turned to the camera and disclosed that he really only told Ronnie how to say, "Isn't this a nice day?" After enough time had passed, he sat back to watch the fun.

GEORGE: I'd better turn on my television set and see how that trick I played on Ronnie is working. He and that French girl must have had lunch and if I know Ronnie, by now he must have found a romantic spot.

The picture on his TV was a secluded park bench, and there sat Ronnie with his arm around his date.

GEORGE: You see, not only do I know Ronnie, I know his spots.

This time, however, George's little plot was foiled. Ronnie did get his kiss because it was the first time the young lady had been on a date in America where the boy had *not* asked for one.

George not only kept tabs on members of his family and neighbors; from time to time, he also looked in on his friend Jack Benny. It was always a treat for the audience as George flipped channels to suddenly see Jack, sitting in a comfortable chair at home. Jack, it seems, was the only person who was aware of this Peeping Tom intrusion, and would greet George's voyeurism with his classic, "Now, cut that out!" George would agreeably change the channel again.

Rod Amateau was instrumental in upgrading the format of film. He made fuller use of the cameras, moving them around the stage to get better angles and a more "four-sided" look to the sets. Also, he and George worked hand in hand creating some of the unique special effects showcased during the last two seasons of "Burns and Allen."

One such effect was a Genie who materialized out of the smoke from George's cigar. George, claiming to be a fairy godmother, had loaned Ronnie thirty-five dollars to take a plain Jane to the prom. Then he turned to the camera:

All right, so I'm the first fairy godmother who smokes cigars . . . you don't believe I am one, huh?

He waved his cigar and poof! a Genie materialized. When he asked George his wish, George asked for his thirty-five dollars back. The Genie just looked at him. "Are you kidding?" and with another puff of smoke, he was gone.

This wasn't the last of the Genie, though. At the end of the episode, George waved his cigar again and the Genie appeared in his den:

GENIE: Yes, master? What is your wish?
GEORGE: Would you like to watch some television with me?
GENIE: Sure, boss.

And they both sat down to enjoy a good cigar and some standard television fare.

Rod Amateau, in his role as producer, made some hardline production changes. The interior of the Burns house had gone through a redecorating process while they were in "New York," and additional sets had been built to depict upstairs hallways and Ronnie's bedroom. The existing sets had begun to look pretty shabby after six years, and Rod sent the following memo to Herb Browar. The fun the staff had with each other is evident, even though the content is very serious business.

MEMO

FROM: ROD AMATEAU   DATE: 8/23/56
TO: HERB BROWAR
      RE: PERMANENCY OF BURNS AND ALLEN
           SETS

Dear Herb,

What follows originally began as a simple request to John Fisher of the paint department to please remove the dirty finger marks from the walls and doors of the B & A set. The topper is they aren't washed off because the paint comes off as well. (John Fisher, you stop buying paint from your brother-in-law!) Upon cooler investigation, I realized that the very capable Mr. Fisher (and his brother-in-law's paint) was only a fragment of the problem that exists.

First, the materials used to construct our set, right down to the paint and hardware, in the movie tradition, are designed for *one shots*. In other words, you use a set for a sequence and then you strike it. This form of thinking, of course, will never carry us through 40 shows with the sets looking as good on the 40th as they did on the first, as indeed, they must.

The situation is not unique to "Burns and Allen" or to me. It occurs on every TV series in which standing sets are used. The materials that are to last a season should be superior to those used on a single picture, otherwise costs of constant repairs might conceivably rival original set costs.

This applies essentially to the portions of the set which operate or receive constant use. I refer to doors, windows, hardware of all kinds and paint. It is difficult enough to shoot a show in one day without the time-consuming problem of a screen door that refuses to swing, a door knob that won't close, etc., etc., etc.

This is by no means a complaint. I'm delighted with the sets, but what is going to happen as the season wears on? Permit me to suggest that a little preventive care at

this time will more than compensate for the frayed
nerves and hysterical repairs during the show.

Very truly yours,
RA

If these kinds of daily production details weren't enough
to keep the staff busy, there were still ongoing surprises for
Gracie. Each year, the local gas company would provide new
appliances for the kitchen set, and take back the old ones.
Gracie owned a big refrigerator at home that she'd had for
years, and George thought it would be nice to give her one of
the later models they'd used on the show. When Herb was
asked to make arrangements to move the new Seville refrigerator into the house, he balked. He knew how much Gracie
loved her old one with its glass partitions for salad crisping
and other extra features. George told him not to worry, just
make the exchange. It took a crew the whole day. The new
fridge was so big it wouldn't fit through the door, and the big
kitchen window had to be removed to get it in her house. A
plumber had to come out to hook it up, and Gracie's old favorite was taken back to the lot for storage. The window was
replaced just in time for Gracie's arrival home. The next morning, George pulled Herb aside. "We have to take it out."
Gracie wanted her old refrigerator back, and they had to go
through the same process all over again. She did keep the new
one, though—in the garage.

"Burns and Allen" repeatedly held its own in the ratings
as well as in the eyes of the press. By now the show was being
seen in other countries, and their critics had equal words of
praise for this U.S. effort. The *Glasgow Evening News* called
it "as important an American import as petrol." In England,
the *Bradford Telegraph* reviewer wrote, "As far as I'm concerned, this is the best comedy film series imported from
America now showing on either BBC or ITV." "Burns and
Allen" was an international success.

20

MEANWHILE,

BACK AT

THE RANCH

*I know very little about being a cow-
boy. I'm not even sure if you're supposed to saddle old paint and ride, or
paint an old saddle and ride later
when the paint dries.*
—GEORGE BURNS,
   TV Guide *(September 28, 1957)*

Cowboys were in. Shoot-'em-ups, box canyons, and hatchet-
waving Indians were on every channel. The 1957–58 television
season had over two dozen Westerns airing in prime time,
offering little variety to its viewers. "Maverick," "The Law-
man," "Yancy Derringer," "Colt .45," "Wyatt Earp," "The
Rifleman," "Cheyenne," "Wanted Dead or Alive," "Have
Gun, Will Travel," "Gunsmoke," "Northwest Passage,"
"Wagon Train," "Bat Masterson," and "Restless Gun" were
only some of the choices that season, with "Burns and Allen"
buried in the stampede of wild mustang hooves.
   But George Burns had yet to face a challenge he couldn't
overcome, and this was no exception. A philosophy of "If you
can't wup 'em, join 'em—but keep it funny" prevailed on the
"Burns and Allen" set. In the opening episode, instead of his
usual dapper suit and tie, George appeared looking like the

original rhinestone cowboy. After a couple of minutes, he stepped aside to explain his unusual attire:

> The situation downstairs has nothing to do with our opening show. . . . We were going to start our new season with a straight Western. That's why I've got this outfit on. This is great. I'm dressed this-a-way, and the plot went that-a-way.

At every opportunity, George remarked on this new phenomenon—occasionally even turning on his TV to show us the competition. At those moments, we were treated to some of the oldest cowboys-and-Indians stock footage in Hollywood. He told us he had rented a ranch and dozens of cowboy actors for his show, and whenever there was a moment to interrupt the plot at hand, George could say: "Meanwhile, back at the ranch. . . ."

The response from the press was as enthusiastic as ever. *Daily Variety*'s was typical (October 2, 1957):

> There will be a lot of joshing on TV's comedy shows this season over the saturation of adult Westerns, but it's doubtful that any will be as masterfully executed as that by "Burns and Allen" in their season opener.

And this, from *Weekly Variety* (September 30, 1957):

> With witty scripting and standout delivery they manage to make the half-hour visit fresh and delightful. Interspersed with a laughable plotline were Burns' cracks about TV's Western rut. He took dead aim at the oaters and shattered them completely. The gunslingers will be in trouble if Burns continues his barbed barrage.

George was constantly refining the series, and the closing routines became a four-minute show all of their own. Each week a lovely young girl, attired in an outfit reminiscent of a drum majorette's, would stand beside an old-fashioned vaude-ville easel where a large sign announced "Burns and Allen." She would smile and tell us, "Yes, they'll be right back and do one of their vaudeville routines for you." A curtain with the names of all the famous circuit theaters would draw back, and, hand in hand, George and Gracie would walk out onto the stage.

In the past season the routines had covered a variety of subjects; now they dealt exclusively with Gracie's "famous" relatives. All George had to say was, "Well, Gracie, which one of your relatives shall we talk about tonight?" and Gracie was off and running, telling us tales of:

"Wyatt Allen"—Western town marshal. He was a per-fect shot—everyone who shot at him, hit him. He had an all-white stallion named "Old Paint" because that was the color he painted it.

"Cousin Robin Allen"—who stole from the rich and gave to the poor. He read someplace that to open a safe, the burglar always sandpapered his fingertips down to where the skin was very sensitive. That's how he got caught. When he touched the dial with those sensitive fingertips, it hurt so much he screamed and woke up the whole neighborhood.

"Great-grandfather Daniel Allen"—pioneer and trail-blazer. A lot of places in history were named after him. He'd ride up to some Indians and whatever he said, the Indians would give it that name. In Arizona alone there's "Where-am-I Mountain," "Where-am-I Canyon," "Where-am-I Creek."

The family tree also contained such noteworthy ances-tors as: "Scoop Allen"—the newspaperman; "Hickok Allen" —the pony express rider; and "Balzac Allen"—the novelist.

In February 1958, two of the biggest surprise episodes of "Burns and Allen" aired. It all began with the writers sitting around in their usual "What if . . . ?" mode, and "What if Gracie were the smartest woman in the world?" was heard. It was an intriguing concept, and before long they conceived a two-part episode in which Gracie is hypnotized and becomes the smartest woman in the world. The plot follows Gracie onto a quiz show while George, now without an act, is reduced to being a house husband. To further complicate matters, George wants his old Gracie back and phones the hypnotist in London, asking him to break the spell. The man agrees, and George sets the phone down and goes to get Gracie. While he is out of the room, Blanche picks up the receiver, and when she hangs up, Blanche is the way Gracie used to be. The poor hypnotist has to fly back to Los Angeles to straighten all this out. Gracie goes on the quiz show and loses, and everyone is back to normal.

The papers went wild with headlines:

WILL GRACIE GET BRAINS?

GRACIE ALLEN HAS ONE SURPRISE LEFT—SHE'S TURNING BRILLIANT!

GRACIE ALLEN TO DON STRAIGHT PERSONALITY

GLIB, GADABOUT GRACIE TO TRY STRAIGHT ROLE

GRACIE SHOWS OFF NEWFOUND BRAIN

GRACIE ALLEN WITH BRAINS? SUCH IS TV MAGIC!

The critics used this opportunity to remind us what a good, straight actress Gracie Allen really was. When she was interviewed on how she felt about being the smartest woman in the world, she batted her eyelashes at the reporters and said, "I always thought I was."

Perhaps we shouldn't have seemed so surprised at this side of Gracie. In early episodes we really did see glimmers of great intelligence:

GRACIE: I love these scientific articles.
GEORGE: You do, huh? What is a volt?
GRACIE: A volt is a unit of electricity.
GEORGE: Hey! This is unbelievable. What is an ohm?

GRACIE: Oh, George, anybody knows that. An 'ome is an 'ouse where an Englishman lives.
GEORGE: I knew it was too good to last.

The writers' imaginations and Rod Amateau's ability to meet any challenge gave us some of the cleverest episodes in the eight-year run of "Burns and Allen." On one of these shows, Bea Benaderet played both Blanche *and* Blanche's mother. Rod explained that in the early days of filmmaking, "split screen" work was done by blocking out half a frame of the film, shooting the entire scene, then winding the film back, blocking out the other half, and shooting the same scene again with the other character. By the 1950s, it was possible to shoot with the entire frame exposed. The same scene would be shot twice, the actor performing first one part, then the other. The two scenes would then be matched up in the lab. It was time-consuming work, and the camera would have to be bolted to the floor to prevent any movement. But the final result was worth the extra effort.

Never one to let anything get past the viewers, George told us at the end of this episode:

See, it's a nice happy ending. Especially for Blanche Morton—she gets two checks this week. One for playing herself, and one for playing her mother. What am I so happy about—I've got to pay her.

Bea was always a professional and always modest when talking about her own accomplishments. In an interview with the *Los Angeles Times* in 1964, she said of working with Burns and Allen, "No one worked harder than Gracie. She was always the first one on the set. She always knew her lines. What little I may know about comedy acting, I got just watching Gracie."

Larry Keating's Harry Morton also continued to develop. The writers must have worn out their dictionaries coming up with speeches like the following:

George, I have long been cognizant that you are a person of inferior caliber, but even I am shocked and appalled to discover that you are so lacking in moral fiber as to approve of your son's reprehensible philandering. Your cynical acceptance of his breach of the ethical code reveals a contempt for integrity that is both revolting to me and deleterious to the social structure of mankind. I feel strongly impelled to thrash you.

And George still, after five seasons, wasn't letting him get away with it:

I'm not worried, Harry. After that long speech, you haven't enough wind left to thrash your grandmother.

It's a shame the speeches were so long; otherwise Harry Morton's love of his profession could have been made into needlepoint samplers to hang in every accounting firm's front office:

In my youth, I might have made a false move. Today, I might find myself trapped in the rut of some dull occupation such as that of airplane pilot or deep-sea diver. Instead, I entered the most thrilling of all professions—Certified Public Accountancy.

Harry Von Zell's character also blossomed, taking advantage of the fine actor that Von Zell was. The season in New York unfortunately offered little for Von Zell to do. His character usually concentrated on his flirtations, with occasional involvement in the plot at hand. Once the series moved back to L.A., Von Zell became the integral part of the show he had been in the earlier episodes.

One of the most remembered aspects of his later character development was his never ending quest for a raise coupled with his ability to get himself fired:

VON ZELL: You've always said that as long as I'm working for you, I could tell you anything that was on my mind and you'd listen.

GEORGE: That's right, and it's too bad you didn't tell it to me while you were working for me.

VON ZELL: You mean I'm . . . I'm fired?

GEORGE: Anyway, until after breakfast.

In another episode, Von Zell, without knowing Gracie has inadvertently helped, finally does get his raise. George is led to believe Von Zell is getting married and therefore needs more money. Each time Von Zell, an inveterate bachelor, tries to explain he doesn't want to get married, George ups the ante. It's beginning to look too good for Von Zell . . . and we're right. In the end George tells him he can't afford him, and once again, poor Von Zell is fired.

Harry Von Zell became the butt of most of George's jokes. His character in the show had asked for more romantic roles and George offered this by way of defense:

It's not that Harry's bad looking. He's not, but he isn't handsome, either. He's like tapioca pudding. Nice, but not exciting. Also a little lumpy.

He used Von Zell to move the stories along:

GEORGE: This story hasn't got enough complications. What can I do to mess it up?

VON ZELL (entering from garden): George?

GEORGE (calls out): In here, Harry . . . (to camera) Here's the perfect mess.

The real Harry Von Zell was a multitalented man, whom George respected greatly. In addition to his acting duties on "Burns and Allen," Von Zell was also a dedicated barbershop quartet aficionado, a ukulele strummer, and a talented script-writer. He had heard that "Wagon Train" was looking for stories about women, and he began writing. When he sent the finished script over, they bought it and asked for more. In a period of about two months, Von Zell wrote four teleplays. All told, he sold five scripts to "Wagon Train" (in one of which he also starred) and two others elsewhere during the last two years of "Burns and Allen."

His Western acting gave the writers of "Burns and Allen" another new gimmick for Von Zell's character. In the last season, he regularly came in to show George what piece of Western business he had perfected that week. Sometimes it was a brawl stunt, other times it was the fast draw. And it didn't matter who else might be with George at the time.

The audience's first encounter with this side of Von Zell was in the opening episode. Von Zell thinks George is going to be doing a Western and desperately wants a part in the show. He has been practicing dying and wants to audition. The staid father of one of Ronnie's friends is trying to have a serious discussion with George, and every other sentence is interrupted by Von Zell—spinning and flopping on the floor. The father doesn't know what to make of all this, and George finally tells him to take his finger, make like a gun and go "bang," and finish Von Zell off. The father, against his better judgment, does, and Von Zell instantly dies. George then picks up their conversation where they left off as if nothing out of the ordinary has happened.

Ronnie's character had also become more active. One of the first things he learned from Gracie was how to get money out of George. Gracie demonstrates this art by telling George she needs to buy a silver spoon for her cousin's baby. George offers her five dollars. Gracie wants more than that and counters:

> Then I'll need $245 for Dr. Neimitz. . . . You know how babies are—they always swallow the spoon and you just can't leave it there.

George has to agree. Gracie then turns to Ronnie, "See how it works?"

George quickly caught on to this new game, but always obliged with a twenty-dollar bill. His standard description of his son was, "You remember Ronnie, my son. Six-foot-one. A tall boy who's always short."

Ronnie spent a good deal of his time on the series covering for his mother. Whenever he thought Gracie was in any kind of trouble with George, he would intervene and try to take the blame himself. For example, Gracie has gotten a traffic ticket (again) and George is trying to find out how. He approaches Ronnie, who is in his room studying:

RONNIE: Hello, Dad. What brings you here?

GEORGE: Just visiting.

RONNIE: That's nice. . . . Er, anything you want to talk to me about?

GEORGE: Just visiting.

RONNIE: If it's about the dent in the fender, I did it when I hit the avocado tree this morning.

GEORGE: Just visiting.

RONNIE: If it's about your new blue suit that's missing, well, Mother didn't send it to Uncle Harvey, I did. Is that it?

GEORGE: Just visiting.

RONNIE: If it's about your electric razor, I'm the one who peeled the potatoes with it. Just visiting?

GEORGE: Mmmmmmm.

RONNIE: If it's about the Mortons' car, it was my idea to drive Mother downtown in it this morning.

GEORGE: End of visit.

The critics were obviously enjoying Ronnie as much as the television audience was. The *Hollywood Reporter* (January 23, 1957) said of his performances:

Ronnie Burns is a definite asset to "The Burns and Allen Show." . . . His double-take looks of compassion for his scatterbrained mother are good fun.

Bob Bernstein's review of the series claimed Ronnie was "a deft comic actor in his own right [and] a welcome regular on the series."

Ronnie was fast becoming one of the most popular teen idols on television. In a 1957 TV magazine survey, he was voted "fourth hottest" star, preceded only by Lawrence Welk, Giselle MacKenzie, and Polly Bergen. (Ricky Nelson, James Arness, Ernie Ford, Tommy Sands, and Dinah Shore finished out the list.)

It would appear that every move he made found its way into the papers. Even the make of the cars he owned was of interest to his fans—his $4,400 1956 Corvette, on which a reporter caught him fixing his headlight with Scotch tape one day, and in 1957 his brand-new Jaguar, license JSV 474. Nothing was sacred—any little anecdote would do. Once, during filming of "Burns and Allen," a missing cake became food for the press. It seems that as the day wore on, it looked like the scene with a cake-cutting sequence might not get shot. Rod Amateau thought he would have to wait and do that particular scene the following week. That was apparently all Ronnie and several others in the cast had to hear. But at the end of the day, Rod realized there was still enough time to go ahead and film the scene. Everyone was ready—but there was no cake. As the press reported, "the culprits were caught with icing all over their faces and the cake was nowhere to be seen."

For a while, it looked like Ronnie had found his niche. He made his feature film debut in 1957 in 20th Century-Fox's *Bernardine* and guested as a murderer in the "Smiling Killer" episode of McCadden's "Panic" series. He started a recording career with Verve records. Although he preferred classical music, for his fans he performed rock 'n' roll songs, appearing on Jack Benny's show and "Dick Clark's American Bandstand." There was even talk of his doing an album with his father called "Sugarthroat and Son Sing Songs."

Ronnie Burns was enjoying his celebrity and became quite a playboy for a while. A running joke among his peers

(*PRECEDING PAGE*) *That's production manager Herb Browar under the beard, as he plays Santa to George at the "Burns and Allen" cast and crew party.* (*Courtesy Herb Browar*)

(*OPPOSITE*) *Family portrait, circa 1955. Back row: son Ronnie, Gracie, George. Seated are daughter Sandra, her husband Young Wilhoite, and baby daughter Lori—the Burnses' first grandchild.* (*Courtesy USC*)

(*ABOVE*) *Ronnie Burns on the General Service Studios lot with his shiny new Corvette. The young costar had a passion for cars and carried many of his fan letters in the glove compartment.* (*Courtesy USC*)

(*TOP*) *Frederick de Cordova, producer/director of "The George Burns and Gracie Allen Show" from 1954 to 1956. (Courtesy USC)*

(*BOTTOM*) *Larry Keating as Robin Hood and Bea Benaderet as Maid Marian in Show #222, "The Costume Party." (Courtesy USC)*

(*OPPOSITE*) *George as Little Lord Fauntleroy, Show #237, concocts a plot to marry off the four daughters of Mr. Jantzen, the plumber. Clockwise from lower left: Mary Ellen Kaye, Jody Warner, Darlene Albert, and Yvonne Lime. (Courtesy USC)*

(LEFT) *The crew takes time out for a group photo. Back row, left, is Joe Depew, assistant director. In front of him is Phil Tannura, head cameraman. Fred de Cordova is seated in the director's chair. George is in the center, and to his right is Hal Hudson, from the CBS network.* (Courtesy USC)

(BELOW) *The 1956 official crew photo on the set of the Burnses' New York apartment. First row, center: Ronnie. Second row, fourth from left: Fred de Cordova, followed by Bea, George, Gracie, Larry, and Harry Von Zell. Back row, directly behind Larry is Al Simon. To the right of him is Herb Browar.* (Courtesy Herb Browar)

(LEFT) Gracie catches Ronnie and a friend (Lisa Gaye) rehearsing a kiss for drama class. Notice the New York scenes through picture windows. (Courtesy USC)

(BELOW, LEFT) George's new toy for the final two seasons of the show—an all-seeing, all-knowing TV set to follow the schemes of Harry Von Zell, Blanche, and Harry Morton. Wonder what Gracie's up to? (Courtesy USC)

(BELOW, RIGHT) A rare photo of George and Gracie kissing, as Blanche and the ladies of their club look on. (Courtesy USC)

(LEFT) *Perky Yvonne Lime was the girl who introduced George and Gracie's vaudeville routines at the end of the show during the last few seasons. She also had an occasional role on the program.* (Courtesy USC)

(BELOW) *George, Gracie, and Harry Von Zell prepare to celebrate the beginning of their eighth season of "Burns and Allen."* (Courtesy USC)

(ABOVE, LEFT) *The long and short of it: Gracie meets Ronnie's college friend Brian McAfee (Robert Easton).* (Courtesy Robert Easton)

(ABOVE, RIGHT) *From Show #243: Gracie comforts Brian McAfee (Robert Easton), who pretends to be injured so he won't have to attend his graduation ceremony.* (Courtesy Robert Easton)

(RIGHT) *Rolf Sedan as Mr. Beeseley, the mailman who always tried to sneak quietly away from the Burnses to avoid Gracie—and never succeeded.* (Courtesy USC)

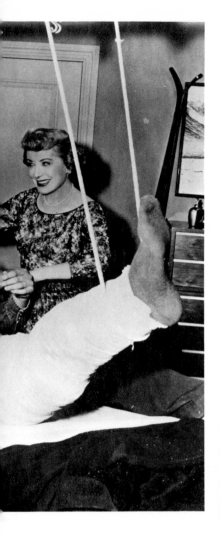

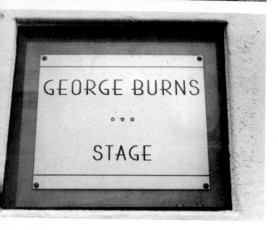

(*LEFT, TOP*) *Opening logo used for the first four seasons. This was not a still photo; George actually stood there, smoking a cigar.*

(*LEFT, MIDDLE*) *The Mc-Cadden logo—an animated "clapboard" opening and closing—was used for the show's end logo.*

(*LEFT, BOTTOM*) *Plaque at the former General Service Studios dedicating Stage 1 as the "George Burns Stage."*

(*OPPOSITE*) *George and Gracie wait tensely backstage to finish filming their last show together. (Allan Grant,* Life Magazine © 1958 Time Inc.)

Their last bow together, The team of Burns and Allen emerges through a curtain covered with the names of the theaters and cities where they played in their vaudeville days. (Allan Grant, Life Magazine © 1958 Time Inc.)

was that he even received his mail at the Luau (a popular restaurant in Beverly Hills). When asked what Ronnie was really like, George once told a *TV Star Parade* reporter, "He's charming, he's diplomatic, but you can't always be sure what he's thinking. And I like that, too. I don't like people whose entire personality is on the surface."

George and Gracie never pushed Ronnie toward show business. Their feeling was if they pushed too hard, he might push back, so they let him work out his career goals for himself. Ronnie did, and his early love of the sea called him back. Today he can be found in the Marina del Rey area of Southern California, where he designs and builds boats.

21

THE HOME

STRETCH

I just get good people together and let them do their job. If I can't help them, I leave them alone.
—GEORGE BURNS,
Variety (*February 7, 1957*)

"The George Burns and Gracie Allen Show" was drawing toward the finish of its eighth season. Besides the series' regulars, new faces had become welcome additions to the cast.

The "Burns and Allen" loyalty extended to rehiring actors whose work they liked—often in different roles with each appearance. We recognized many familiar faces from the early shows when these actors became recurring characters in the later episodes. Grandon Rhodes was cast in several different roles before settling into the part of Mr. Vanderlip, the Burnses' banker. Hal March, who was the original Harry Morton, reappeared as Morton's business partner, Casey, and when that character was dropped, Hal continued to make guest appearances in assorted roles. Many actors, such as Douglas Dumbrille, Joe Kearns, Rex Evans, Jan Arvan, and

Verna Feldon popped up frequently in a variety of disguises. After a succession of actors played the mailman, the returning role of perpetually perplexed Mr. Beeseley went to Rolf Sedan. And James Flavin was the perfectly panicked Detective Sawyer whenever the precinct phone rang and Gracie was on the other end.

Judy Boutin (who later billed herself as Judy Meredith) played Bonnie Sue McAfee, one of Ronnie's girlfriends, and sister of his pal Brian. Judy and Ronnie originally met while Ronnie was working at the Pasadena Playhouse, and prior to her recurring role as Bonnie Sue, Judy portrayed a variety of young women involved with Ronnie.

Jody McCrea (Joel's look-alike son) was Lew, a friend of Ronnie's at USC, and Bob Ellis played Ralph, Ronnie's best friend.

Robert Easton was the tall, blond, gangly Texan, Brian McAfee. Whereas Brian was in his tenth year of college, still trying to graduate, Bob Easton was one of the original Quiz Kids on radio, and his exceptional performance on his college entrance exams allowed him to take his freshman, sophomore, junior, and senior courses concurrently! (You might also remember Bob's portrayal as the bird-watching boyfriend of Shultzy on "The Bob Cummings Show.") Today, Robert Easton is still working in Hollywood, but behind the cameras as the world's foremost dialect coach—the Henry Higgins of Hollywood. His list of clients includes Al Pacino (Cuban dialect for *Scarface*), Charlton Heston (Scottish burr for *Mother Lode*), Gregory Peck (German for *The Boys from Brazil*), and several hundred others.

Jacqueline Beer played Yvette, a young Frenchwoman, in several early episodes, and later turned up as Marie, the pretty cigarette girl at the St. Moritz.

Howard McNear has one of those wonderful faces you always recognize, but can't seem to place. He was delightful as Gracie's plumber, Mr. Jantzen.

The "Burns and Allen" format did not call for major guest stars the way their original radio series had. Jack

Benny was the most frequent celebrity guest, and he could get away with it as George's best friend. Occasionally the real mayor of Los Angeles might show up, or such luminaries as Francis X. Bushman and Charles Vidor. Several actors cast in minor roles later became highly recognizable celebrities: Steve Reeves, Richard Deacon, Sheldon Leonard, Marion Ross, and Ronald Reagan, to name a few.

In addition to the cast of "Burns and Allen" growing by leaps and bounds with all of Ronnie's school chums, McCadden Productions was going full bore as well. The crews were pulling double duty by crisscrossing from one McCadden show to another, and so were the casts. Bob Cummings would drop in on "Burns and Allen," and George, Gracie, Bea, and Larry (in character) all guested on one episode of "The Bob Cummings Show."

McCadden Productions was a booming industry with four series on the air: "Burns and Allen," "The Bob Cummings Show," "The People's Choice," and "Panic." Also, in preparation were series to star Margaret O'Brien, Carol Channing, Marie Wilson, and June Havoc, and discussions were going on to develop one for Hermione Gingold. *Variety* (August 26, 1957) stated, "Not that Burns has lost his faith in male comics, but he feels that among the femmes in his future there may be another Gracie."

At one point in the filming of "Cummings," McCadden got "two for the price of one" when they did an episode that focused on Chuck (Dwayne Hickman) going to college, and used it as a pilot for a series to star Dwayne. (Unfortunately, that series didn't sell; but Dwayne Hickman later went on to star in "Dobie Gillis" for 20th Century-Fox.) George did find one male comic who gave McCadden another hit series—Alan Young, starring in "Mr. Ed."

Al Simon was instrumental in developing many dramatic pilots for McCadden, and George was deeply involved in the writing, casting, and filming of all the McCadden shows, as well as his constant supervision of "Burns and Allen." If this weren't enough, McCadden's commercial division was continually adding new advertisers to its client list. More than three hundred people were on McCadden's payroll, and its yearly gross was approaching $7 million.

George and Gracie's lives were being overrun with personal appearances and product endorsements. Their faces were seen hawking everything from Zenith Televisions to Stauffer Home Plan exerciser/recliner boards, to American Airlines DC7 Mercurys—Nonstop to L.A. Even their grocery shopping was an opportunity for publicity. An announcement in the *Hollywood Reporter* (August 23, 1956) stated:

GEORGE BURNS
BOUGHT TOMATOES
AT McDANIEL'S MARKET
"Grocery Store of the Stars"
325 N. Canon Dr., Beverly Hills
BR 2-6271

In addition, George and Gracie guested on such shows as "I've Got a Secret," and George was center stage one night on "This Is Your Life."

Although "Burns and Allen" never received ratings that put them in the top five shows, they did enjoy consistently high Nielsen numbers. George steadfastly claimed that the "show worked because we didn't tell jokes. It was situation comedy, it was story. And all the humor was attached to a story."

From their beginning, "I Love Lucy" was "Burns and Allen" 's biggest competition. By 1958, Lucy and Desi were only doing occasional specials, often preempting "Burns and Allen" and sweeping the ratings for the night. George told the *Call Bulletin* in San Francisco, "I have a joke about it. They say being on TV once a week is too much, being on every two weeks is better and once a month is even better. That means if you're not on at all, you've got to be a screaming success."

But they were on, and the awards they received proved the people's adoration. The show was still going strong in 1958, and the TV critics' poll voted George and Gracie the best comedy team over Lucy and Desi, copycatting a 1957 *Fame* magazine poll. Over the course of their eight-year run, "Burns and Allen" received a total of twelve Emmy nominations—six for Gracie as best actress/comedienne, two for Bea as supporting actress, and four for "Burns and Allen" as best comedy series. In 1957, George ran the following ad in the "trades":

I'M PAYING FOR THIS AD,
SO I CAN SAY WHAT
I WANT.

I think my wife, GRACIE ALLEN, is a great artist and deserves an Emmy.

My son, RONNIE BURNS, is a promising young actor and should get an award, too . . . next year.

BEA BENADERET deserves an award as a supporting actress.

LARRY KEATING deserves an award as a supporting actor.

HARRY VON ZELL should have gotten an award years ago.

My writers, KEITH FOWLER, HARVEY HELM, NORMAN PAUL and WILLY BURNS should get an award.

ROD AMATEAU, my director/producer should get . . . two awards.

As for me, I'm pathetic. Vote for Jack Benny.

                                        GEORGE BURNS

Unfortunately, critics and viewers don't get to vote for their choice for Emmys, and the results were the same as the previous years—not one winner.

As early as 1955, Gracie had begun to feel the strain of a weekly show. She told the *Los Angeles Examiner* (January 23, 1955): "I'll say one thing, and I'll say it right out loud. I liked television better when I did one live show every two weeks. It gave me a breather. Now we film the show, but I have to do it every week. I think I felt fresher when I had a little time to myself."

Three years after that comment, Gracie made a startling announcement.

22

THE LAST

GOOD NIGHT

Gracie deserves a rest. She's been
working all her life and her lines
were the toughest in the world to do.
—GEORGE BURNS,
Los Angeles Times

It seemed to come so swiftly, out of nowhere. The press as
well as the American public was shocked and upset when
columnist Louella O. Parsons, longtime "voice" of Hollywood,
made the preliminary announcement in mid-February 1958.
Gracie's fans waited, praying it wasn't true, but in Louella's
March 2 column she made it official:

> Gracie Allen has announced her decision to retire from
> show business after 35 years as a member of the famed
> Burns and Allen comedy team. . . . Gracie just couldn't
> separate from her George, professionally, that is, and
> leaves a vacuum that cannot be filled in the entertain-
> ment world. The hold that Gracie, the fluttery rattlebrain,
> the queen of the non sequitur, has on her public has never
> been equalled by any woman in show business. Without

her cheerful inanities Monday night just won't be Monday night on TV.

Other reporters were petulant. "Don't leave your nutty nest, Gracie," wrote William Ewald of the *Oakland Tribune*. He went on to say that "the announcement she won't be back on TV next season is mournful news. She deals in a special brand of uncalculated nuttiness and happy incomprehension that no other funny lady is able to match. . . . Come on back, Gracie." The newspapers were full of stories, all saying the same thing: "TV without Gracie? Take away the set!" "Gracie, stay! George, do something!!"

But George wouldn't force his wife to work. He told Louella, "The decision was entirely up to Gracie. I agree with her—what's so strange about a normal, charming woman, after 35 years, wanting to enjoy her home, children and friends?"

Gracie had wanted to retire for a number of years prior to the actual announcement. "Every year," said Rod Amateau, "she told George it was the last." Gracie explained in *TV Guide* (June 14, 1958):

I wanted to retire for the last three years, but George always beat me to it by signing the contracts for the following season, but he finally began to catch on. Last spring he was in Palm Springs with Jack Benny when the option for this season was picked up. He turned to Jack and said he didn't have the heart to call and tell me. Would Jack do it for him? Well Jack, of course, just fell on the floor. He thought it was the funniest thing in the world that any performer would be afraid to tell his partner that their option had been picked up. So this spring, George finally asked me in advance if I really wanted to retire and I said yes. You see, he wanted the sponsors to know ahead of time so they'd know what they'd be getting if they renewed.

She was tired of being Gracie Allen. Now she could become simply Mrs. George Burns, wife, mother, grandmother. Up until now, she'd had no free time for these things. She told *TV Guide:*

I have one darned appointment after another. Dress fittings for one thing. It's hard to believe how tiring they can be, and I have two a week just for the show. Every Thursday I'm supposed to be free, but it never works out that way. That's the only day I have to go to the dentist, for instance, and that's the day everybody says, "Gracie's free today—this will be a good time to get that interview, or take those pictures, or have her go to that nice business luncheon." So you see, it's seven days a week.

That Gracie needed a rest was evident not only from her hectic work schedule, but from her health. Although she was only fifty-two years old, an age that seems premature for retirement to most people, she privately suffered from a heart ailment, violent migraines, and was fast approaching a state of total exhaustion from overwork. Asked what she planned to do with her newfound free time, she told a *Time* magazine reporter, "I'm going to sleep for six months." Then she added, "I'm going to invite people in to dinner and visit my grandchildren. And I'm going to clean out the bureau drawers." Like a teenager with her first charge account suddenly turned loose, she made elaborate plans for shopping in Saks and Magnin's, two large Beverly Hills department stores. She told Louella, "Think of the fun I'll have when I can shop for my clothes without thinking about how the dress will look for the TV cameras. And afternoons when I can play gin rummy if I feel in the mood for cards without a couple of comedy writers under the table. Best of all there's sleeping late—as late as I like without waking up with a script under my pillow!"

The final episode of "The Burns and Allen Show" was filmed on June 4, 1958. After this, there would be no more scripts for Gracie.

There was nothing exceptional about that script. It dealt primarily with Ronnie worrying that he was going to lose his girlfriend to a handsome foreign exchange student. No monologue, short aside, or even closing routine mentioned that this was the last show they would ever shoot. George had always been very honest with his audience in the past, and this was the first time he chose *not* to inform us of any change. Perhaps because he knew that "Burns and Allen" would continue in reruns, it seemed wise to let the show run in perpetuity with no mention of this being the last original episode.

The filming day was just like any other, with only a brief moment backstage where George and Gracie held hands and fought back tears before coming through the curtain to do their closing routine. As soon as Rod Amateau said, "Cut. That's a wrap!" the crew burst into applause and gave Gracie a standing ovation. Champagne was poured into paper cups, and everyone toasted her, laughed, and recounted memorable moments during the eight years of working together. "Everybody was happy," recalled Rod. "Sure we all lost jobs; but we all felt so protective about Gracie, and because Gracie wanted it, everybody was happy for her."

It was late by the time all the tearful farewells were said. Arms laden with bouquets of flowers, George and Gracie headed home after their last performance together as a team.

23

BURNS WITHOUT

ALLEN

*I'm happy and flattered to appear on
one of George's shows. Also, I'm curious. Burns without Allen? What can
he pay me?*
—JACK BENNY,
IN A GUEST APPEARANCE ON
"THE GEORGE BURNS SHOW"

Rumors immediately began circulating that George didn't
want Gracie to retire. *Life* magazine speculated, "George has
not altogether written Gracie off as a partner. 'Maybe after
six months one of the kids will spill a glass of milk on her,'
he says hopefully. 'Then maybe she'll retire from the kids
too.' " But George insisted that "no one so richly deserves
it. . . . Her kind of work takes a lot out of you." He added, "I
can always keep busy as both an executive and a performer."

George wasted no time in fulfilling the "show must go
on" tradition. On February 20, 1958, he disclosed plans for a
new pilot, a show in the "Burns and Allen" genre, without
Gracie. It was to be called, naturally, "The George Burns
Show." "If they like my pilot," he stated in *Daily Variety*,
"that's fine. If they don't, I'll start smoking smaller cigars. At
62, I'm too old to retire."

The new show seemed like a natural. It had all the original cast of "The Burns and Allen Show," minus Gracie. There were new settings. George was now a producer in a Beverly Hills office building; Harry Morton had a C.P.A. office down the hall; Blanche Morton became George's secretary, with her character now taking on the added role of George's watchdog on behalf of Gracie, "protecting" him from the steady parade of young starlets streaming through his office. Ronnie Burns and Harry Von Zell were also on hand, as were a number of well-known guest stars such as Bob Cummings, Carol Channing, Peter Lawford, Phyllis Kirk, and of course George's old pal Jack Benny. George always had an eye for talent, and some not-so-well-known people just starting out in the business were given their first breaks on this show. Actress Suzanne Pleshette, poet and singer Rod McKuen, and an up-and-coming actress named Mary Moore (sans the middle name "Tyler") were all billed as guests.

"We can go anywhere with this format," George declared in *TV Guide* (October 25, 1958), "do anything, use almost any guest star perfectly legitimately. In fact, when Gracie saw the pilot film she turned to me and said, 'You know, I didn't miss me at all.' Nobody did, because nobody had ever been accustomed to seeing Gracie in these new surroundings." And George insisted that there would be no Gracie-type female replacement. "If an imitator were to come along," he said, "the audience would miss her more than ever."

"The George Burns Show" premiered on Tuesday, October 21, 1958, from 9:00 to 9:30 P.M. on NBC. For the first time in thirty-five years, George stood alone in the spotlight. He was funny, his timing was impeccable as always, the writers had pushed themselves to the limit, and the script reflected the enormous amount of labor that went into its planning. But without Gracie, the show had lost its center. Desperately searching for some magic formula that would make the show work, in December, less than two months after the premiere, the writers revamped the format to include a live variety show within almost every episode. Nevertheless the ratings remained low, and the last show was telecast April 14, 1959.

Twenty-twenty hindsight makes it all so clear now. You can't make "Burns and Allen" without Gracie Allen any more than you can make "M*A*S*H" without Alan Alda (remember 1984's "AfterMASH"?). George later admitted, "It didn't take a genius to figure out what was wrong. Sure, we had the same people, but any minute you expected Gracie to come through the door. It was like having dinner; we had the soup, the salad, and the dessert, but the main course was home playing with her grandchildren."

Rod Amateau thought that George's show might have succeeded if George had gone it alone, the way he did years later. "If he had made a clean break and played God or whatever . . . he would have been a hit. He was just as talented then as he is now. George was insecure. He thought he needed that support system."

Perhaps he had the notion in the back of his mind that Gracie would rush out of retirement and save the day. But she didn't. Not only was she burned out, she was also in poor health and was content to watch George from the sidelines as she had done so long ago that evening in New Jersey when they first met. Now George would have to work as a single, something he hadn't attempted in decades. "Here I was," he said, "a kid of sixty-two, struggling to get into show business."

He sat down with his writers and planned his next career. They put together a monologue, some amusing stories and jokes, a few songs, and launched George on the nightclub circuit. His first appearance was at Harrah's in Lake Tahoe, Nevada, and his dependency on a support system was still evident because he brought along Bobby Darin, the DeCastro Sisters, and a dancing act. He opened nearly a year after Gracie's retirement and remarked that the first time he walked out on that stage alone, it was a very strange feeling.

Soon George began to realize what audiences had known all along—he was a talent in his own right. After his hit performance at Harrah's, he moved to the Sahara in Las

Vegas for a four-week stand. Other nightclub appearances followed, and he added female partners, including Carol Channing and Ann-Margret (his protégée), Jane Russell, Connie Haines, and Beryl Davis.

George continued on the nightclub circuit until 1964, when he felt he was ready for a return to television. He began preparation of a new series called "Wendy and Me" (with Connie Stevens as Wendy). However, before the show had even premiered, the greatest tragedy of his life struck.

24

THE ACT IS

OVER . . .

The whole world loved Gracie.
—JACK BENNY, IN HIS EULOGY FOR
GRACIE ALLEN

"Wendy and Me" was in full production during the summer of 1964, and George was once again totally involved in a television series, his first since the unsuccessful "George Burns Show."

Three years earlier Gracie had suffered a severe heart attack. She recovered but had been on medication ever since. Thursday night, August 27, George came home from the studio, tired but feeling good about his new series. A short while after dinner, Gracie started having chest pains. When she failed to get any relief from her pills, George knew something was drastically wrong, and she was rushed to the hospital. Gracie Allen was admitted into Cedars of Lebanon at 10:25 P.M., and by 11:15 she was gone. A stunned George slowly left her side for the last time.

The next morning millions of people read the tragic news

on the front page of their local paper. The *Los Angeles Times* ran one of its rare headlines above their logo: RADIO-TV'S GRACIE ALLEN DIES. Gracie's life, death, and impending funeral were the subject of front-page stories for the next two days. From the *L.A. Times*, August 29, 1964:

> RADIO-TV COMEDIENNE GRACIE ALLEN, 58, DIES
> HUSBAND-PARTNER GEORGE BURNS AT BEDSIDE
> FUNERAL MONDAY—HEART ATTACK
>
> Funeral services will be conducted Monday for Gracie Allen, the smartest dumbbell in the history of show business. Her zany chatter has been stilled by a heart attack at the age of 58. . . . Named pallbearers were Jack Benny, George Jessel, Edward G. Robinson, Mervyn LeRoy, Dr. Rexford Kennemer, and Mike Connolly.

Variety's obituary a week later revealed that her retirement only six years before had been on doctor's orders—but she had never made the news public. The weekly newspaper editorialized with glowing praise for Gracie Allen, something rarely done in an obituary:

> The millions who followed [Burns and Allen] through all their years of radio, pictures and television were intrigued by her personal charm and love of people. The word "beloved" has been over-worked, especially in obits, but those who knew her best reserved the word for her.

The article went on to describe the funeral service that had been held at the Church of the Recessional at Forest Lawn:

> George Jessel spoke for all show biz in his brief eulogy at the service . . . attended by the great and not-so great and several thousands of her public who assembled outside. . . .

Jessel, a lifetime friend of both Gracie and George Burns . . . paid highest tribute to the talent and sincerity of the comedienne, saying . . . , "The act is over, the bow music has faded, the billing will have to be changed—the next stage manager will have to be told 'George N. Burns, in one alone.' " So be it. The passing of this sweet girl who never seemed to grow older is again something which cannot be challenged. The hope of mankind must be in the faith that the play is never over—when the curtain falls, it rises again. . . ."

Benny, moved by grief, in his eulogy said: "I was afraid I might not be able to say these few words. I was afraid it might be too difficult . . . but I was encouraged by George. . . . Mary and I have lost one of our two closest friends. . . . The whole world loved Gracie . . . all of us will miss her so very, very much. . . . We'll never forget her, ever."

George, rocked by Gracie's death, handled his grief by immersing himself in his only other love—his work. At first it was difficult, and he began having chronic insomnia. After experiencing many bouts of sleeplessness, he discovered the problem. "We had twin beds the last years she was alive because of her bad heart. So, finally, I decided to change over and sleep in her bed, and it worked. There was something warm about that."

Gracie was buried in Forest Lawn Memorial Park in Hollywood. George has been quoted as saying he still visits her grave once a month. When asked if he tells her what's been going on, he often replies, "Sure. Why not? I don't know if she hears me, but I've got nothing to lose. And it gives me a chance to break in new material."

25

IN ONE ALONE

GRACIE: *He's been entertaining people for forty years, and nobody
ever knew it.*
—FROM AN EARLY "BURNS AND ALLEN"
EPISODE

It is ironic that Gracie's passing was followed barely two weeks later (September 14, 1964) by the premiere of George's long awaited new television series, "Wendy and Me." In that series, set in a Southern California apartment house, Connie Stevens played a slightly fuzzy, mixed-up young bride of an airline pilot (Ron Harper). George played the building owner. He purchased the property to have a place to practice vaudeville routines in case anyone should ask him to perform again. No one ever did, but that didn't keep him from rehearsing. And he wisely had a clause put in the tenants' leases that said they couldn't evict the landlord. His singing, as usual, was not greatly appreciated. He also stepped out of the action from time to time, à la "Burns and Allen," to narrate the happenings and puff on his cigar.

The show wasn't a huge success; the last episode aired

exactly one year later, September 6, 1965. "The problem was the competition," mused George in a recent *TV Guide* interview (September 15, 1984). "Andy Williams was on one channel, and he sang better than I did. And on the other channel was Lucille Ball, who was a smash. Plus, color was just coming in. It's bad enough to be against Andy Williams and Lucille Ball, but to have to fight with color, too, we didn't have a chance."

Be that as it may, a large part of the problem would seem to be that ever since Gracie's retirement, George had been searching for a replacement, cast in her mold. None of the feminine partners he worked with could duplicate Gracie's style or success. Connie Stevens was the last of a long line of blondes, including Carol Channing and Dorothy Provine, who partnered with George on TV and in his nightclub act. Eventually George sized up the situation and moved on.

Over the next ten years, George found himself with a number of new careers. He produced the "No Time for Sergeants" TV series at Warner Brothers for ABC-TV, and the "Mona McCluskey" TV series for United Artists and NBC. In addition, he helped to develop the "Mr. Ed" television series, now in syndication.

He guested on numerous television shows, performed in nightclubs, on college campuses, and made personal appearances from Las Vegas to Carnegie Hall.

Then, in 1975, fate stepped in to hand him a third career —motion picture actor. George's best friend, Jack Benny, had signed to costar with Walter Matthau in Neil Simon's *The Sunshine Boys* for M-G-M. But, sadly, Jack passed away shortly before the film was to begin production. George was touched when he was asked to assume what would have been Jack's role. It was his first feature film since 1939, and when the film was released, the audiences ate it up. *Newsweek* raved, "If George Burns didn't exist, Neil Simon might have had to invent him—and in a sense he has." The Academy of Motion Picture Arts and Sciences members loved it too and voted him the Oscar for Best Supporting Actor of 1975. In his acceptance speech, George quipped, "If you stay in the business long enough and get to be old enough, you get to be new again."

Two years following the success of *The Sunshine Boys*, George Burns became God. He was cast in the role of the Supreme Being in the Warner Bros. comedy, *Oh, God!*, an unlikely but perfectly believable sort of Deity given to wearing golf hats, tennis shoes, and windbreakers. (Actually, he had had years of practice for the role—on "The Burns and Allen Show" he portrayed an omniscient character who watched from on high—his den—via his all-seeing TV.)

In *Time* magazine, Richard Schickel described the casting as "inspired, in the largest sense of the word. . . . Burns' impeccable—and legendary—timing [is] a quality as essential to working miracles as it is to telling jokes. Burns maintains a reserve, a dignity, that must surely be appreciated in heaven."

A sequel, *Oh, God! Book II*, followed, but it wasn't quite the hit the first one had been. Other films since then included *Sgt. Pepper's Lonely Hearts Club Band* (Universal, 1978); *Movie Movie* (Warner Bros., 1978); *Just You and Me, Kid* (Columbia, 1979); and a highly praised dramatic performance as the mastermind of a senior citizens' bank robbery in *Going in Style* (Warner Bros., 1979).

In 1984, at the age of eighty-eight, George made the third "God" picture for Warners', called *Oh God! You Devil*, in which he played opposite himself as both God *and* the Devil. Director Paul Bogart had these words of praise for his star: "He makes it look easy. . . . Few actors could pull it off with such honesty. George has such good instincts for the truth of a character and a situation, he goes beyond what we usually call 'acting.' " The movie did well at the box office, and George received his customary raves. Arthur Knight, in the *Hollywood Reporter*, wrote:

My biggest complaint about Warners' *Oh, God! You Devil* is that even though George Burns plays both of the

title roles, we don't really see enough of him. Whether
being celestial or satanic, he's a sheer delight with his
perfectly timed delivery and his spare, fine-honed body
language. He even gets in a little soft shoe routine, and,
in his devilish persona, croaks out a chorus of "That Old
Black Magic" in his inimitable style.

In addition to his films, George continues to play Las
Vegas—one show a day and two shows on Saturday nights—
singing, joking about his age, and even delighting the audience with a few dance steps. He makes numerous television
appearances each year on such talk shows as "The Tonight
Show" and "The Phil Donahue Show." On them, he promotes
his books—he's written seven so far: *I Love Her, That's Why,
Living It Up, The Third Time Around, How to Live to Be
100, Dr. Burns' Prescription for Happiness, Dear George,*
and *Gracie: A Love Story.*

In 1985, *People* magazine voted him one of the busiest
people in the world. "Burns prides himself on never taking a
vacation," they noted, then went on to divulge his hectic
schedule for a typical year: two to three months writing a
book, two to three on a movie, four to six weeks on a TV
special, six weeks in Vegas and Tahoe, and six more in concert. The rest of the year is spent writing new material.

He can also be seen in numerous print ads and television
commercials. And, of course, some of his time is devoted to
his two children, four granddaughters, three grandsons, and
one great-granddaughter.

In his "spare" time, he is working on a project to persuade the U.S. Post Office to issue a Jack Benny commemora-
tive postage stamp. Jack was his closest friend, and nothing
would please George more than this tribute to his memory. "I
think of Jack constantly," he once said. "I'll always think of
him. Not only me—the whole world thinks of Jack. Nobody
will forget Jack." In working for this goal, George heads up
a committee that includes former President Gerald Ford,
Norm Crosby, Irving Fein (Jack's manager, who now works

with George), Charlton Heston, Bob Hope, Gene Kelly, Jack
Lemmon, Jimmy Stewart, Gregory Peck, Frank Sinatra, and
other prominent Hollywood personalities.

In September 1985 "George Burns' Comedy Week," a
short-lived half-hour television anthology program, debuted
with George as the weekly host. Actor/comedian Steve Martin was the executive producer.

How does George explain his remarkable stamina and joie de
vivre? "I love show business and I'm lucky to have spent my
whole life in it," he mused. "I think that's really the secret to
a long life. I would rather be a failure in something that I love
than be a success at something that I hated to do. . . . You
can't help getting older, but you don't have to get old. . . .
Never retire! Retire? I'm doing better now . . . I'm making old
age fashionable. People can't wait to get old."

The nonagenarian continued philosophically, "There's
nothing you can do about dying. Like in vaudeville, if they
didn't like your act, they'd cancel you. The manager would
knock on your door and give you back your pictures if you
were canceled. Well, when the guy knocks on my door, I'm not
going to answer! Let them keep the pictures. I can't die—I'm
booked." And, in fact, he is—in 1996, when he will be one
hundred, George is booked in to the Palladium in London.

George Burns still lives in the same house on Maple Drive
in Beverly Hills that he and Gracie bought when they first
came to Hollywood. He seldom looks backward, preferring to
concentrate on the present and future. But once, when reflect-
ing on his successful thirty-eight-year marriage to Gracie,
George said simply: "We made each other laugh."

How fortunate for us that we were able to share some of
that laughter.

EPILOGUE

It has been more than three and a half decades since the debut of "The George Burns and Gracie Allen Show." After the series went off the air, most of the cast and crew continued to have successful careers in television and motion pictures. Sadly, many of them have passed away. But their legacy, the 291 episodes of "Burns and Allen," will live forever.

BILL GOODWIN had his own show on NBC and received a number of film offers. In 1956 he bought the Nooks Hotel in Palm Springs and was on a constant shuttle between there and Hollywood. In 1957 he had a radio show on KFI in Los Angeles, and soon after that he became host of "Colgate Theatre" on KTTV in L.A. He died of a heart attack in 1958; he was survived by his wife and four children.

HARRY VON ZELL made a number of motion pictures throughout his career, including *Uncle Harry, I Can Get It for You Wholesale,* and *Boy Did I Get a Wrong Number.* His later years saw him as the commercial spokesman for Home Savings and Loan in Los Angeles. He died of cancer at the age of seventy-five in 1981, and was survived by his wife, son, daughter, four grandchildren, and four great-grandchildren.

BEA BENADERET went on to play Wilma, the housekeeper on "Peter Loves Mary," and was cast by Paul Henning in "The Beverly Hillbillies" as cousin Pearl Bodine. When Paul became producer of "Petticoat Junction" in 1963, Bea received the starring role of Kate Bradley. She also dubbed the voice of Betty Rubble in "The Flintstones" for many years. Bea succumbed to lung cancer at the age of sixty-two in 1968, and was survived by her husband, daughter, son, and granddaughter.

HAL MARCH served as host of TV's "The $64,000 Question" for three years. After that, Broadway beckoned, and he replaced Henry Fonda in *Two for the Seesaw.* He starred in Neil Simon's *Come Blow Your Horn,* and then turned to stock, motion pictures, and television. Among his film credits were *The Eddie Cantor Story, A Guide for the Married Man,* and *Nobody Loves an Albatross.* His last assignment was as host of the KNBC (Los Angeles) game show "It's Your Bet." He died at the age of forty-nine in 1970, from pneumonia following lung cancer, and was survived by his wife, three sons, and two daughters.

JOHN BROWN was one of the founders and an active participant in the American Federation of Radio Artists. He did a number of character roles in radio, television, and motion pictures and also did character portrayals on the New York stage. He died of a heart attack at the age of fifty-three in 1957, and was survived by his mother, his wife, a daughter, a son, three sisters, and a brother.

FRED CLARK continued a career in legitimate theater, starring on the London stage in *Never Too Late* and on Broadway in *Romanoff and Juliet* and *Absence of a Cello.* He appeared in twelve episodes of "The Milton Berle Show" before going on to star in the television series "The Secret Life of Henry Phyfe." He died in 1968 at the age of fifty-four, and was survived by his second wife and his mother.

LARRY KEATING costarred as Alan Young's neighbor Roger Addison in the "Mr. Ed" TV series for over three years, and although suffering from leukemia during the last six months of filming, he worked until the week preceding his death. He died in 1963 at the age of sixty-four.

WILLIAM (WILLY) BURNS went on to write for several TV series, including "Mr. Ed," "Wendy and Me," "No Time for Sergeants," "Panic," and "Mona McCluskey." He died at the age of sixty-three in 1966, and was survived by his wife, three daughters, three sisters, and three brothers, including George Burns.

HARVEY HELM wrote for "Burns and Allen" for twenty years, both in radio and TV. He died in 1965 at the age of sixty-six and was survived by his wife, daughter, brother, and sister.

KEITH FOWLER was one of Hollywood's busiest comedy writers. After "Burns and Allen" he wrote for "Hazel," "The Farmer's Daughter," "The Addams Family," and "Dennis the Menace." He died of diabetes at the age of sixty-six in 1973.

JESSE GOLDSTEIN continued writing for TV comics such as Ed Wynn, Alan Young, Victor Borge, and Joan Davis, eventually joining the staff of "The Red Skelton Show." He worked with Skelton for over four years until his untimely death at the age of forty-three in 1959. He was survived by his wife and five children.

NORMAN PAUL continued his successful writing career, eventually landing an assignment for the highly popular TV show "Get Smart." He died in 1979 at the age of sixty-six.

SID DORFMAN continued his writing career until his death from a heart attack in October, 1988. He was seventy-two.

NATE MONASTER one of the original "Burns and Allen" writers, is still working in Hollywood today.

In June 1958, McCadden Productions found itself with a shelf full of unsold pilots. Among these were a new solo George

Burns outing entitled "The XYZ Project"; "Theodora," starring Hermione Gingold; "Women"; "Flight"; "21 Beacon Street"; and "Mr. Ed," the talking horse series (which eventually was sold to Filmways). With the final episode of "The George Burns and Gracie Allen Show," the only McCadden series to pick up a renewal was "The Bob Cummings Show."

At the same time, George Burns and McCadden sold the "Burns and Allen" rights to Columbia Pictures' video arm, Screen Gems, for a reported $4.5 million. The show is still being syndicated by Columbia today, rekindling fond memories for the first generation of television viewers while treating a new younger audience to the magic that is Burns and Allen.

APPENDIX 1

CAST LIST

George Burns	HIMSELF
Gracie Allen	HERSELF
Blanche Morton	BEA BENADERET
Harry Morton	HAL MARCH
	JOHN BROWN
	FRED CLARK
	LARRY KEATING
Ronnie Burns	HIMSELF
Bill Goodwin	HIMSELF
Harry Von Zell	HIMSELF

REGULAR CHARACTERS

Detective Sawyer	JAMES FLAVIN
Jane *(wardrobe woman)*	ELVIA ALLMAN
Mr. Vanderlip	GRANDON RHODES
Mrs. Vanderlip	KAY REIHL
Emily Vanderlip	ELINOR DONAHUE
Mr. Beeseley	ROLF SEDAN
Phillips *(the gardener)*	BOB SWEENEY
Casey *(Morton's partner)*	HAL MARCH
Yvette	JACQUELINE BEER
Mr. Boardman	FRANK WILCOX
Jim Boardman	HART SPRAEGER
Mrs. Sohmers	DORIS PACKER
Clara Bagley	IRENE HERVEY
Marie	JACQUELINE BEER
Ralph	BOB ELLIS
Brian McAfee	ROBERT EASTON
Bonnie Sue McAfee	JUDY BOUTIN (MEREDITH)
Joyce	JACKIE LOUGHRY
Kathy	KATHY MARLOWE
Mr. Jantzen	HOWARD MCNEAR
Jean Jantzen	JODY WARNER
Joan Jantzen	MARY ELLEN KAYE
June Jantzen	DARLENE ALBERT
Joy Jantzen	YVONNE LIME
Lew	JODY MCCREA
Mr. McAfee	RALPH DUMKE
Alfred	HOOPER DUNBAR

SPECIAL GUEST STARS

JACK BENNY—*as himself*
HENRY JONES—*as an encyclopedia salesman*
SHELDON LEONARD—*as Silky the gangster*
MAYOR BOWRON—*as himself*
RONALD REAGAN—*as himself*

BOB FOSSE—*as himself, a dancer, on early live shows*
JACK BENNY'S DOG, SUZETTE—*as herself*
JACK ALBERTSON—*as Bozo*
MARY LIVINGSTON—*as herself*
FRANCIS X. BUSHMAN—*as himself*
STEVE REEVES—*as Foley*
RICHARD DEACON—*as Mr. Dayton*
DR. FRANK BAXTER (OF U.S.C.)—*as himself*
BOB CUMMINGS—*as himself*
CHARLES "KING" VIDOR—*as himself*
MARION ROSS—*as Dixie (She later became famous as Mrs. Cunningham on "Happy Days")*
HAYDEN RORKE—*as a psychiatrist (he later went on to star in "I Dream of Jeannie" as the psychiatrist, Dr. Bellows)*

EMMY NOMINATIONS *(no wins)*

1951 BEST COMEDY SHOW

1952 BEST SITUATION COMEDY

1953 BEST SITUATION COMEDY

   Bea Benaderet—BEST SUPPORTING ACTRESS (SERIES)

1954 *Burns and Allen*—BEST COMEDY SERIES

   Gracie Allen—BEST ACTRESS (SERIES)

   Bea Benaderet—BEST SUPPORTING ACTRESS (SERIES)

1955 *Gracie Allen*—BEST ACTRESS (SERIES)

   Gracie Allen—BEST COMEDIENNE

1956 *Gracie Allen*—BEST ACTRESS (COMEDY SERIES)

1957 *Gracie Allen*—BEST ACTRESS (COMEDY SERIES)

1958 *Gracie Allen*—BEST ACTRESS (COMEDY SERIES)

APPENDIX 2

SYNOPSES, FIRST SEASON—1950–51

PRODUCER/DIRECTOR: Ralph Levy
WRITERS: Paul Henning
Sid Dorfman
Harvey Helm
William Burns

NOTE: These were all live shows, preserved as kinescopes, and are not in syndication.

#1 AIR DATE: OCTOBER 12, 1950

In his opening monologue George explains being a "straight man." He introduces the cast, explains the show's format, and sings with the Skylarks. In the story, the boys (George and

Harry Morton) want to go to the fights; the girls (Gracie and Blanche) want to go to the movies. George tries to trick the girls with a fictitious card game called "Kleebob," but Gracie instantly catches on and wins the game. The husbands give in and take them to the movies.

#2 AIR DATE: OCTOBER 26, 1950

After a visit to an art museum, Gracie decides to become a great artist. At home she attempts a portrait of George. It's awful, but when she starts crying, everyone tells her it's great. Gracie knows it's a masterpiece. She has been told that to be a good artist you must suffer. She's been wearing size-two shoes and her feet are killing her.

#3 AIR DATE: NOVEMBER 9, 1950

The Mortons and Burnses are going to a football game together. But when Gracie discovers a dent in the fender, she tries to get them to walk to the game so George won't discover the dent. Finally George admits he was the one who dented the fender.

#4 AIR DATE: NOVEMBER 23, 1950

Harry Morton has a new secretary, so naturally Blanche and Gracie are certain it's a pretty young girl. George tries to tell them it's a man, but the two women won't believe him, until Harry finally arrives and convinces them that it is indeed a man. Everybody has Thanksgiving dinner at the Burnses' house, and George "treats" them to a song.

#5 AIR DATE: DECEMBER 7, 1950

Gracie returns George's Christmas presents before he's seen them, because every year George exchanges his presents, and this year she's saving him the trouble. Vanderlip the banker complains to George about Gracie's strange system of check writing, and he and Gracie go to the bank, where she convinces George she'd be better off without an account.

#6 AIR DATE: DECEMBER 21, 1950

A show centering on the Christmas holidays. Gracie buys a tree and thoroughly confuses the tree salesman. The tree is delivered, and, as they decorate it, some children sing carols. They exchange presents and Gracie tells about the Christmases she remembers as a child.

#7 AIR DATE: DECEMBER 28, 1950

The first one from CBS, Hollywood.
      The Mortons and the Burnses are going to a party, so Gracie hires an Arthur Murray instructor to give them rumba lessons. George and Harry Morton begin to limp and complain about their "old football injuries"—until the beautiful female instructor arrives. But then a man arrives and he turns out to be the teacher—the girl only plays the records. Suddenly the boys' old football injuries return.

#8 AIR DATE: JANUARY 4, 1951

Gracie can't remember why she circled a date on the calendar. It must mean something, so she throws a party. The guests all arrive with their congratulations, although no one is sure what for, until Jack Benny arrives. The date on the calendar was to remind George and Gracie that *Jack* was giving a party.

#9 AIR DATE: JANUARY 18, 1951

It's the boys versus the girls again, as George and Harry Morton want to go duck hunting and Gracie and Blanche want to go to Palm Springs. George hires a "doctor" to phone

Gracie and tell her he can't go anyplace hot and sunny because it will make his blood pressure go up. The "doctor" gets
drunk, can't make the call, and they all end up going to Palm
Springs.

#10 AIR DATE: FEBRUARY 1, 1951

Gracie finds a stray St. Bernard dog. She brings him home and
uses George's golf clubs to teach the dog how to fetch. This
dog is really putting George's patience to the test, and when
a boy finally shows up and claims the mutt, George pays *him*
a twenty-five-dollar reward!

#11 AIR DATE: FEBRUARY 15, 1951

Blanche discovers Harry has been holding out twenty dollars
a week from his paycheck to go to the racetrack. She leaves
and goes to stay with Gracie. Helpful George tells Blanche
that Harry had really been holding out the money to buy a fur
coat for her. Harry arrives to take her back, but he's too late
—Blanche is already out spending the nonexistent money for
a fur coat.

#12 AIR DATE: MARCH 1, 1951

Hadley, the income-tax man, spends a frustrating day up
against Gracie's inimitable logic when he questions her about
her tax deductions.

#13 AIR DATE: MARCH 15, 1951

Gracie tries to get the Mortons invited to the Vanderlips'
party, but they can't invite them because they don't have
enough room at the table. Gracie and George decide not to go
without their good friends, so they cancel out. Of course the
Vanderlips now have room, and naturally they invite the Mortons to dinner.

#14 AIR DATE: MARCH 29, 1951

Gracie is a witness to an automobile accident involving gangster Johnny Velvet. Velvet and his attorney threaten her,
trying to get her to go to court and testify in his favor. In
court, Gracie tells the truth in her best form; Johnny Velvet
is found guilty and sentenced—he must spend one whole day
with Gracie.

#15 AIR DATE: APRIL 12, 1951

Poor sick George. Well-meaning people keep bringing him
food to help him get over his bug, but everyone taste-tests the
food for him, while George gets nothing to eat.

#16 AIR DATE: APRIL 26, 1951

While the Vanderlips are out of town for a few days, their
teenage daughter is staying at the Burnses'. Gracie decides
to help her with her schoolwork. Little did Emily dream how
confused she could become in such a short time!

#17 AIR DATE: MAY 10, 1951

Mr. and Mrs. Anderson, a couple from Minnesota, make a
real-estate deal with Harry Morton and buy the corner lot in
the Burnses' neighborhood. All goes well until they hear
George singing in the shower while he's shaving. Gracie promises them they can look forward to this treat every morning.
The Andersons tear up the contract and head back to Minnesota.

#18 AIR DATE: MAY 24, 1951

The Vanderlips plan a lavish costume party, so Gracie naturally goes to a travel agency to get ideas for costumes from
the brochures. Vanderlip's wife has rented him a Buster

Brown outfit complete with teddy bear and straw sailor hat, and he calls off the party, since this outfit isn't dignified enough for a bank president.

#19 AIR DATE: JUNE 7, 1951

Gracie's school chum Mamie Kelly has come to visit the Burnses and ends up staying two weeks. She keeps missing the bus, the train, the plane; she just can't seem to leave, much to George's dismay. At last her husband shows up, but since she's finally left, he decides to stay on with George and Gracie while he waits for Mamie to return.

#20 AIR DATE: JUNE 21, 1951

Harry Morton wants to go fishing and Blanche wants him to go to her mother's. Harry tries to scheme his way out of it, but he gets caught in a lie, which only gets him in deeper trouble with Blanche—now he has to buy her a fur coat as an apology. Gracie bawls out George because he never lies to her.

#21 AIR DATE: JULY 5, 1951

George thinks he and Gracie have been seeing too much of the Mortons. They decide to trick the Mortons into leaving town for the weekend so they can use their pool alone. When the Mortons say they'll stay home, the Burnses try to sneak away, but are caught in the act. Both couples end up sharing their weekend at the beach.

#22 AIR DATE: JULY 19, 1951

A petition is being circulated to keep the notorious gangster Silky Thompson from moving into the neighborhood. However, after three hours with Gracie, Silky signs the petition to keep *himself* out of the neighborhood.

#23 AIR DATE: AUGUST 2, 1951

Gracie and Blanche go on a health kick when they read a diet book. They invite the author to speak at a meeting of their club, the Beverly Hills Uplifters Society. After the speech, they serve their husbands nothing but vegetables, until both men are totally fed up.

#24 AIR DATE: AUGUST 16, 1951

Mamie Kelly and her three children park their trailer in the Burnses' backyard. The kids raise hell, shooting their BB guns, breaking a window, and leaving their skates where George can trip over them. George attempts to get them to leave, but to no avail.

#25 AIR DATE: AUGUST 30, 1951

Harry Morton has a real-estate client whom he's trying to woo, and he tells Gracie that she can order new appliances through the client—wholesale. Gracie orders all sorts of unnecessary things, but George makes her send everything back. No more buying wholesale! So Gracie goes out and buys all the same things—retail.

#26 AIR DATE: SEPTEMBER 13, 1951

Gracie is having a wedding at their home for Mrs. Nelson's daughter to repay Mrs. Nelson for a tremendous favor she once did Gracie. After George spends thousands of dollars for the wedding, we learn what the tremendous favor was—Gracie's car had stalled and Mrs. Nelson was kind enough to give her a push.

SYNOPSES, SECOND SEASON—1951–52

PRODUCER/DIRECTOR: Ralph Levy
WRITERS: Paul Henning
          Sid Dorfman
          Harvey Helm
          William Burns

#27 AIR DATE: SEPTEMBER 27, 1951

Blanche is having bad dreams and is afraid to see a psychiatrist, so Gracie goes in her place, pretending to be Mrs. Morton. Harry hears that his wife has gone to a shrink, thinks she must be crazy, and starts treating Blanche nicely. Gracie, trying to convince George that she's crazy so he'll be extra nice to her, ends up acting *normal* for Gracie.

#28 AIR DATE: OCTOBER 11, 1951

Gracie and her Uplifters Society are locked out of their clubroom because she forgot to pay the rent. She spent the money for a wall safe to protect their money. George finally gives the money to the girls to get them out of the house.

#29 AIR DATE: OCTOBER 25, 1951

The Burnses and the Mortons have each bought four tickets to the football game, so they discover they have extra tickets to sell. After Gracie gets arrested for "scalping," the cops buy a ticket to get rid of her. Then the couples discover they have no tickets because they've sold them all. Finally, Gracie gets tickets at the box office and they all get to go to the game.

#30 AIR DATE: NOVEMBER 8, 1951

Gracie plans a surprise party for George's birthday. George is supposed to invite everybody to the Mocambo and they are all supposed to decline. But when everyone does take him up on his offer, George ends up with the bill. Surprise!

#31 AIR DATE: NOVEMBER 22, 1951

Gracie is hostessing Thanksgiving dinner for some friends, including Harry Morton's partner, Casey. Casey's new wife is named Linda Lee; so is a horse that Casey thinks must be a sure bet. Blanche tells Gracie that Linda Lee is a horse, and Gracie thinks she's insulting Casey's new wife. All gets straightened out as they sit down to dinner and football.

#32 AIR DATE: DECEMBER 6, 1951

The Uplifters Society is having a concert and the girls want new dresses, but of course their husbands refuse to buy them. Harry thinks George has bought Gracie a new dress so he gets one for Blanche. Gracie then pleads with George that since Blanche has a new dress, she should have one too. George relents, and she rushes to the closet to get the dress she's already bought.

#33 AIR DATE: DECEMBER 20, 1951

Their second Christmas show. Mamie Kelly and her children spend the holidays with the Burnses. George dresses up and plays Santa for the children and Gracie tells the story of "A Christmas Carol," which emerges as a cross between "Goldilocks," "Cinderella," and several other fairy tales.

#34 AIR DATE: JANUARY 3, 1952

Gracie has a storeroom built so she can store home-canned fruits and vegetables. When the project gets out of hand, George hires someone to pretend he's a building inspector to tell her she doesn't have a permit and will have to tear the storeroom down. Gracie obliges, then goes to City Hall and gets a permit, so they have to build it all over again from scratch.

#35 AIR DATE: JANUARY 17, 1952

Blanche Morton is running against Mrs. McAviddy for president of the Beverly Hills Uplifters. Blanche and Harry quarrel over her candidacy, and she leaves him. Mrs. McAviddy is elected president, but leaves her husband because he didn't want her elected either. Gracie chimes in and pretends to leave George so she won't feel left out.

#36 AIR DATE: JANUARY 31, 1952

The Vanderlips are invited over to the Burnses' for dinner. George and Harry Morton dread looking at Vanderlip's home movies once again, and they both take sleeping pills so they'll doze off early. But Vanderlip's wife is out of town, and he shows up ready to watch the fights on TV with the boys. George and Harry stagger around slapping their faces so they can wake up and watch too.

#37 AIR DATE: FEBRUARY 14, 1952

Gracie has dented the fender on the car *again*. She schemes to get it fixed without telling George about it. But all her elaborate plotting was unnecessary, and George finally 'fesses up—he knew about it all the time.

#38 AIR DATE: FEBRUARY 28, 1952

George and Gracie are going to Palm Springs to rehearse with Jack Benny for his next TV show. Blanche wants to go, but Harry won't let her. Blanche pretends she has a cold and needs to be where it is warm. Finally Harry gives in to Blanche because he wants to go on a hunting trip anyway.

This episode used a background projection process to depict movement in the scene involving travel in the car.

#39 AIR DATE: MARCH 13, 1952

Gracie loses her engagement ring. George finds it, but decides to teach her a lesson and doesn't tell her. A detective brings over the notorious pickpocket Fingers Leeds as a possible suspect. Fingers deftly lifts the ring from George, but finally brings it back after he sees how small it is.

#40 AIR DATE: MARCH 27, 1952

Jane the wardrobe woman tells Gracie that Jane's brother is mixed up with a gold digger named Flossie Hardwick. Gracie fixes Flossie up with Harry Von Zell instead. The show ends in a pie-throwing fest, as a pie promoter tries to show George a new gimmick for improving his show.

#41 AIR DATE: APRIL 10, 1952

Barney Dean, a producer making a film about vaudevillians, stops by the house to interview George and Gracie. He sends over a photographer to take some pictures of them with various props, and while the two pose, they reminisce.

#42 AIR DATE: APRIL 24, 1952

Jack Benny guest-stars. He and George have been feuding— George claims Jack stole a joke from him up in San Francisco, and the two comedians now aren't speaking. During George's monologue, Jack stands at the opposite end of the proscenium and the camera swings back and forth between the two of them—sort of "dueling comedians." Everyone has a hand in trying to get them to make up. Finally Gracie and Jack's wife, Mary, get them to apologize to each other, and they drink a toast to their friendship.

#43 AIR DATE: MAY 8, 1952

Gracie wants to redecorate, and tricks George into taking Harry Morton fishing, telling him Blanche wants to redecorate and he has to get Harry out of town. But Harry backs down and Gracie goes to great lengths to try to think of ways to get George out of the house. She manages to get him to go to the Mortons' for two days, but it's obvious George knows what's up.

#44 AIR DATE: MAY 22, 1952

Mamie Kelly and her kids move into the Burnses' backyard with their trailer while they house-hunt. The kids drive George crazy playing "Space Patrol," and he has difficulty doing his work. One of Mamie's children falls in the pool and George (stunt double) rescues her. Finally George puts on one of the kids' space helmets to get some privacy.

Show ended with special announcement by Harry Von Zell: "And now, Carnation's own contented couple, who have been honored this week with the Sylvania Pioneer Award for their work in radio and television."

#45 AIR DATE: JUNE 5, 1952

Gracie goes to a swami, who tells her that she's going to be married twice. She knows she could never be happy with anyone but George, and she hires a lawyer so she can divorce and remarry him. George and Harry Von Zell pretend to be swamis so they can persuade Gracie not to go through with it. During this, the police show up looking for the original swami, who is a bookmaker, and George, Harry, and the original swami are carted off to jail.

#46 AIR DATE: JUNE 19, 1952

Two slick promoters have conned Harry Von Zell into invest-
ing five thousand dollars in a new musical. They promise
George the starring role, and he also writes them a check.
George does finally get his money back, and then he makes
everyone listen to him sing by holding them at bay with a
shotgun.

#47 AIR DATE: JULY 3, 1952

George buys a new secretary/desk and Gracie thinks he's
getting a gorgeous woman to work for him. She hires a detective to follow him, but the man mistakenly follows Harry
Morton. The detective, thinking Harry is George and George
is Harry, tells Blanche her husband is having an extramarital
affair with Gracie, which makes for more confusion when
Blanche gets jealous.

#48 AIR DATE: JULY 17, 1952

Gracie convinces a recording company that she can deliver the
Great Gazatti, a renowned Italian singer, if they'll agree to
sign George. They sign George, but Gazatti signs with another company and they fire George. George sings mer-
rily anyway—"I'd love to call you rose dear, but roses fade
away. . . ."

#49 AIR DATE: JULY 31, 1952

George doesn't want to go to the Happy Time Lodge with the
Mortons, so he invents a story that he needs fifty thousand
dollars by that evening or he can't go. Thinking they are
broke, Gracie tries to raise the money by renting out their
spare room to boarders. George is forced to admit he made it
all up.

#50 AIR DATE: AUGUST 14, 1952

Gracie goes to the racetrack and is talked into buying a horse. The horse traders move in with the Burnses, and George pays them $150 to leave. The police trace the horse to the Burnses' house, and George is arrested for horse theft—the horse was stolen. Once again, it's off to jail for George.

#51 AIR DATE: AUGUST 28, 1952

When George tells Gracie he ran into Georgie Jessel at the Friars Club, she misunderstands and thinks George needs glasses. She connives to get an eye doctor over to the house to test George's eyes. But the doctor needs glasses more than George does, and falls into the pool when he leaves.

#52 AIR DATE: SEPTEMBER 25, 1952

The girls want to have their houses redecorated, but George and Harry cook up a scheme to trick them out of it. Gracie learns of the plot and hires the best decorator in town. To get George out of the house for two weeks, she invites her relatives to come and stay for a second honeymoon. Therefore, Gracie tells George, they will have to go to Las Vegas. George knows what's up, but he agrees to the trip.

This was the last live show.

SYNOPSES, THIRD SEASON—1952–53

NOTE: All remaining shows are on film.

PRODUCER/DIRECTOR: Ralph Levy
WRITERS: Sid Dorfman
Harvey Helm
Nate Monaster
Jesse Goldstein
William Burns

#1 AIR DATE: OCTOBER 9, 1952

Gracie's wardrobe woman, Jane, wins a free trip to Hawaii. Gracie contacts a marriage broker to find Jane a husband to take on the trip, not realizing the woman is already married.

#2 AIR DATE: OCTOBER 16, 1952

Gracie is giving a dinner party for a famous atomic scientist who usually turns down dinner invitations. But when he learns that George was in Las Vegas at the time of the atomic tests, he thinks George is a fellow scientist and accepts. The man leaves when he learns George isn't a scientist after all, and the Burnses and Mortons enjoy each other's company, since Gracie forgot to mail the invitations to the other guests.

#3 AIR DATE: OCTOBER 23, 1952

When George rehearses sneezing for an upcoming show, Gracie thinks he needs a doctor. Since she doesn't want George to know about the doctor, she has herself examined instead and does her best to imitate George's symptoms. The doctor naturally recommends a psychiatrist. Gracie tells George she thought the sneezing was brought on by his scripts, so she burned them.

#4 AIR DATE: OCTOBER 30, 1952

Harry Morton and Von Zell think George should buy a boat so they can all use it. They try to convince him he's overworked and needs a hobby. They all decide that the best way to convince him he's cracking under pressure is to make him think he's someone named Charlie Cochran. George as usual has the last word—he buys the boat and signs the contract "Charlie Cochran."

#5 AIR DATE: NOVEMBER 6, 1952

Gracie decides to surprise George with a portrait of himself. She hires a famous artist, then hides him in the closet so he can paint George secretly. George is onto Gracie, and tells her a portrait painted in the closet won't be any good. If it is, he'll live in the closet for a month. The portrait is wonderful, and George dutifully steps into the closet and closes the door.

#6 AIR DATE: NOVEMBER 13, 1952

Gracie and Blanche want a night on the town, but husbands George and Harry aren't interested. The girls dress up in fancy evening gowns and drop hints, to no avail. As a last resort, they hire gigolos to take them out, and the plan seems to be working when their husbands show up dressed in their tuxedos. Actually, they had planned all along to take their wives out for a night on the town.

#7 AIR DATE: NOVEMBER 20, 1952

Blanche and Gracie want George to sponsor a famous ballet troupe, but George isn't interested. Gracie arranges to bring the ballet to him by having its two stars pose as their new maid and butler. George enjoys their pirouetting and arabesques as they do their work, but he still refuses to sponsor the troupe. Gracie manages to trick him into buying tickets when she tells him the man selling the "boxes" is a funeral director.

#8 AIR DATE: NOVEMBER 27, 1952

George and Gracie's old friends from vaudeville, the Skating Pearsons, come to visit. Their son Joey wants to be in show business, and the Pearsons hope George and Gracie can talk him out of this risky profession. George and Gracie succeed.

Joey is ready to go back to school when his parents get an
offer to appear in a show—and it's back to the boards for Joey.

#9 AIR DATE: DECEMBER 4, 1952

Gracie tries to sell swampland of Harry Morton's so he'll buy
Blanche a TV, and Harry ends up thinking there's oil on the
property.

#10 AIR DATE: DECEMBER 11, 1952

Gracie writes "My Life with George Burns" for *Look* magazine and makes up a story about George beating up a gangster—who decides to set the record straight.

#11 AIR DATE: DECEMBER 18, 1952

When Gracie finds a line of George's dialogue to be memorized, she thinks it's a suicide note. Everyone is extra nice and
tries to keep George happy so he won't do himself in. Rather
than correct them, George uses their misconception to keep
Gracie's mother from visiting.

#12 AIR DATE: DECEMBER 25, 1952

Having Harry Von Zell and Harry Morton as good friends is
an invitation for trouble when Gracie tries to help Von Zell,
who has just discovered he's been dating a married woman.
The Harrys get confused in the translation, and the woman's
jealous husband thinks it's Harry Morton who's been seeing
his wife.

#13 AIR DATE: JANUARY 1, 1953

Gracie has never met her Uncle Clyde the paper-tearer, but
he's coming for a visit—against George's wishes. She tries to
fool George by pretending her uncle is just a stranger renting

the room, not knowing he really *is* a stranger—a friend of Harry Von Zell's. By the time her real uncle does show up, everyone is confused as to who's who.

This show is introduced with Ronnie and Sandy Burns sitting in the living room about to watch the show with parents George and Gracie.

#14 AIR DATE: JANUARY 8, 1953

Harry Morton tries to hide his anniversary present for Blanche at the Burnses' house. When Gracie finds it, she mistakenly thinks he's fallen in love with her. The only way she can think of discouraging him is by preparing indigestible food, like tuna-fish-and-rubber-band sandwiches.

#15 AIR DATE: JANUARY 15, 1953

When Harry Morton trades their house for one across town, Gracie tries to prevent the move so she won't lose her best friend, Blanche. She does her best to convince the new neighbors that she and George wouldn't be suitable next-door neighbors. She hires a woman who does vocal impressions to make animal sounds from the basement, baby cries from next door, and screams from the attic. None of this works until the buyers hear George singing in the kitchen, and they flee in terror.

#16 AIR DATE: JANUARY 22, 1953

Gracie is convinced that she and George aren't legally married when she sees a judge in a movie who resembles the one at their wedding. Since their marriage license was burned in a fire, George has to bring in guest star Jack Benny as a witness to prove to Gracie they're really married.

#17 AIR DATE: FEBRUARY 12, 1953

On the train home from visiting her folks in San Francisco, Gracie thinks one of the passengers is going to murder his wife. When she reports it, the police think Harry Morton has done away with Blanche, who has really just gone shopping.

#18 AIR DATE: FEBRUARY 5, 1953

George loans Georgie Jessel fifty dollars to buy a teddy bear from a gorgeous cigarette girl and give her a big tip. Jessel gives George the teddy and keeps the girl. Gracie reads a gossip column story about a well-known star giving a fifty-dollar tip to a cigarette girl, and when George shows up with the bear, he has a hard time convincing Gracie the story was about Jessel, not him.

#19 AIR DATE: JANUARY 29, 1953

When Gracie gets a $2.38 tax refund, she invites Mayor Bowron to dinner and tries to return it, feeling the government needs it more than she does.

Los Angeles's Mayor Bowron appeared as himself, and in the middle of the show he did a pitch for the March of Dimes, which needed contributions to help develop a vaccine against polio.

#20 AIR DATE: FEBRUARY 19, 1953

When Harry Von Zell tells Gracie he could save three thousand dollars on his income tax if he had a wife and three kids, Gracie thinks he's going to pay her the money to find him a family. She runs an ad in the paper and she and Blanche make plans to buy a car with the money. Fortunately, George figures out what she's up to just in time.

#21 AIR DATE: FEBRUARY 26, 1953

Harry Morton has a piece of swampland he's sure he could sell, if only he had the right party. So Gracie decides to throw that party for him.

#22 AIR DATE: MARCH 5, 1953

When Harry Morton stumbles downstairs to turn off his car's headlights late at night, George and Gracie think he's a prowler. Each time George looks, Harry's gone. Then Blanche hears George and thinks *he's* a prowler. Detective Sawyer is summoned and ends up nabbing Harry Von Zell, who had insomnia and stopped by for a chat.

#23 AIR DATE: MARCH 12, 1953

Gracie thinks George wants to buy a ranch, so she starts investigating the market. George gets Harry Von Zell to pretend he's a doctor who'll convince Gracie that George can't live on a ranch. Harry Morton has a hot client eager to sell a ranch and gets his partner Casey (played by Hal March) to play doctor and convince Gracie that George *must* live on a ranch.

#24 AIR DATE: MARCH 19, 1953

George hasn't been sleeping well, so Gracie enlists him in the Army Reserve for three weeks. An Army doctor comes to give George his physical, but by mistake he examines Harry Morton, who has been waiting for his insurance exam, and Harry ends up in the Army. George has no intention of going but at the end of the show the M.P.s come and take both men away for being AWOL. George ends the show by stepping in front of the curtain and saying, "You're right, they got me out."

#25 AIR DATE: MARCH 26, 1953

When someone whistles in George's dressing room, Gracie believes the old show-biz superstition that it means three days' bad luck for George. Gracie hides the car so he can't drive to Palm Springs for a writers' meeting. George reports the car stolen, but eventually gets it back and starts the drive to Palm Springs. But he's arrested soon after—the car was still on the "hot" list. Gracie tells the police to keep him; she'll pick him up after the three days go by.

#26 AIR DATE: MARCH 30, 1953

A college student wanting to impress his girlfriend's parents asks Gracie to pose as his mother. Gracie agrees, but George will have none of it. Harry Von Zell is innocently roped into being the "father"; at the same time Harry Morton, at Blanche's urging, arrives to play the part. Confusion reigns until George admits he's Gracie's husband. (See also #278.)

The names of the college boy and girl were "Ronnie" and "Sandy"—the real names of the Burnses' own kids.

#27 AIR DATE: APRIL 6, 1953

Harry Von Zell is planning to buy a mountain cabin, not from Harry Morton, but from another real-estate agent. The agent calls Gracie for a reference, and she thinks George is buying a cabin. The Mortons are furious at George for buying from someone else, so he agrees to buy a cabin from Harry M. After George has signed the contract, Blanche finds it and tears it up, not knowing it was Harry's.

#28 AIR DATE: APRIL 13, 1953

Blanche secretly buys a fur stole and asks Gracie to hide it from Harry. George finds it and thinks Gracie has bought a stole. He takes it to Harry to hide, hoping to teach Gracie a lesson. She reports the fur stole stolen, while to Blanche's horror, her fur has turned up at her house. The stole keeps house-hopping as George keeps taking it back and Blanche keeps returning it to Gracie.

#29 AIR DATE: APRIL 20, 1953

Gracie and Blanche are taking Spanish lessons from a friend of Harry Von Zell. The instructor informs the girls that he will be deported in three days unless he has a relative in this country who can vouch for him. Gracie tells the immigration officer that George is Juan's uncle. When the officer shows up at the Burnses', George is wearing a poncho and strumming a flamenco guitar, getting into the spirit of the Spanish lessons. The officer thinks George is an illegal alien, and George is nearly deported.

#30 AIR DATE: APRIL 27, 1953

Gracie overhears the Vanderlips' maid saying that their cook told her that on Vanderlip's wife's birthday, he gave her a fur and a diamond. Gracie thinks Vanderlip gave these gifts to the cook, and, hoping to make Vanderlip jealous, she sets about turning the tables on the two-timer by convincing him his wife is seeing Harry Von Zell.

#31 AIR DATE: MAY 4, 1953

Harry Von Zell's old sweetheart comes to town. Harry thinks she's married, and doesn't want her to know he never married. So Gracie pretends to be his wife.

#32 AIR DATE: MAY 11, 1953

George mistakenly thinks he's invited to lecture at UCLA. Actually, they wanted him to enlist his colleagues Jack Benny and Georgie Jessel as speakers. But he doesn't learn this until he's dressed in his formal suit, ready to leave for the college. Embarrassed, he continues out the door, but spends the two hours going on rounds with the mailman.

#33 AIR DATE: MAY 18, 1953

When Harry Morton doesn't show up for lunch, Blanche jokes that he must have been kidnapped. Gracie takes this literally and reports Harry missing. But Harry was down at the office playing cards, and later takes Blanche to lunch at the Brown Derby. The investigator spots Harry with Blanche and reports to Gracie, who's convinced he's two-timing Blanche. All gets straightened out and everyone goes off to the movies.

#34 AIR DATE: JULY 6, 1953

The gang plans a surprise party for Harry Morton—but Gracie thinks it's for George. It's another classic mix-up when Harry is upset because he thinks everyone's forgotten his birthday. And to top it off, he gets to spend the afternoon in a sanitarium, courtesy of his friends, who want him out of the way while they plan a surprise dinner at his club.

#35 AIR DATE: JULY 13, 1953

Two sneak thieves introduce themselves as cousins, and Gracie invites them to stay. After they clean out the entire neighborhood, and the cops finally come and take them away, Gracie admits they aren't *her* cousins—she never said that; just that they were *cousins.*

#36 AIR DATE: JULY 20, 1953

Gracie gets her wires crossed when she finds an old telegram of George's requesting him to perform on Broadway—without his partner. She doesn't want to hold George back so she sends herself a telegram asking her to be in a film without him. That way he won't feel guilty about doing the Broadway show. George eventually pins Gracie down about sending the wire to herself, and everyone goes out to dinner.

#37 AIR DATE: JULY 27, 1953

Blanche and Harry are planning a trip to New York, so Gracie tries to persuade George to let them go along. The trip is on again, off again. A steady stream of visitors drops by to use the Burnses' pool in their absence—except that they finally decided not to go, and George, relaxing by his pool, is suddenly in the midst of a small mob.

#38 AIR DATE: AUGUST 3, 1953

Gracie witnesses a bank hold-up involving Johnny Velvet (Sheldon Leonard). He kidnaps Gracie so she can't testify, but after a few hours with her he's glad to release her. He decides to hold George hostage instead, but keeps getting the wrong person.

Ronald Reagan makes a small appearance as himself on the show in a subplot involving a dinner for him with George as guest singer—and no one will buy tickets.

#39 AIR DATE: AUGUST 10, 1953

Gracie and George return late one evening to find themselves locked out of the house. They wake the Mortons and call for a locksmith, and then the Mortons then get locked out. (See #294.)

#40 AIR DATE: AUGUST 17, 1953

When Gracie trips and falls in a department store, the store tries to settle with her. But she thinks they are suing *her* for the small hole in the carpet. When the insurance adjuster meets Gracie, he's sure she's suffered a head injury and the store is in big trouble. (See #272.)

SYNOPSES, FOURTH SEASON—1953–54

PRODUCER/DIRECTOR: Frederick de Cordova
WRITERS: Sid Dorfman
       Harvey Helm
       Keith Fowler
       William Burns

Note: There were no new shows numbered 41 through 52. These numbers were assigned to twelve reruns.

#53 AIR DATE: OCTOBER 5, 1953

Harry Morton pays two hundred dollars for an iron deer for his lawn. When Gracie shows it to George and tells him how much Harry paid for it, George says he can't see it. Gracie, taking him literally, thinks George must need glasses.

This show introduced Larry Keating as Harry Morton, and marked the debut of Frederick de Cordova as producer/director of the series.

#54 AIR DATE: OCTOBER 12, 1953

When it looks as though a prospective client of Harry Morton's is going to deal with another accountant—a swinging bachelor—Gracie tells the client that Harry is getting a divorce. Then she learns that he liked Harry's stability after all, so Gracie pretends to be Blanche Morton and tells him that their marriage is terrific.

#55 AIR DATE: OCTOBER 19, 1953

When Gracie gets a summons for jury duty, she hires an attorney to instruct her in proper court behavior. Blanche, Harry Morton, Von Zell, and even Mr. Beeseley all go independently to the judge to try to get her off. Ultimately all of them end up being summoned for jury duty, including George, who had nothing to do with it. And Gracie is excused!

#56 AIR DATE: OCTOBER 26, 1953

To teach Gracie a lesson, George hides her watch in Blanche's sugar bowl. Gracie finds it and suspects that Blanche is a kleptomaniac. When Blanche tells Gracie she's "picked up" two new dresses, Gracie suspects the worst and returns them to the store. Blanche thinks her dresses have been stolen and calls in Detective Sawyer. Gracie finally learns the whole story from Blanche, and George buys Gracie a new watch, thinking the old one was really stolen. But Gracie has her old one, and happily gives her best friend the new one.

#57 AIR DATE: NOVEMBER 2, 1953

Gracie misinterprets a remark made by Harry Morton to George, and thinks Harry is saying terrible things about her husband. This leads to a major rift between the two couples. Von Zell tells Gracie they'd like each other again if they both had someone else to hate—and, thanks to Gracie, Von Zell becomes that someone.

#58 AIR DATE: NOVEMBER 9, 1953

When George complains that Gracie is overspending, she decides to hire a business manager. Confusing a hobo with a financial expert recommended by Harry Morton, she invites the tramp into her home. It's another case of confused identities when Harry M. tries to toss out the imposter and the real expert shows up and thinks Harry is George Burns.

#59 AIR DATE: NOVEMBER 16, 1953

Blanche wants to get rid of Harry's old raccoon coat, but he won't hear of it. She gives it to Von Zell to give to Gracie to hide. Von Zell hangs it in Gracie's closet, where she finds it and gives it to her gardener. Realizing her mistake, she borrows a coat from a friend of the mailman's, and it too is accidentally given to the gardener, whose wife plans to cut them into little coats for their children. At the last moment the gardener brings the coats back—they scared the children.

#60 AIR DATE: NOVEMBER 23, 1953

Gracie gets the mistaken idea that Harry Von Zell is in financial straits and decides to give a benefit party for him. When Von Zell overhears Gracie and Blanche talking about their plans, he thinks it is Harry Morton who needs the money.

#61 AIR DATE: NOVEMBER 30, 1953

Gracie plans to visit her mother in San Francisco for a week, and Blanche decides to go with her. Meanwhile, George and his friends plan to get together for an evening of singing in her absence. But a telegram arrives announcing Gracie's mother's train arrival time—Gracie had forgotten who was to visit whom. George threatens to move out to the Y, but when all the visitors begin singing in harmony, George naturally can't resist and joins in.

#62 AIR DATE: DECEMBER 7, 1953

Gracie overhears a phone conversation and thinks George is planning to retire from show business. She arranges to trade their beautiful home for a run-down mountain cabin as a retreat for George's inactive days. When she realizes her mistake, hasty plans are made to keep their home and discourage the new owners.

#63 AIR DATE: DECEMBER 14, 1953

Gracie and George are given five tickets to a movie premiere. They each give away two of the tickets, unaware that the other is doing the same. It looks like everybody's going except

George or Gracie, until the producer sends over two more tickets and once again, they each give one away.

#64 AIR DATE: DECEMBER 21, 1953

When Jane, the wardrobe woman, confides to Gracie that her husband is jealous because Jane earns more than he does, Gracie is at a loss for advice, since that's not a problem she and George have. She decides the only way to help is to call her agent and request bookings without George, so she can earn more money. Jane and her husband work out their differences, and George is left to untangle Gracie's new career.

#65 AIR DATE: DECEMBER 28, 1953

Gracie decides to take flying lessons when she overhears George ordering a plane on the phone. She thinks it's a surprise anniversary present. Actually, George was talking to the hardware store, ordering a plane to shave down a door that was sticking.

#66 AIR DATE: JANUARY 4, 1954

Gracie's Uncle Harvey invents a tonic that he says will make plants grow to gigantic proportions. She pours some of the stuff into a vase of carnations, and when her back is turned, George innocently comes in, tosses out the old flowers, and replaces them with a bouquet of white mums. Everyone thinks the magic potion works. Even Harry Morton is willing to mortgage his house to buy in, until George discovers another use for it—it makes a great martini mix.

#67 AIR DATE: JANUARY 11, 1954

George is trying to study a play before a London producer arrives. Blanche and Harry are fighting, and Von Zell helps cook up a scheme to make Harry jealous. You guessed it:

when the producer arrives, Harry thinks he's Blanche's lover. It's all explained over dinner and everyone goes home happy.

#68 AIR DATE: JANUARY 18, 1954

A lovelorn mechanic comes to Gracie for help. His girlfriend only wants to marry a man who's in show business. Gracie tries to tell the girl how miserable it is being married to an actor. The girl changes her mind and decides to marry her mechanic boyfriend—not because Gracie's talk worked, but because she saw how really happy George and Gracie were, and that persuaded her to marry the man she loves.

#69 AIR DATE: JANUARY 25, 1954

Gracie reads a magazine article that says that one out of every five men has a secret vice. Her calculations find George to be the fifth man in her life, and she's determined to find out what his vice is. Meanwhile, George is concerned with getting Blanche and Gracie off to the movies so he can go to the fights. The famous "Kleebob" card game is played again here. (See Live Show #1.)

George and Gracie do their famous "lamb chops" routine.

#70 AIR DATE: FEBRUARY 1, 1954

Gracie misunderstands a fire inspector's order to get rid of some flammable rubbish that's in the garage. Gracie thinks she has to get rid of the car—fast—and tries to sell it. Everyone believes the car is "hot" until George straightens it out. They end up still having to pay the fine because no one got rid of the trash in the garage.

#71 AIR DATE: FEBRUARY 8, 1954

When a radio quiz program calls Gracie, she hangs up, looks up the answer, and calls them back. Then she thinks she's won a TV set, gives their old one to the mailman's daughter, and rushes to the store to pick out her new set. Fortunately, George saves the day by buying her a new TV.

#72 AIR DATE: FEBRUARY 15, 1954

Gracie feels sorry for George because he never gets any fan mail. She writes a glowing letter and signs it with a name from the phone book—Violet McGonigle. George thinks Von Zell is playing a joke on him, looks up the number, and calls Violet, reaching instead her jealous husband, who comes gunning for George. No one will confess to being George. Mr. McGonigle has heard George sing, so Morton, Von Zell, and George all sing for him. Then the neighbor's dog howls, and McGonigle, convinced he's found George Burns, heads off for the neighbor's house.

#73 AIR DATE: FEBRUARY 22, 1954

Vanderlip invites the Burnses and Mortons to share their box at the opera. But George doesn't want to go. One at a time the Mortons and Von Zell try to persuade him. He still refuses, but gives in when he sees how great he looks in his formal attire.

#74 AIR DATE: MARCH 1, 1954

Blanche goes out to a movie one evening while Harry goes on to a business appointment. But his car breaks down, so he gets a ride and comes home early. He's sound asleep when Blanche returns and, not seeing his car, phones her neighbors. They finally discover Harry asleep, but Von Zell has already hired a detective, who spots Harry out with a blonde the next day at lunch. The blonde is Blanche, but the rumor reaches Gracie, who sends for a marriage counselor to try to save her friend's marriage.

#75 AIR DATE: MARCH 8, 1954

When Blanche has a recurring nightmare, Gracie goes to a
psychiatrist on her behalf. The psychiatrist thinks Gracie is
Blanche, calls Harry, who then worries about his wife and
brings home flowers. Gracie sees all the attention Blanche is
enjoying and decides to make George think *she's* crazy. But
George is so used to Gracie that he thinks nothing's new. (See
Live Show #27.)

George and Gracie introduced Sandra Burns to the audience at the end of the show; she plays the psychiatrist's receptionist.

#76 AIR DATE: MARCH 15, 1954

When Gracie plays hostess to a basketball team coach,
George is embarrassed by his lack of athletic prowess. Gracie
borrows Harry Morton's trophies to impress the coach, and
Blanche and Harry think the trophies are stolen and report
the theft. George sees the trophies on the mantel and thinks
the coach is too ostentatious, so he puts them in the man's
suitcase. Gracie and Blanche discover the suitcase full of trophies and think he must need money, so they fill up the bag
with silverware.

#77 AIR DATE: MARCH 22, 1954

Gracie gets a traffic ticket, which George gives to his business
manager to get "fixed." Meanwhile, Gracie tries to enroll
George in college. When he lands in jail over the ticket, she
thinks he's in school, gathers all her friends, and goes to visit
him there.

#78 AIR DATE: MARCH 29, 1954

When a motion-picture company decides to make the life story
of George and Gracie, all their friends try to get into the act,

including Von Zell, the Mortons, and the butcher's daughter. Everyone tries to bribe George with the exact same gift—golf clubs. But the picture is called off because Gracie confuses the writers too much.

#79 AIR DATE: APRIL 5, 1954

Gracie dents the car's fender and tells George an elephant sat on it. Nobody believes her. The manager from the elephant's circus comes out and writes Gracie a check for one hundred dollars, but George thinks it's a joke and tears it up. George calls a meeting of everyone, and they all manage to convince George that the car really was sat upon by an elephant.

#80 AIR DATE: APRIL 12, 1954

George has a black eye from walking into a door. His production manager (named "Al Simon") comes by to file an insurance claim for his brother, an employee who has been injured in a skiing accident. Gracie hears them arguing and thinks George and Al have had a fistfight. Confusion abounds when the insurance claims adjuster tries to settle.

#81 AIR DATE: APRIL 19, 1954

When an old flame and former vaudeville partner of George's appears on the scene, Gracie fears there will be a renewal of the old romance. In order to thwart any thought of possible romantic notions, Gracie hires two professional child actors to pose as their children and prove that their home life is a happy one.

#82 AIR DATE: APRIL 26, 1954

Gracie overhears Mr. Vanderlip making a call to a personal shopper for a surprise gift of a negligee for his wife. Gracie suspects the worst, so she makes up a story telling Vanderlip that his wife is involved with a handsome young dentist.

#83 AIR DATE: MAY 3, 1954

Gracie finds a gift Harry Von Zell has left in the house, and thinks George is giving her a present for some occasion she's forgotten. She decides to throw a party for George so he won't know she can't remember. George can't figure out what's going on, but he buys Gracie a present anyway.

#84 AIR DATE: MAY 10, 1954

George plans to spend twenty-four hours in bed so he'll be completely rested for a physical he has to pass for an insurance policy. Determined to keep the house quiet, Gracie has Harry Morton disconnect the doorbell—fouling up the entire wiring system in the house. She even takes the phone off the hook. An electrician and telephone repairman arrive to try to straighten this all out, and Harry Von Zell comes over to act out his new dramatic role. Naturally most of this takes place in George's bedroom, but in spite of all the confusion he does manage to pass his exam.

#85 AIR DATE: JULY 12, 1954

An astrologer tells Gracie it's a good day for George in business, so she buys him twenty thousand dollars' worth of terrible old films for possible sale to television. George has just advised Harry Morton and Harry Von Zell against buying these same films, and when the Harrys hear that George has bought them, they think he's double-crossed them.

#86 AIR DATE: JULY 5, 1954

Gracie mistakenly thinks Harry Morton has only a week to live. She tries to comfort Blanche, who thinks it is George who has only a week to live. George finally straightens it all out, and he and Gracie end the show with a tap dance.

#87 AIR DATE: JULY 26, 1954

Gracie mistakenly thinks the Beverly Hills League of Women Voters wants her to run for city council. She decides to campaign by pulling a publicity stunt—breaking up a gambling house (hers), but accomplishes the feat of putting George in jail again. He's freed, of course, when the mistake is discovered, and Gracie decides not to run because she heard a daffy lady is running and the voters might think it is she.

Marion Ross, who later went on to star in "Happy Days," plays the role of Dixie.

#88 AIR DATE: JULY 19, 1954

Gracie makes plans to help the Vanderlips' daughter with her elopement—except the girl doesn't have any such plans. To placate Gracie, she and her boyfriend pretend to elope, but actually they go bowling.

#89 AIR DATE: AUGUST 9, 1954

When Gracie sets out to get a new toaster, she learns that she can save money if she buys it from a friend of George's who can get it wholesale. She is ecstatic when she learns she can save lots more money with each appliance purchase—so she orders hundreds of dollars worth of new appliances—and begins totaling up her "savings."

#90 AIR DATE: AUGUST 2, 1954

George and Gracie find that a simple evening at the movies can cause confusion when everyone they know decides to join them. No one can agree on a picture that everyone hasn't seen; as soon as they think they've found a show, along comes

someone else to join the party, and it's back to the newspapers.

#91 AIR DATE: AUGUST 23, 1954

When George tries to show Gracie the pitfalls of spreading
rumors, he is caught in his own snare. Much to his surprise,
George later learns from someone else that he has been gambling in Las Vegas and has won a huge sum of money. He has
to convince everyone, including Gracie, that he was really
with Jack Benny in Palm Springs.

#92 AIR DATE: AUGUST 16, 1954

Gracie suggests the Mortons and their New York friends
swap houses for a month. Then Harry Morton cancels the trip
at the last minute. But the Gibsons are happily ensconced in
the Mortons' home, making long-distance calls to all their
friends back East. The Gibsons end up as George and Gracie's
houseguests. Harry Von Zell moves in after he offers the
Gibsons his apartment, and George and Gracie head for the
car to sleep.

SYNOPSES, FIFTH SEASON—1954–55

PRODUCER/DIRECTOR: Frederick de Cordova
WRITERS: Keith Fowler
         Norman Paul
         Harvey Helm
         William Burns

NOTE: There were no new shows numbered 93 through 104.
These numbers were assigned to twelve reruns.

#105 AIR DATE: OCTOBER 4, 1954

George and Gracie start their fifth season by inviting some reporters over to see a telecast of the "show." George hopes to establish good relations with the press and rehearses Gracie in the proper things to say. Gracie, in order to get some general input, invites strangers home to join the viewing. George and the reporters move from room to room trying to get some peace and finally end up at the local bar to watch the broadcast.

This was the only show filmed in color, although it is being syndicated in black and white.

#106 AIR DATE: OCTOBER 11, 1954

Gracie attends a do-it-yourself show and purchases a power machine so that George can build her a dresser. When George refuses, she hires a carpenter. But just as George is about to take the credit, a cop shows up because the neighbors complained about the noise. All the men—George, Harry, and Von Zell—are hustled off to jail to pay fines of ten dollars each.

#107 AIR DATE: NOVEMBER 29, 1954

When Blanche weighs herself on a supermarket scale, the card says she will run into a stranger who loves her deeply. Gracie thinks it's the man who bumped into her in the market, and calls his wife. The woman thinks her husband is having an affair with Blanche. Gracie invites the couple over and straightens it all out at dinner.

#108 AIR DATE: NOVEMBER 22, 1954

A shoplifter steals a ruby clip and plants it in the purse of Mrs. Vanderlip. Gracie, observing this, believes Mrs. Vanderlip is involved in the theft and covers for her. Later, Blanche goes to Mrs. Vanderlip's house to loan her a book. She's not

home, so Blanche leaves the book, then spots a ruby clip like
the one in the store. Thinking it's stolen, she returns it to
Saks. Then Blanche and Gracie learn Mrs. Vanderlip had purchased it a week ago, so Gracie enlists Von Zell to help her
steal it back from the store. Mrs. Vanderlip arrives and explains that the store has already returned it to her.

#109 AIR DATE: OCTOBER 18, 1954

Gracie owes a favor to a lady and holds a wedding in her home
for the woman's daughter and bridegroom as repayment. The
favor: when Gracie's car got stuck, the woman gave her a
push. (See Live Show #26.)
    Ronnie Burns makes an appearance as Jim, the groom.

#110 AIR DATE: OCTOBER 25, 1954

Gracie and Blanche arrange a surprise baby shower for Mr.
Beeseley's daughter. She isn't the only one surprised. George,
trying to be a good husband, wants to surprise Gracie and has
the shower catered at their home, only to learn, after no one
shows up, that she had the party at the Brown Derby.

#111 AIR DATE: NOVEMBER 1, 1954

Gracie has a busy day, starting at the department of motor
vehicles to get her license renewed and leaving some very
confused people in her wake. Then she hurries home to help
George, who is in the throes of writing his first book. She's
almost too helpful for poor George, but he does make the sale
based on his first three chapters.

#112 AIR DATE: NOVEMBER 8, 1954

It's time for George's annual physical. Gracie wants to keep
him calm, but disappearing car keys make it impossible.
Harry Morton needs a lift to a client's, and each time George

gets out of the running car to see what's keeping him, Gracie finds the keys and brings them back in the house. By the time they're ready to leave, George is out of patience and the car is out of gas. A cab arrives just in time to save the day.

#113 AIR DATE: NOVEMBER 15, 1954

A CBS executive from the East Coast is coming to see George, and Gracie fears they will have to move to New York. The only way she can think of keeping George in town is to say that he's the only witness to a crime she read about in the newspaper. George now believes the criminals are after him, but they end up turning themselves in, and Gracie learns that they're not moving to the East after all.

#114 AIR DATE: DECEMBER 6, 1954

George tries a new ploy in getting out of going to a concert. He buys a jigsaw puzzle for Gracie, hoping she'll become so engrossed in it that she'll forget the time. To his surprise, she shows no interest in it as he works away at the puzzle, trying to make the pieces fit. It's almost time to leave, and George tells Gracie he'll go just as soon as he finishes this fun puzzle. Gracie walks over, and—one-two-three—simply fits in the remaining pieces, as a very puzzled George puts on his coat to go.

#115 AIR DATE: DECEMBER 13, 1954

George learns a lesson when he tries to teach Gracie to write down phone messages. She tells him "Victor" called about some films, but she didn't take the number. George thinks it's a movie offer, and makes her promise to write down future messages. Victor calls again, and she dutifully writes it down, but when George calls and she writes *that* down, he says she doesn't have to—she can tear up the message. So she tears up Victor's message. But George need not fear for his career:

Victor works at the local drugstore and he's been calling to let Gracie know the photos she was having developed are ready.

#116 AIR DATE: DECEMBER 20, 1954

Harry Morton needs a master of ceremonies for his college fraternity reunion. Gracie helps by lining up Von Zell, not realizing that Harry wanted George. George thinks Harry doesn't want him, and stops speaking to his neighbor. Gracie manages to get the fraternity to agree to use George—whom they wanted all along. But now George refuses, until Harry and Gracie straighten him out.

#117 AIR DATE: DECEMBER 27, 1954

Bob Cummings makes a special appearance, dropping by to play golf with George. Gracie overhears Bob telling George, "I'm in love with your wife." What she doesn't know is that Bob was reciting lines from his new drama, and she thinks Bob is in love with her. She tries to discourage him by acting "tough." It works, and Bob leaves, a very confused man, while George has his Gracie back.

#118 AIR DATE: JANUARY 3, 1955

Gracie helps a woman in the post office who is trying to get back a letter she wrote her husband asking for a divorce because he wouldn't let her mother visit. Von Zell overhears this and thinks it was Gracie who wrote the letter. He anxiously tells George he should let Gracie's mother come for a visit. George agrees, Gracie is very happy, and when George realizes what happened, Von Zell is in the doghouse again.

#119 AIR DATE: JANUARY 10, 1955

Gracie helps George's press agent cook up a publicity gimmick involving George and a famous pilot. George doesn't
want to go on any stunt flights, and to get out of it, he fakes
a sprained ankle. But the press agent keeps phoning and
insists he still has time to make the rendezvous. George
finally limps on down to the runway in time to realize that
when Gracie said "shake hands" that's all she meant. The
only thing that took off in this episode was George's imagination.

#120 AIR DATE: JANUARY 17, 1955

Gracie can't get Blanche, Harry, and the Bagleys into an
exclusive Friars Club dinner party through regular channels,
so she borrows waiters' and cigarette girls' costumes to get
them in. At the last minute, George's publishers and wives
can't make it, and the seats are available anyway.

#121 AIR DATE: JANUARY 24, 1955

Warmhearted Gracie offers sanctuary to Blanche and Clara
Bagley, who are feuding with their husbands. But George
says, "Out!" and he and Von Zell return the girls' suitcases
—to the wrong homes. Blanche and Clara then get suspicious
when they see the strange suitcases in their bedrooms, and it
takes a while till everyone gets straightened out.

#122 AIR DATE: JANUARY 31, 1955

Gracie hires a valet to assist George with his personal needs,
but George is anything but overjoyed. The valet quits because
of Gracie's strange way of laundering George's socks—with
the toes sewn together so they won't get lost in the wash. Unaware that he's quit, Gracie decides to try to get him to leave
and dresses up Blanche as a French maid who flirts with him.

#123 AIR DATE: FEBRUARY 7, 1955

Gracie doesn't know that George has volunteered to baby-sit the Vanderlips' pet parakeet, and she frees it from its cage. When she learns of her error, she replaces it with one from a pet shop and must teach it to say "Hi, Poopsie" before Vanderlip returns. Harry Von Zell finds the lost bird, and he and Gracie return the substitute to the pet store. George hears about Gracie's first scheme, sees the real bird in the cage, and thinks it's the replacement. Vanderlip arrives in time to learn that his pet has flown the coop, and he tells George to release this imposter. He does, and as the bird flies off, they are astonished to hear it cry, "Hi, Poopsie"! Finally, Vanderlip finds his pet in the bushes and places it safely back in the cage, ending the "fowl-ups."

#124 AIR DATE: FEBRUARY 14, 1955

Blanche's lazy brother Roger arrives and sponges off George until George puts his foot down. Then Gracie undertakes the task of getting a job for Roger. She lands him a job; but, to avoid having to work, he decides to go to Seattle and visit his mother.

#125 AIR DATE: FEBRUARY 21, 1955

George's publisher needs some of his baby pictures, so George searches frantically through his old vaudeville trunks. He's also lost five dollars, and Gracie thinks his anxious behavior is because of the money. His friends all try to help by "finding" the five dollars, and George makes an unanticipated profit. Finally, the publisher arrives and returns the five dollars George had loaned him. George finds the pictures, and everyone lines up to get his money back—with Gracie going through the line twice!

#126 AIR DATE: FEBRUARY 28, 1955

Gracie visits an art museum and, impressed by the prices of the paintings, decides to take up dabbling in oils. She's only going to paint masterpieces, however—they're worth more. (See Live Show #2.)

#127 AIR DATE: MARCH 7, 1955

Gracie doesn't think it's such a good idea when George brings home a new trombone, so she gives it away. Then George tells her it was "solid gold," so she sets out to raise ten thousand dollars to get it back. They finally get the worthless trombone back and return it to its original owner, to whom it's worth a fortune—in memories.

#128 AIR DATE: MARCH 14, 1955

Countess Braganni has bought the house next door to the Mortons, and word has it she's seeking husband number five. Blanche is convinced she's after Harry, so Gracie goes to the countess's hotel suite to call her off. The countess agrees, but mistakes George for Harry and decides she won't move in after all.

#129 AIR DATE: MARCH 21, 1955

Gracie overhears Emily Vanderlip and Blanche's freeloading brother, Roger, discussing wedding plans—for Emily and her college fiancé. Gracie thinks Roger and Emily are planning a wedding. Roger certainly wouldn't mind this, and he accepts Mr. Vanderlip's offer of a job. George offers him one thousand dollars not to marry Emily, and this he also accepts, but eventually they all shoo him out of town.

#130 AIR DATE: MARCH 28, 1955

Gracie agrees to hide a puppy as a favor to young Joey Bagley. She tells George that Uncle Harvey is in the guest room. Then she gets in trouble with the police when the dog terrorizes the neighbors, especially Harry Morton. Clara Bagley relents and says Joey can have the dog because her son's been spending so much time at the Burnses' that she never sees him anymore.

#131 AIR DATE: APRIL 4, 1955

To get out of a yachting trip, George has Harry Von Zell send a telegram saying Gracie is ill. Then Gracie comes to the erroneous conclusion that she's not long for this world and, ever thoughtful, she looks for a wife for widower George.

#132 AIR DATE: APRIL 11, 1955

Gracie receives a traffic citation that she feels was unjustly issued. George tries to get the ticket fixed, and winds up in the slammer—again.

#133 AIR DATE: APRIL 18, 1955

Gracie presents George with a wall safe and, for added security, locks the combination inside it. To open it she seeks the aid of a skilled safecracker. George gets the combination, memorizes it. Then Von Zell burns it and George forgets it. Fortunately, the safecracker still remembers it.

#134 AIR DATE: APRIL 25, 1955

Gracie appears on a TV show on behalf of a remarried girlfriend who has discovered her former husband is alive. The Mortons see the program and feel obliged to tell George that Gracie has been married before! Actually, the friend's

first husband has also remarried, so it all works out successfully.

#135 AIR DATE: MAY 2, 1955

George refuses to allow Gracie to paint their home coral, but
she goes ahead and hires painters anyway. She can only afford
to paint half the house but figures George will see how pretty
it is and paint the other half. George has secretly ordered the
painters to paint half a house too—and they end up with a
half-coral/half-white house.

#136 AIR DATE: MAY 9, 1955

Gracie turns talent scout when the substitute delivery boy
gives an ad-lib performance. When George agrees to audition
the boy, the wrong one shows up. Eventually, George gets to
hear the right kid, who impresses George with his impressions of him.

#137 AIR DATE: MAY 16, 1955

When George announces he has an appointment at the beach,
Gracie decides to have an impromptu picnic, and invites all her
friends.
     The first "AFTERPIECE" followed this show. Title:
"Beach—Gracie's Family."

#138 AIR DATE: MAY 23, 1955

Gracie gives Harry Von Zell and Harry Morton the mistaken
impression that George owns a huge uranium mine. Actually,
he's discussing a script possibility on the phone with writer/
brother Willy. Gracie borrows some real uranium samples;
Harry Morton finds them and thinks they are from George's
mine.
     No AFTERPIECE with this show.

#139 AIR DATE: MAY 30, 1955

Blanche has left Harry again, and brother Roger comes down from Seattle to help her. Blanche and Roger stay at the Burnses', while George goes to live with Harry. George meets a friend of Von Zell's, a divorce lawyer, and thinks Gracie wants a divorce. It all gets straightened out, with no one actually getting a divorce.

AFTERPIECE: "Auction Routine."

#140 AIR DATE: JUNE 6, 1955

Gracie becomes suspicious of George when she discovers an old picture of him in a striped prison suit. Actually, it was he and his old vaudeville partner in an act called the Jolly Jailbirds. Now the partner is in town, and George plays a joke by hiding him in the closet. The Mortons hold him at bay, thinking he is a wanted criminal, and the cops are summoned. When the police learn it's all a joke, everyone is hustled off to jail.

AFTERPIECE: "Driver's License Routine."

#141 AIR DATE: JUNE 13, 1955

Gracie tangles with the immigration authorities in an attempt to help a friend from France get an extension on her visa. She tries to get Von Zell to marry her so she can stay, but he says he's already engaged to Alice. Alice introduces the Frenchwoman to her kid brother Jim; they get married; and the woman can stay in the country.

AFTERPIECE: "Uncle Harvey and Crowd."

#142 AIR DATE: JUNE 20, 1955

Just as Blanche's brother Roger is about to leave for good, he develops amnesia. Gracie tries to help by pretending she has amnesia and going to a doctor. Roger hires a friend to play doctor, but George gets wise to him.

AFTERPIECE: "Sister Hazel's Eyesight."

#143 AIR DATE: JUNE 27, 1955

The Vanderlips' new barbecue is being delivered to the Burnses' house, and Gracie promises to keep the surprise a secret. George thinks Gracie is having a barbecue party for thirty people and doesn't believe her when she denies it. Thirty people show up on a tour bus and George feeds them —with expensive food he has to order from Chasen's.
AFTERPIECE: "Aunt Clara Moves into a New House."

#144 AIR DATE: JULY 4, 1955

The Mortons have plans to go to Hawaii, when Roger shows up. George doesn't want him as a houseguest either, so they all make plans to go to Hawaii. Unfortunately, Roger ends up on the ship with them.
AFTERPIECE: "Shoe Store Routine."

SYNOPSES, SIXTH SEASON—1955–56

PRODUCER/DIRECTOR: Frederick de Cordova
WRITERS: Harvey Helm
    Norman Paul
    Keith Fowler
    William Burns

NOTE: There were no new shows numbered 145 through 156. These numbers were assigned to twelve reruns.

#157 AIR DATE: OCTOBER 3, 1955—"THE BURNSES AND MORTONS GO TO NEW YORK"

The Burnses and Mortons are en route to New York. Harry has been offered a new job, and Gracie goes along because she can't bear to be separated from Blanche. George goes along because where Gracie is, the show is. Traveling incognito on the train is the world's foremost atomic scientist. Von Zell's idea to get him and Gracie together for a publicity photo backfires. While he and George end up wining and dining a traveling salesman, Gracie is happily playing gin rummy with the scientist.

AFTERPIECE: "Bus Routine."

#158 AIR DATE: OCTOBER 10, 1955—"RONNIE ARRIVES"

Ronnie Burns joins the cast when he arrives in New York to surprise George and Gracie. The bigger surprise is that he wants to study serious acting—not comedy—and he's embarrassed by the fact that his parents do a television comedy show. When he does a scene from *Picnic*, everyone agrees he's a good actor and George pays for Ronnie's tuition.

AFTERPIECE: "Hunting Routine."

#159 AIR DATE: OCTOBER 17, 1955—"RONNIE MEETS SABRINA"

Ronnie is hoping to be cast in a play about a young man in love with an older woman. For the sake of realism, he starts dating an older woman, who, George finds out, is really after George and Gracie's money. His parents save Ronnie in the nick of time, and to help him with his research, they suggest he date Blanche instead.

AFTERPIECE: "Uncle Otis—Explorer."

#160 AIR DATE: OCTOBER 24, 1955—"CHANGING NAMES"

When Gracie learns Ronnie is afraid his last name will hinder his acting career, she changes hers so he won't have to alter his. George starts getting charge slips signed "Lola E. Benedict" (Gracie got the inspiration for her new name from the menu in the coffee shop), and Ronnie thinks his father is seeing another woman. To protect Gracie, Ronnie insists Lola is his new girlfriend. George knew it was Gracie all along, and in the end nobody has to change his name.

AFTERPIECE: "Cousin Louise's Wedding."

#161 AIR DATE: OCTOBER 31, 1955—"HARRY
      MORTON'S COCKTAIL PARTY"

It's the day George's book *I Love Her, That's Why* goes on sale. Gracie and Blanche head for the bookstore to help out, and in the crowded confusion, Blanche accuses an innocent man of being a masher. To compound matters, he turns out to be an important client of Harry's who's coming to dinner that night. The dinner guests wind up with Gracie as Harry's wife, the Swedish maid as "Mrs. Burns," Blanche as the maid, and Ronnie trying to figure out who his parents are. Blanche finally calls a halt to the deception, explains what happened, and it's a happy ending for all.

AFTERPIECE: "Uncle Harvey Getting Jobs."

#162 AIR DATE: NOVEMBER 7, 1955—"THE MUSICAL
      VERSION"

They're going to make a Broadway musical based on George's book. George and Gracie depart from their usual format to take a tuneful excursion into the past. Joined by songwriter Mac Gordon, the former vaudeville team sings and dances to "I Love Her, That's Why," "Never in a Million Years," "Stay as Sweet as You Are," and others. Meanwhile, oblivious to all this frivolity, Ronnie and his girlfriend, Velma, try to study a very dramatic script.

AFTERPIECE: "Gracie's Father."

#163 AIR DATE: NOVEMBER 14, 1955—"RONNIE
      MOVES TO THE VILLAGE"

In order to be a serious actor, Ronnie feels he should move into a Greenwich Village apartment with his friend, Jim

Boardman, and his artist father. Everyone thinks Ronnie is living in poverty, when actually Jim's father is very rich and famous. When George and Gracie, dressed as beatniks, come to visit bearing gifts of food and socks, they are greeted by a butler. Everyone plays along and has a good laugh. Afterward, Ronnie decides it's more fun to live at home after all.

AFTERPIECE: "Aunt Clara's Husbands."

#164 AIR DATE: NOVEMBER 21, 1955—"GRACIE HELPS LOLA"

Gracie helps a waitress friend with love troubles by taking her shift so the girl can spend the day at the beauty parlor. Meanwhile, Ronnie is getting ready for an important lunch meeting with George and the dean of his school. Naturally, Gracie ends up as their waitress, and when all is revealed, the dean feels so sorry for Ronnie, he personally takes him under his wing.

AFTERPIECE: "Aunt Clara's Husbands."

#165 AIR DATE: NOVEMBER 28, 1955— "ANNIVERSARY PARTY"

It's George and Gracie's anniversary. Mr. Boardman and his wife are quarreling, and Gracie, trying to straighten out their lives, unstraightens everyone else's. They all manage to put their lives together in time to don party hats and help George and Gracie celebrate a happy anniversary.

AFTERPIECE: "Shopping At Macy's."

#166 AIR DATE: DECEMBER 5, 1955—"GEORGE BECOMES A DICTATOR"

George thinks he's helping Ronnie by getting him a booking on "The Jackie Gleason Show." Ronnie, who's up for a part in a serious drama, thinks this is an act of treachery. He asks Gracie to get him out of it, and Gracie misunderstands and gets him out of the drama. George comes to Ronnie's rescue by getting him out of the Gleason show and back into the drama, and the night his drama is on the air, Gracie, thinking she's watching Ronnie on the Gleason show, is upset because Ronnie "isn't very funny."

AFTERPIECE: "Sightseeing Tour."

#167 AIR DATE: DECEMBER 12, 1955—"RONNIE'S ENGAGEMENT"

Marie, the cigarette girl at the hotel, asks Gracie to give a message to Ronnie about two tickets to Connecticut. Gracie thinks Marie and Ronnie are eloping and alerts Marie's parents. They arrive, ready for a confrontation, and Ronnie comes in just in time to explain the tickets were for him and Jim Boardman to see a play.

AFTERPIECE: "Doctor's Office."

#168 AIR DATE: DECEMBER 19, 1955—"COMPANY FOR CHRISTMAS"

Blanche's brother Roger is coming, and the St. Moritz Hotel is full. Gracie pretends to be a maid and makes life unbearable for one of the guests, hoping he will leave so there will be a room for Roger. Further confusion is added when Mr. Morton, Harry's father, also decides to pay a visit. Gracie never does get the innocent guest to vacate, but fortunately the Mortons' relatives decide not to visit after all. Unfortunately for George and Gracie, Gracie told an elderly honeymoon couple they could have the Burnses' suite.

AFTERPIECE: "Christmas with Gracie's Family."

#169 AIR DATE: DECEMBER 26, 1955—"GRACIE PAWNS HER RING"

Ronnie's friend has written a play and hopes George will finance it. George doesn't think it's very good and declines.

Gracie tries to help by pawning her diamond ring for one thousand dollars. When the boys realize the play really isn't any good after all, Ronnie gives George the one thousand dollars to buy back Gracie's ring. George hands Gracie the money and she hands him the pawn ticket.

AFTERPIECE: "Insurance Company Routine."

#170 AIR DATE: JANUARY 2, 1956—"APPEARANCES ARE DECEIVING"

The puritanical father of a drama classmate of Ronnie's, believing the city is no place for his daughter, is coming to New York to take her home. He arrives to find Ronnie and her rehearsing a love scene, and he won't listen to any explanations. Gracie and Blanche devise a scheme to catch him in a compromising situation that is really innocent. The scheme backfires, and Harry Morton ends up with water spilled all over him and his shirt off. But the point is made, and the father realizes he made a mistake and his daughter really is in good hands.

AFTERPIECE: "Post Office—Hazel's Cake."

#171 AIR DATE: JANUARY 9, 1956—"LET'S DANCE"

To help Ronnie with ticket sales for the school dance, Gracie promises each prospective male customer a date with Marie. When all the young men arrive to pick up Marie, they find out the girl is Ronnie's date, and George has to give everyone his money back.

AFTERPIECE: "Uncle Otto's Farm."

#172 AIR DATE: JANUARY 16, 1956—"GEORGE GOES SKIING"

Gracie learns that Jim Boardman's father does everything with his son and convinces George he should be a better pal to Ronnie. George learns how to ski so he can join Ronnie on the slopes, only to discover Ronnie wants everything to stay exactly the way it's been.

AFTERPIECE: "Drugstore."

#173 AIR DATE: JANUARY 23, 1956—"RONNIE GETS AN AGENT"

Ronnie invites his girlfriend's parents to dinner, promising them that show people are no different than any other people. Meanwhile, an agent who wants to represent Ronnie hopes he can get his other clients on George and Gracie's show. The dinner party turns into a three-ring circus when all the acts show up to audition. Even Jack Benny makes a cameo appearance in a pyramid of tumblers.

AFTERPIECE: "Fishing Routine."

#174 AIR DATE: JANUARY 30, 1956—"POLITENESS NEVER PAYS"

Gracie tries to get some attention from George by becoming more alluring. When that fails, she hires a gigolo. Harry Morton's father comes to visit and Gracie mistakes him for her date. In the end, George lets Blanche have the gigolo to show Harry how to treat a woman.

AFTERPIECE: "Gracie's Musical Family."

#175 AIR DATE: FEBRUARY 6, 1956—"ALICE GETS MARRIED"

Harry Von Zell learns his old girlfriend, Alice, is coming to New York and feels his bachelor status is threatened. Gracie comes to his rescue by broadcasting that Von Zell is married to Ronnie's girlfriend, Marie. Now everyone thinks Ronnie is dating a married woman. After all this, it turns out Alice was coming to tell Von Zell that *she* is the one who got married.

AFTERPIECE: "Pet Shop Routine."

#176 AIR DATE: FEBRUARY 13, 1956—"GEORGE
   NEEDS GLASSES"

Gracie's gone shopping again and George pretends not to see
the packages because he wants her in a good mood when he
tells her he's going to California to visit the Friars Club.
Gracie ends up thinking George needs glasses. When she
believes his vanity is keeping him from going to a doctor, she
buys three dozen pair of glasses for everyone around him to
wear, so he won't feel bad if the doctor says George must
wear them, too.

AFTERPIECE: "Gracie's Athletic Family."

#177 AIR DATE: FEBRUARY 20, 1956—"THE INDIAN
   POTENTATE"

Gracie is curious about a mysterious guest of the hotel—a
maharaja who insists on seclusion. In order to get one little
peek, she disguises herself as an Eastern princess. It turns
out she didn't have to go to all that trouble. Ronnie is dating
the maharaja's daughter, and his whole family is invited for
dinner.

AFTERPIECE: "Aunt Clara's Husbands and Redecorating."

#178 AIR DATE: FEBRUARY 27, 1956—"THE LADIES'
   CLUB"

Harry Morton's new client's wife is head of an elite women's
club. He's afraid that if Gracie joins, it will ruin his career. The
women arrive to interview Gracie and find Ronnie studying
the Stanislavsky method (he's acting out scenes without using
any props). The women decide Gracie's family doesn't suit
their criteria and don't want Gracie in their club. Just as well,
George and Gracie aren't sure they want anything to do with
the women either.

AFTERPIECE: "Nature Studies."

#179 AIR DATE: MARCH 5, 1956—"CYRANO DE BERGERAC"

In order to study *Cyrano*, Ronnie has been lip-synching to José Ferrer's reading from a record. Ronnie's worried that he's not very good, and George thinks it's because he's been listening to the best. He makes his own recording for Ronnie and when the school president overhears the record, he thinks *that's* what Ronnie has been studying and belittles George's reading. Ronnie defends his father with all the style of Cyrano and gets the part.

AFTERPIECE: "Fortune Teller."

#180 AIR DATE: MARCH 12, 1956—"THE STOLEN PLANTS"

Gracie takes home some jonquil bulbs from Central Park. When she realizes it was stealing, she turns herself in, ready to go to jail. The commissioner says she can buy the two bulbs for twenty-five cents—then she'll be an honest woman again. The next day Gracie shows up back in court. She wants to buy a whole carton of bulbs she's dug up.

AFTERPIECE: "Grand Central Station."

#181 AIR DATE: MARCH 19, 1956—"THE ENGLISH PLAYWRIGHT"

Gracie thinks she's helping Ronnie win a part in a play when she meets the playwright and pretends to be a widow, telling him Ronnie is her only means of support. Her plan backfires when the writer becomes enamored of her, inviting her for an intimate dinner for two. When he sees how protective Gracie's family becomes, he can only laugh—and his romantic interlude turns into dinner for five.

AFTERPIECE: "Gracie's Mother."

#182 AIR DATE: MARCH 26, 1956—"A WEEKEND ON
    LONG ISLAND"

The students in Ronnie's drama class want to give a surprise
party for their teacher, Mr. Canning, in the Burnses' apartment. Gracie is afraid that George will want to monopolize the
party by singing, so she tries to find ways to get George out
of town. But George isn't buying it, and he ends up singing
at the party—and everyone seems to love it.
    AFTERPIECE: "The Zoo."

#183 AIR DATE: APRIL 5, 1956—"THE NEWLYWEDS"

Emily Vanderlip comes to visit George and Gracie in their
New York hotel. She is secretly married to an Air Force man
from the nearby base, but doesn't want to tell Gracie because
she's afraid Gracie will tell Emily's mother. George finds out
the secret and they try to hide it from Gracie. Emily's groom
ends up with George for a roommate, while Emily is "pro-
tected" by Gracie. Eventually everyone learns the truth, and
even Emily's mom is happy.
    AFTERPIECE: "Easter Parade."

#184 AIR DATE: APRIL 9, 1956—"NIGHT OF
    VAUDEVILLE"

Ronnie's drama school is losing money, so Gracie talks them
out of doing their usual performance of *Othello* in favor of
a vaudeville night. They enlist George to direct, and Gracie
emcees, and of course it's a huge success.
    No AFTERPIECE.

#185 AIR DATE: APRIL 16, 1956—"BURLESK"

Following the previous week's successful vaudeville show,
Ronnie and his friend decide to try out for a burlesque theater
opening. Ronnie is accepted, but his gifts seem to lie in an-

other field of show biz. When George and Gracie pay a call to the theater to try to talk to Ronnie out of this new career, they learn he's already been fired—by a boss who turns out to be an old vaudeville pal of George—and the two reminisce.
AFTERPIECE: "Travel Bureau."

#186 AIR DATE: APRIL 23, 1956—"THE RIGHT PEOPLE"

Ronnie is dating the daughter of a prominent New York socialite, Mrs. Sohmers, and Gracie mistakenly thinks they are going to get married. The girl's mother looks down her nose at the Burnses because they are "show people." But when a famous horse breeder stops in to get Gracie's autograph, Mrs. Sohmers is impressed. However, Ronnie isn't at all interested in marriage—he was merely giving the girl advice about another suitor with whom she's in love.
AFTERPIECE: "The Library—Lucy Crown."

#187 AIR DATE: APRIL 30, 1956—"THE MAGIC ACT"

Gracie is under the impression that George has been offered a part in a movie—without her. She doesn't want to stand in his way, so in order to convince him of her sincerity, she becomes a partner in a magic act, and we see her actually perform as a magician's assistant. When George realizes her mistake, he tells her it wasn't him, but Ronnie, that they want for the part.
AFTERPIECE: "Aunt Bridget—The Artist."

#188 AIR DATE: MAY 7, 1956—"THE PARIS CREATION"

Gracie remarks to George that she doesn't like a bow on a dress she has, so George tells her he'll take it to the dressmaker to have it removed. He didn't know the *designer* was from Paris. So our whole cast takes off for France. The de-

signer happens to be on the same plane over, and his initials
—G.B.—are the same as George's. Their briefcases get mixed
up, and neither man realizes it until after they've landed, but
they straighten it all out at the American Express office.
AFTERPIECE: "The Auto Show."

#189 AIR DATE: MAY 14, 1956—"BACK FROM PARIS"

Gracie and Broussard, the Paris dress designer, have an ar-
rangement for her to take twenty-four of his creations back
to the States and sell in a shop she plans to open in New York.
She goes to great lengths to hide this from George, but he
finds out about it anyway.
   This show had elaborate Parisian sets.
AFTERPIECE: "The Backyard Circus."

#190 AIR DATE: MAY 21, 1956—"THE TWENTY-FOUR
   DRESSES"

Gracie has brought back from Paris twenty-four designer
originals that she intends to sell in a dress shop. But first, she
needs George to loan her one hundred dollars to open the
store. George refuses and tries to get her to send the dresses
back. Ever resourceful, she borrows the money from Mrs.
Sohmers, sells all her own clothes, and has twenty-four new
dresses for herself.
AFTERPIECE: "The Flower Show."

#191 AIR DATE: MAY 28, 1956—"RONNIE IS
   LOVESICK"

When Gracie overhears Ronnie practicing his lines for a
movie about the French Foreign Legion, she thinks he's pin-
ing for Yvette, his French girlfriend, who's gone home. When
his uniform arrives, Gracie is even more upset, until he finally
explains it's a costume for the movie.
AFTERPIECE: "The Beauty Show."

#192 AIR DATE: JUNE 4, 1956—"THE NIGHT OUT"

George has loaned his topcoat to Harry Von Zell, who takes
a young lady to the Stork Club. Then George gets locked in
a steam room and doesn't get home until the next morning.
The hatcheck girl from the Stork Club returns his coat at the
same time, and Gracie suspects the worst. To convince Gracie
he's telling the truth, George brings over the janitor, the
policeman and all the other people who saw him at the steam
room.
    AFTERPIECE: "Gracie's Family Graduating."

#193 AIR DATE: JUNE 11, 1956—"QUESTIONS AND
        ANSWERS"

Blanche has become a member of the Ladies of Oyster Bay
Literary Club, but in order for Gracie to join, she must pass
a test of her literary knowledge. The president of the club
tries to help by supplying her in advance with the answers,
which Gracie learns, then has trouble fitting them to the right
questions. But the ladies find her delightful and let her into
the club anyway.
    AFTERPIECE: "The Beach."

#194 AIR DATE: JUNE 18, 1956—"THE TRIPLE
        SURPRISE PARTY"

Blanche plans to give husband Harry a surprise birthday
party in the Burns apartment. At the same time, Ronnie's
acting class has completed the term, and Gracie plans a surprise party for him. Harry Von Zell is celebrating his fifth
anniversary with George. When he learns George has purchased a pipe for "Harry" he assumes it's for him and expects
a surprise party. Gracie discovers Harry Morton's surprise
gifts in the closet, thinks they're all wrong for Ronnie, and
exchanges them. In the end, *everyone's* surprised.
    AFTERPIECE: "Uncle Harvey—The Repair Man."

#195 AIR DATE: SEPTEMBER 17, 1956—"MRS.
    SOHMERS NEEDS A PSYCHOLOGIST"

Mrs. Sohmers goes to a psychologist because Gracie is driving
her bananas. The doctor asks her to send in her friend Mrs.
Morton so they can discuss Gracie. Blanche has a hair appointment, so Gracie goes in her place. The psychologist, thinking
Gracie is Mrs. Morton, phones Harry to tell him his wife needs
help. Harry starts treating Blanche with extra kindness. Everyone gets straightened out except the poor doctor, who is
totally confused. (See also Live #27 and #75.)
    AFTERPIECE: "Cowboys and Rodeo."

#196 AIR DATE: SEPTEMBER 24, 1956—"THE SWITCH-
    BOARD OPERATORS"

In order to prevent Harry Morton from receiving a call about
a job Blanche doesn't want him to accept, she and Gracie take
over the hotel switchboard and create havoc for Harry and
everyone else. Harry, concerned over not receiving his call,
discovers what Blanche is up to and tells her that he had
already decided not to take the job.
    AFTERPIECE: "Superstition and Astrology."

SYNOPSES, SEVENTH SEASON—1956–57

PRODUCER/DIRECTOR: Rod Amateau
WRITERS: Norman Paul
        Harvey Helm
        Keith Fowler
        William Burns

NOTE: There were no new shows numbered 197 through 208.
These numbers were assigned to twelve reruns.

#209 AIR DATE: OCTOBER 1, 1956—"RETURN TO
    CALIFORNIA"

George, Gracie, Harry, and Blanche return unannounced to
Beverly Hills from New York, expecting to find an empty
house. Instead, they find Ronnie has also returned, and has
turned the Burns home into a fraternity house, while the
Mortons' place has become a sorority house for some of
Ronnie's college classmates. The adults end up having to
grin and bear it, staying at a hotel until Ronnie can evict
his friends.
AFTERPIECE: "The Pioneer in the Allen Family."

#210 AIR DATE: OCTOBER 8, 1956—"THE
    SHAKESPEAREAN PAPER"

Ronnie has to write a paper on the subject of his favorite
Shakespearean play, so Gracie visits his professor at USC,
noted authority Dr. Frank Baxter (who makes a guest appearance). She learns that Dr. Baxter's favorite play is *King Lear*,
and proceeds to change all references to "Julius Caesar" in
Ronnie's essay to "King Lear." Naturally Ronnie gets an *F*.
Later Dr. Baxter learns that Ronnie's mother is Gracie Allen
and understands why the paper was so strange. They find the
original copy and Ronnie gets an *A*.
AFTERPIECE: "The Political Allens."

#211 AIR DATE: OCTOBER 15, 1956—"THE WOMAN IN
    THE CAR"

Gracie borrows the Mortons' car when her own car has a dent.
She gets a parking ticket and puts it in the glove compartment. The officer has written on the ticket, "Woman in car
very cooperative." Blanche finds this and accuses Harry of
having an affair with another woman.
AFTERPIECE: "Home Remedies."

#212 AIR DATE: OCTOBER 22, 1956—"THE
    INTERVIEW"

A *TV Guide* reporter tries to get a story about the Burnses'
"normal" home life—amidst Ronnie and his friends' cheer-
leading practice, stuntmen auditioning for George, a surprise
visit from Francis X. Bushman (who plays himself)—and of
course Gracie, just being herself.
AFTERPIECE: "Halloween."

#213 AIR DATE: OCTOBER 29, 1956—"THE
    INITIATION"

Mrs. Sohmers, Blanche's friend from New York, decides to
buy a house in Pasadena. Gracie thinks the Mortons are moving to Pasadena, and tells Mrs. Sohmers she can buy the
Burnses' house so she and George can move to Pasadena to
be near the Mortons. During this, Ronnie's college friends
subject him to a fraternity initiation—he must say and do the
exact opposite of what people expect, and it's like having two
Gracies around the house.
AFTERPIECE: "Gracie Goes to Western Union."

#214 AIR DATE: NOVEMBER 5, 1956—"RONNIE'S
    BASHFUL"

When Ronnie's girlfriend goes on a trip out of town, he promises not to go to the dance with someone else. Gracie thinks
he's staying home because of bashfulness and has his fraternity brothers send over a blind date. Instead, they send *three*
girls. Ronnie's friend Carol returns in time, however, and
Gracie and the girls all go to the theater together.
AFTERPIECE: "Uncle Ben at County Fair."

#215 AIR DATE: NOVEMBER 12, 1956—"THE BIG
STAMP ROBBERY"

In her haste to mail a letter, Gracie borrows a three-cent
stamp from Harry Morton's collection, not realizing it's a
rare, valuable stamp. Harry thinks Blanche's lazy brother
Roger stole it. When Gracie asks George to mail her letter, he
sees the rare stamp on it and hides the letter. Relishing his
small victory, George invites everyone over and puts up a
reward for whoever finds the stamp, knowing he'll win. The
others add to the pot, and Roger—who had found the letter
earlier—scoops up all the money. Harry gets his stamp back,
and George has been outsmarted again.

AFTERPIECE: "Uncle Fred's Winter Resort."

#216 AIR DATE: NOVEMBER 19, 1956—"GEORGE'S
GRAY SUIT"

Gracie mails George's favorite suit to Blanche's brother, then
finds out George wouldn't approve. George knows (via his
magic TV) that the suit hasn't left the post office yet and gets
the package back. Gracie decides to tell George his suit was
stolen so he won't be angry. The police arrive, and the detective asks how all this happened. George starts to tell him
about the writers coming up with this story, how they had no
ending . . . and slowly the screen starts to iris out to black.

AFTERPIECE: " 'Scoop' Allen, Newspaperman."

#217 AIR DATE: NOVEMBER 26, 1956—"VON ZELL'S
RAISES"

Harry Von Zell has been trying again to get a raise from
George, while Gracie is trying to find a chaperone for Ronnie's ski weekend. She figures Von Zell could chaperone if he
and his girl were married and thinks the reason they're not
is that Harry doesn't have enough money. She tells George,
who gives Harry a raise, thinking he's getting married. Harry

has no intention of getting married, but each time he tries to tell George, George gives him another raise, until George finally says he can't afford him. Harry is fired—once again.
AFTERPIECE: "Daniel Allen, Trailblazer and Pathfinder."

#218 AIR DATE: DECEMBER 3, 1956—"THE REFRIGERATOR SALESMAN"

Ronnie has a Christmas job selling electric shavers. Gracie learns that the commission isn't much on shavers and has him transferred to the refrigerator department. George needs presents for his staff, and, at Von Zell's suggestion, phones Ronnie. Thinking Ronnie is still selling shavers, George orders seven. When everyone calls George to thank him for the refrigerators, it's too late to back out, and Von Zell quickly disappears.
AFTERPIECE: "Uncle Waldo in the Foreign Legion."

#219 AIR DATE: DECEMBER 10, 1956—"THE GIRL BEHIND THE PERFUME COUNTER"

Ronnie leaves his coat at the home of his new girlfriend, Madeline, who works at the same store he does. When the girl's mother returns the coat the next day, Gracie fears Ronnie is in love with an older woman and decides to get Ronnie fired so he won't be near her. Gracie inadvertently tells the young girl that her son Ronnie is seeing an older woman. Madeline is outraged. George catches the action on his magic TV, phones Madeline, and straightens it all out.
AFTERPIECE: "The Volunteer Fire Brigade."

#220 AIR DATE: DECEMBER 17, 1956—"RONNIE QUITS COLLEGE BECAUSE HIS FATHER GOES BROKE"

To persuade Ronnie to finish his education, Gracie tells him that his father has gone broke because he didn't go to college.

Upset that they are now poor, Ronnie vows to quit school to support the family. George learns via his TV set that he's "broke" and decides to go along with it. Gracie hears the rumor and takes in boarders. George finally admits to her that they're not penniless, Gracie says good, because Romanoff's is catering for the boarders. George laments, "Now we *are* broke."

AFTERPIECE: "The Ferryboat Pilot."

#221 AIR DATE: DECEMBER 24, 1956—"CHRISTMAS IN JAIL"

The story is told in flashbacks, as George—in jail—recalls why he's there for Christmas. George buys Gracie a pearl necklace for Christmas, and hides it. Ronnie needs money for a gift, so when Gracie finds the necklace, she pawns it to get the money for Ronnie, and replaces the real pearls with a $1.98 version. Ronnie takes the loan and buys Gracie a gift— a pearl necklace. Discovering this, George decides he will exchange the pearls he's bought for Gracie. When he tries to return the cheap imitation, he's tabbed as a con man and arrested. At the jail, Gracie persuades the desk sergeant to let her spend Christmas with George in his cell. The whole cast shows up with a decorated tree, and they all sing carols.

AFTERPIECE: "Christmas Eve with the Allens."

#222 AIR DATE: DECEMBER 31, 1956—"THE COSTUME PARTY"

George and Harry Morton need a loan from Vanderlip the banker for a property deal, so the Burnses throw a dinner party. Ronnie suggests a costume party, and George mistakes the Vanderlips for Blanche's ne'er-do-well brother Roger and his date. George throws out the Vanderlips and makes a fuss over Roger, until the party crasher is unmasked and the Vanderlips are called back by a sheepish George.

AFTERPIECE: "Relative Who Is a Cab Driver."

#223 AIR DATE: JANUARY 7, 1957—"GRACIE AND
    THE BULLFIGHTER"

When Ronnie returns from Tijuana, Gracie thinks he's taken
up bullfighting, and that as a parent she should have an interest in her son's hobby. She gets Harry Von Zell to drive her
to Tijuana, where they meet a famous bullfighter and bring
him home to meet Ronnie. They even get George to wear a
bullfighter's outfit. But Ronnie's hobbies are fleeting, and by
now he has a new interest—modern dancing, and the pretty
modern-dance teacher.
    AFTERPIECE: "Cousin Nelson—Northwest Mountie."

#224 AIR DATE: JANUARY 14, 1957—"THE UGLY
    DUCKLING"

Ronnie and his friend Ralph study with Mildred McCoy, a
brainy plain-Jane. Gracie decides to help transform the girl so
Ronnie will take her to the prom, and even George kicks in
thirty-five dollars. Gracie turns the ugly duckling into a swan,
and Mildred lands her own date—one of the real "catches" on
campus.
    This was the show with the "magic genie" special ef-
fects.
    AFTERPIECE: "Let's Talk About Your Family."

#225 AIR DATE: JANUARY 21, 1957—"THE APTITUDE
    TEST"

When George seems moody, Gracie thinks he must be in the
wrong profession and has a psychologist give him an aptitude
test. George knows Harry Von Zell is hiding in the closet
and pretends to hire the psychologist as his new announcer.
He even sprays the closet for moths—with poor Harry still
in it.
    AFTERPIECE: "Casey Allen, the Railroad Man."

#226 AIR DATE: JANUARY 28, 1957—"GOING TO PALM SPRINGS"

Ronnie and his friend Ralph plan a trip to Palm Springs for a rest—and a week with seven girls. Gracie's afraid he won't get any rest, and promises Ronnie she'll send George down there so he can keep the girls away. Ronnie pleads with George not to go, and George promises he won't. Gracie and George do end up in Palm Springs, but agree to stay at a different hotel from Ronnie.

AFTERPIECE: "Cousin Philo, Private Eye."

#227 AIR DATE: FEBRUARY 4, 1957—"THE MATRIMONIAL BUREAU"

When Ronnie's friends turn twenty-one and get married, Gracie fears Ronnie has only four months of bachelorhood left. She goes to a marriage bureau to find him a girl, but mistakenly thinks they want a photo of George. The bureau sends George a potential wife and he pretends to make a pass at her. Gracie phones the agency and insists they send her a prospect for a new husband. The two single people then meet at the Burnses' and fall for each other.

AFTERPIECE: "Wyatt Allen, Western Town Marshal."

#228 AIR DATE: FEBRUARY 11, 1957—"THE FORTUNE TELLER"

In a tearoom, a gypsy tells Gracie that her husband is going to acquire a fortune, so she immediately buys Ronnie a convertible as a gift for passing his exams. Harry, Blanche, and Von Zell are furious because George didn't tell them the secret of his "fortune." Gracie goes back to the tearoom to find out how George made his money. George, watching his magic TV, learns what's going on and phones the gypsy, who comes to the house so George can explain to his friends about his "fortune."

AFTERPIECE: "The Veterinarian."

#229 AIR DATE: FEBRUARY 18, 1957—"FIGHTING
    FOR HAPPINESS"

When Gracie hears that fighting in a marriage leads to great
makeups, she decides to try to provoke George into a fight.
Nothing seems to work, not even telling him he has a terrible
singing voice. Ronnie finally explains to George what Gracie
is after. When George picks the fight, Gracie tells him she
won't forgive him and leaves.
AFTERPIECE: "Doc Allen, Medicine Man."

#230 AIR DATE: FEBRUARY 25, 1957—"THE
    TERMITES"

Gracie wants to redecorate their bedroom and surprise
George, but she can't get him out of the house. She finally
resorts to having Ronnie's friend wire the house to make it
appear that termites are devouring the place. George is on to
the scheme, but goes along with it, telling her they'd better go to Palm Springs so the exterminator can come
while they're gone, and maybe the bedroom could be redecorated too.
AFTERPIECE: "Robin Allen, Incompetent Burglar."

#231 AIR DATE: MARCH 4, 1957—"THE $15,000
    ERROR"

The decorator calls and asks Gracie if she can pay the bill a
little early because there's a once-in-a-lifetime chance to buy
an art collection he wants. How much? Fifteen thousand dollars. Gracie knows she'll never get George to sign a check for
that much, and Von Zell tells her she'll have to mortgage the
house. Fortunately, the decorator comes by and explains what
happened, and George happily gives him a check for eight
hundred dollars.
AFTERPIECE: "Cecil B. Allen, The Movie Director."

#232 AIR DATE: MARCH 11, 1957—"THE RING"

When Gracie tells George her engagement ring slipped down the drain, he hires a plumber to tear out the kitchen drain pipe. What George doesn't know is that Gracie loaned the ring to Ronnie so he could become engaged to his girlfriend. The girl realizes it's Gracie's ring and gives it back to her.

Harry Morton is not in this show; dialogue discloses he's away on a business trip.

AFTERPIECE: "The Cruise Hostess."

#233 AIR DATE: MARCH 18, 1957—"THE PLUMBER'S FRIEND"

Mr. Jantzen, the plumber, is on his way to San Diego to meet a widow and asks Gracie to baby-sit his four daughters. Gracie says yes, and four beautiful girls, ages seventeen to twenty-one, arrive. Meanwhile, Ronnie and his fiancée, Kathy, have a fight because she is always so jealous. Ronnie's fed up with girls—until he comes home and sees his houseguests. Eventually it's straightened out and Ronnie, Kathy, and the four girls all go to dinner.

Harry Morton missed this show, too—still away on business.

AFTERPIECE: "Edward R. Allen, News Analyst."

#234 AIR DATE: MARCH 25, 1957—"GOING TO HOUSTON"

In an attempt to convince the father of Ronnie's college friend Brian McAfee that the boy should complete his education, Gracie, Ronnie, Blanche, and later George all head for Houston. Ronnie meets Bonnie Sue McAfee in this episode—she later becomes his semi-steady girlfriend. Harry Morton is still "out of town."

AFTERPIECE: "Henry Wadsworth Allen, Poet."

#235 AIR DATE: APRIL 1, 1957—"THE STRAY DOG"

When she arrives in Houston, Gracie checks into a hotel that absolutely forbids pets. This, of course, does not deter Gracie from befriending a stray French poodle whom one of the guests has lost. The guest buys another to trick his wife, and both dogs end up with Gracie. Eventually the owner gets his original dog back.

AFTERPIECE: "Thomas A. Allen, the Inventor."

#236 AIR DATE: APRIL 8, 1957—"RONNIE GETS A MOVIE ROLE"

Ronnie's part in the movie *Bernardine* requires him to be on the set early in the morning. Fearing that George will not approve of the interruption in his son's college curriculum, Gracie attempts to keep Ronnie's movie work a secret. Harry Von Zell pretends to be Ronnie, sick in bed, but George doesn't buy it.

AFTERPIECE: "Bowling."

#237 AIR DATE: APRIL 15, 1957—"THE PLUMBER'S UNION"

Gracie learns that Mr. Jantzen, a widower with four daughters, is looking for a wife. She volunteers to place an ad in the personals column. Unfortunately, a very young lady shows up, and it is evident that Gracie has stretched the truth quite a bit. George has some fun by dressing in a Little Lord Fauntleroy suit to try to impress the young Jantzen girls.

AFTERPIECE: "Wilbur Orville Allen, Barnstormer."

#238 AIR DATE: APRIL 22, 1957—"HARRY'S HOMECOMING"

Gracie and Blanche have been complaining that their husbands have lost their romantic spark. George decides to teach

them a lesson and persuades Harry Morton to disguise himself as an amorous Frenchman to test Blanche. George lets Blanche in on the scheme, and Blanche pretends to fall for the "Frenchman." Gracie thinks Blanche is having an affair and sends Von Zell over to pose as competition.
AFTERPIECE: "Deep-Sea Doodle Allen, Diver."

#239 AIR DATE: APRIL 29, 1957—"THE PUBLICITY ROMANCE"

Ronnie is having trouble explaining to his girlfriend, Kathy, that the big romance between him and an Italian starlet is just a publicity stunt. Gracie tries to help by having Harry Von Zell pose as the girl's outraged father. Just when Ronnie is about to lose Kathy for good, the starlet arrives in tears with her jealous boyfriend. He doesn't understand publicity stunts either. The four of them go out together.
AFTERPIECE: "Atlas Allen, Strong Man."

#240 AIR DATE: MAY 6, 1957—"THE TEXAN LADY MACBETH"

One of Ronnie's classmates, Brian McAfee, is upset when his sister in Texas decides to come to Hollywood to be an actress. He asks Gracie to convince the girl that life on stage is not as glamorous as it looks. When Bonnie Sue does her rendition of Shakespeare, proud that she's lost her Texas accent, George saves the day by telling her the studio is going to be looking for a Texas girl for a new movie. She rushes home to recapture her accent and practice for the audition.
AFTERPIECE: "Clyde 'Bring 'Em Back Alive' Allen, Animal Tamer."

#241 AIR DATE: MAY 13, 1957—"RONNIE'S BOAT"

Ronnie uses the money from his first movie role for the down payment on a boat, but he needs George to cosign the loan. George would rather Ronnie invested it in an annuity. Gracie comes to Ronnie's rescue by trying to convince George that Ronnie needs the boat for "health" reasons. George relents, but then he was going to let Ronnie have it all along.

AFTERPIECE: "Boulder Allen, Construction Engineer."

#242 AIR DATE: MAY 20, 1957—"A TRIP TO TAHITI"

Ronnie and Ralph are all set for a sea cruise to Tahiti on Ronnie's new boat when the four Jantzen girls come by, and the boys realize what they'll be missing. Gracie has already prepared an explanation to give George *after* the boys have left. Before that can happen, Ronnie begs his father to convince his mother that they don't want to go.

AFTERPIECE: "The Process Server."

#243 AIR DATE: MAY 27, 1957—"THE HOME
      GRADUATION"

Brian McAfee's father is in town from Texas to attend Brian's graduation. After nine years of college, the lad will finally get his B.A., only Brian thinks he hasn't passed. Gracie has a plan: if Brian pretends to be sick, "Dean" Von Zell can give him his diploma at home, and his father will think it's official. The plan is set into motion, but at the last minute George arrives with the real dean. It seems Brian finally passed after all.

AFTERPIECE: "The Lifeguard."

#244 AIR DATE: JUNE 3, 1957—"BLANCHE'S MOTHER
      ARRIVES"

Harry Morton has to go on a business trip, making this the perfect time for Blanche's mother to visit, since she and Harry don't get along. When Harry's trip is canceled at the last minute, Gracie says Blanche's mother can stay with her. At the same time, Marie, a foreign exchange student, is visiting Ronnie. Harry Von Zell hears there's a French girl at Gracie's, and confuses her with Blanche's mother.

Bea Benaderet played a dual role, appearing as both Blanche Morton and Blanche's mother.

AFTERPIECE: "The Camp Counselor."

#245 AIR DATE: JUNE 10, 1957—"THE WADING POOL AT ACAPULCO"

Ronnie and Ralph accept summer jobs as lifeguards at a hotel in Acapulco. Gracie and Blanche want George and Harry to go too. The only way the men can get out of it is to beat the boys to the swimming test, pretend to be Ronnie and Ralph, and fail. George and Harry Von Zell go to a lot of trouble, only to find out afterward that Ronnie and Ralph didn't want the jobs after all—it was for a children's wading pool.

AFTERPIECE: "The One-Man Post Office."

#246 AIR DATE: JUNE 17, 1957—"THE MARITAL MIX-UP"

Gracie tries to fix up her plumber, Mr. Jantzen, with one of her friends, but the prospective bride mistakes Harry Von Zell for her groom-to-be. Harry thinks she's offering him a job and he tears up his contract with George. Once again George makes him suffer to the bitter end before straightening things out.

Bob Cummings makes a special appearance as "Bob Collins" in a photo session with Jantzen's daughters.

AFTERPIECE: "The Mountain Climber."

#247 AIR DATE: JUNE 24, 1957—"A PAIN IN THE BACK"

Gracie and Blanche are concerned because they're such good friends and their husbands are not. They decide the best way for them to like each other is for the two men to go camping together. Neither George nor Harry wants to go—they like their relationship just the way it is. George tells Harry he has a bad back, and Harry says fine—he's done his duty by asking. Then, to avoid a massage by the Rams' trainer, George says he'll go. Harry says he can take Blanche—she's wanted a second honeymoon anyway.

AFTERPIECE: "The Allen Annual Picnic."

#248 AIR DATE: JULY 1, 1957—"RONNIE'S TWENTY-ONE"

Ronnie's just had his twenty-first birthday, and his first present is a marriage proposal from Marie, the French exchange student. She asks Ronnie to marry her so she can stay in the country, since her visa expires in six days. Ronnie thinks he said no, but Marie took it as yes. Gracie tries to help by getting Ronnie's birth certificate changed, and she succeeds, only to find out Marie was just teasing Ronnie.

AFTERPIECE: "The Butler."

SYNOPSES, EIGHTH SEASON—1957-58

PRODUCER/DIRECTOR: Rod Amateau
WRITERS: Keith Fowler
Harvey Helm
Norman Paul
William Burns

NOTE: There were no new shows numbered 249 through 260. These numbers were assigned to twelve reruns.

#261 AIR DATE: SEPTEMBER 30, 1957—"THE GENERAL"

A friend of Ronnie's gets married, and Gracie agrees to help the newlywed couple keep their marriage from the groom's father, an Army general who had a West Point career in mind for his son. Gracie tells the general that the young bride he meets is Ronnie's wife. No one has the courage to tell the regimental general the truth—until George comes to the rescue and explains.

No AFTERPIECE.

#262 AIR DATE: OCTOBER 7, 1957—"TOO MUCH POT ROAST"

Ronnie is so distracted by his girlfriends, he's neglecting his studies. Gracie thinks the "too much of a good thing will result in boredom with it" philosophy is what Ronnie needs. She hires four beautiful girls (Miss Universe contestants) to come to the house and pretend to be the new maid, chauffeur, gardener, and chef. The plan backfires—Ronnie is even more smitten. The girls tell him what his mother's plan was, and Ronnie agrees to study from nine to three, with the rest of the day for all his girlfriends.

AFTERPIECE: "Balzac Allen, The Novelist."

#263 AIR DATE: OCTOBER 14, 1957—"THE TEXAN ITALIAN"

Gracie tries to help Bonnie Sue McAfee get into the movies by transforming the Texas beauty into "Tina Caccitori," an Italian actress. To cover her accent, Gracie tells her to just keep eating grapes whenever anyone talks to her, since she won't be expected to answer while eating. Ronnie asks George to help, and when George comes up with a part for her, it's for a young girl from Texas.

AFTERPIECE: "The Bus Driver."

#264 AIR DATE: OCTOBER 21, 1957—"AN ENGLISH TEA"

Gracie goes all out to impress the English dowager mother of one of Ronnie's girlfriends. George, not being very cultured, is not invited, while Harry Morton is—and he bores everyone to tears.

AFTERPIECE: "Noah Allen, The Zookeeper."

#265 AIR DATE: OCTOBER 28, 1957—"SEPTEMBER AND MAY"

Gracie is asked to intervene in a budding romance. The plumber's daughter, June, saw her father out with a very young woman and she fears the relationship will get serious. George wishes Gracie had kept out of it when her heart-to-heart talk with the plumber ends up costing George six hundred dollars for new pipes.

AFTERPIECE: "Mississippi."

#266 AIR DATE: NOVEMBER 4, 1957—"THE STAR MAKER"

Brian McAfee knows he's going to flunk his exam and goes to Gracie for help. She enlists the aid of the smartest boy in class, Alfred. First she tells him not to wear his glasses because he looks so handsome without them; next she instructs him to change his name—to Brian McAfee. Just before the big test, Brian tells Gracie it's okay: the professor didn't want him to take the test, in order to keep the class average up.

AFTERPIECE: "The Press Agent."

#267 AIR DATE: NOVEMBER 11, 1957—"THE AFRICAN HUNTER"

George promises Ronnie when he brings his new girlfriend home for dinner that all will be normal. What George doesn't know is that Gracie has invited an African big-game hunter to dinner, who arrives complete with a witch doctor.

AFTERPIECE: "The Psychiatrist."

#268 AIR DATE: NOVEMBER 18, 1957—"ONE LITTLE
    FIGHT"

Ronnie and his friend Ralph are not speaking to one another
because Ronnie thinks Ralph stole his girlfriend. Gracie and
Blanche stage a mock fight to show the boys how foolish it is
to fight with your best friend. Gracie doesn't know the boys
have already made up, and her quarrel with Blanche results
in everyone else's fighting.
    AFTERPIECE: "The Old Prospector."

#269 AIR DATE: NOVEMBER 25, 1957—"WITH OR
    WITHOUT GLASSES"

Ever since Gracie convinced Ronnie's classmate Alfred that
he is more handsome without his glasses, he hasn't worn
them. Consequently, he hasn't been able to see, and is now in
danger of flunking. While Gracie tries to persuade Alfred to
put them back on, Ronnie confides to Von Zell that he, too, is
having trouble in school. Von Zell pretends to be Ronnie's rich
uncle who will buy the school a new gym if Ronnie passes.
George arrives to straighten everybody out.
    AFTERPIECE: "Mozart Allen."

#270 AIR DATE: DECEMBER 2, 1957—"A BOX OF
    CIGARS"

Ronnie and Ralph are campaigning for their candidate for
homecoming queen. Gracie wants to help, and tries to talk
George out of a box of his cigars to hand out to voters. It
turns out Gracie didn't have to go to all that trouble—Ronnie
gave out kisses instead, and the girl won.
    AFTERPIECE: "Mozart Allen, Part II."

#271 AIR DATE: DECEMBER 9, 1957—"MISERY
    LOVES COMPANY"

Ronnie's friend Ralph is miserable because his girlfriend left
him for a football player. Gracie tries to cheer him up by making everyone as miserable as he is, and Ronnie almost loses
his own girl. In the end, Ralph's girl comes back to him after
realizing that the ballplayer really didn't care about her at all.
    AFTERPIECE: "The Psychiatrist."

#272 AIR DATE: DECEMBER 16, 1957—"A HOLE IN
    THE CARPET"

Gracie stumbles in a department store and tears her nylons.
When the claims adjuster comes to settle for damages, Gracie
thinks the store is going to sue her, instead of the other
way around. After a discussion with Gracie, the adjuster
leaves, very worried that Gracie also suffered a head injury. (See #40.)
    AFTERPIECE: "Florence Allen, Nurse."

#273 AIR DATE: DECEMBER 23, 1957—"HOW TO
    WRAP A MINK"

Gracie and Blanche both think their husbands are getting
them mink coats for Christmas, while the men had something
much less expensive in mind.
    AFTERPIECE: "The Bird-Lover."

#274 AIR DATE: DECEMBER 30, 1957—"INVITATION
    TO THE PARTY"

When the Mortons receive an invitation to an exclusive party,
Harry can't wait to tell George. Then Blanche discovers they
actually received George and Gracie's invitation by mistake.
Gracie straightens it all out by getting the hostess to invite
the Mortons too.
    AFTERPIECE: "The Sculptor."

#275 AIR DATE: JANUARY 6, 1958—"THE STOLEN
   CAR"

Gracie tries to help Ronnie get a job on the school paper by
concocting a surefire scheme. She gets Brian to hide his father's new car in the Mortons' garage so she can report it
stolen and give Ronnie "the scoop" on finding it. The police
discover the stolen car before Ronnie does, but when they
learn Gracie Allen is involved, they leave, letting Ronnie get
the story.
   AFTERPIECE: "The Lover."

#276 AIR DATE: JANUARY 13, 1958—"RONNIE FINDS
   A FRIEND AN APARTMENT"

Ronnie helps a friend and his new family find an apartment.
When Gracie arrives to check it out and talks with a baby-
sitting neighbor, she leaves thinking the young baby is Ronnie's. Finally she meets the real father, and Ronnie's life is
back to normal.
   AFTERPIECE: "Soldier of Fortune."

#277 AIR DATE: JANUARY 20, 1958—"McAFEE AND
   THE MANICURIST"

Brian and Bonnie Sue's father falls for the hotel manicurist.
Bonnie Sue thinks she's after her father's money and goes to
Gracie for help. Gracie gets Von Zell to pose as an even
wealthier Texan, thinking the girl will drop him. Meanwhile,
Bonnie Sue has persuaded Harry Morton to pretend to be her
boyfriend, hoping her father will see the comparison. What
she doesn't realize is, he's already decided he was too old for
the young manicurist.
   AFTERPIECE: "The Plantation Owner."

#278 AIR DATE: JANUARY 27, 1958—"TOO MANY FATHERS"

One of Ronnie's friends has fallen for a girl from a wealthy background. He asks Gracie to pose as his mother for her visiting parents. George won't go along with it, and both Von Zell and Harry Morton show up to help Gracie out. (See #26.)
AFTERPIECE: "The Taxi Dancer."

#279 AIR DATE: FEBRUARY 10, 1958—"THE ACCIDENT"

Gracie is riding with Harry Morton and they have a small accident. Gracie is ready to testify on Harry's behalf, when Ronnie gets a crush on the pretty girl driver of the other car. Gracie is caught between her friends and her family until she solves the problem by having Von Zell impersonate Harry Morton and talk to the girl's father.
AFTERPIECE: "The Poll Taker."

#280 AIR DATE: FEBRUARY 17, 1958—"THE JAPANESE TEXAN"

Texas-born Bonnie Sue wants the part of a Japanese girl in a movie. Gracie goes out of her way to help land Bonnie Sue the role, only to discover that the movie will be filmed in Japan, and Bonnie Sue doesn't want to leave Ronnie.
AFTERPIECE: "Judge of the Old West."

#281 AIR DATE: FEBRUARY 24, 1958—"HYPNOTIZING GRACIE"

A hypnotist promises the press that he can turn Gracie into the smartest woman in the world. At first everyone *but* Gracie succumbs to his hypnotic technique—Harry Morton becomes charming, and Harry Von Zell keeps barking like a dog. Finally he gets to hypnotize Gracie, and she astounds the press with her erudite statements. Then the hypnotist leaves for England, and no one can snap Gracie out of it. Her new-found intelligence even carries over into the Afterpiece. Without Gracie in the act, George asks Ronnie to help him tell "cousin" jokes, but it doesn't work.

AFTERPIECE: "Gracie Won't Do Jokes."

#282 AIR DATE: MARCH 3, 1958—"GRACIE IS BRILLIANT"

Gracie has been turned into a "brain" by a hypnotist and is cleaning up on a quiz show. Without her, George has no act, and is reduced to the role of house husband—cooking, cleaning, baking cookies, etc. The professor tries to break the spell over the phone from London, but while George goes off to bring Gracie to the phone, Blanche picks up the receiver and becomes like the old Gracie. The hypnotist finally flies over from England and straightens it all out. Gracie loses on the quiz show, which is all right because it saves the Burnses money in taxes.

AFTERPIECE: "Uncle Barnum, Circus Owner."

#283 AIR DATE: MARCH 10, 1958—"RONNIE'S FAN CLUB"

Edie Westrope, a fourteen-year-old fan, has a crush on Ronnie. She sends him a letter saying she wants to start a fan club for him, but her nineteen-year-old sister comes to the Burnses' house and is mistaken for the younger sister. Ronnie later phones for a date with her, but gets the younger girl on the phone, and, thinking she's the older one, makes a date. He ends up doubling with Ralph and the older sister.

AFTERPIECE: "The Diplomat."

#284 AIR DATE: MARCH 17, 1958—"FROZEN
     PASSION"

George is interested in producing a feature film, and everyone
wants a part in it. Gracie sees a bogus script and begins
thinking of casting it—Ronnie and Bonnie Sue for the leads;
also parts for Harry Von Zell and Blanche. They all get out
the script for the director, and he flees in haste.
AFTERPIECE: "The Horticulturist."

#285 AIR DATE: MARCH 24, 1958—"HIGH BLOOD
     PRESSURE"

All George wants to do is play a little golf, but everyone keeps
detouring him. Mr. Jantzen the plumber arrives and is supposed to be examined for an insurance policy. He tells Gracie
he always flunks because of his high blood pressure. Gracie
tells the doctor that George is the plumber, but George tells
him where the real plumber is. Jantzen fails the test, and
Gracie thinks George has high blood pressure. Everyone goes
out of his way to be extra kind to poor "ailing" George.
AFTERPIECE: "Rhinestone Lil."

#286 AIR DATE: APRIL 7, 1958—"SOFTENING THE
     PROFESSOR"

Ronnie and Ralph cut classes for two days, and George convinces them they are about to be suspended from school.
Actually the professor himself has missed class because he's
just gotten married. His call was not to suspend the boys, but
to invite them to a reception. Gracie doesn't know he's married and vows to introduce him to a young lady. She does—
to his own wife, whom Gracie mistakes for Harry Von Zell's
girlfriend Mimi. When the professor and the young lady invite
them all to a wedding reception, Gracie is convinced she's a
great matchmaker.
AFTERPIECE: "Annie Allen, Sharpshooter."

#287 AIR DATE: APRIL 14, 1958—"THE PUBLICITY
  MARRIAGE"

To get Edie, the fourteen-year-old president of Ronnie's fan
club, off his back, Gracie has her publicist plant a story about
Ronnie and Bonnie Sue's "marriage." Edie gives up on Ronnie
and goes back to her old boyfriend, Malcolm. Bonnie Sue is
now convinced Ronnie wants to marry her. Gracie manages
to persuade Bonnie Sue she'd be giving up a great career as
an actress if she got married. Soon Edie learns it was a trick
and dumps Malcolm, and Ronnie is stuck with the lovesick
teen again.
  AFTERPIECE: "Old-time Motorcycle Cop."

#288 AIR DATE: APRIL 21, 1958—"BLANCHE GETS A
  JURY NOTICE"

Blanche has been called for jury duty, and Harry Morton has
all kinds of exciting plans during her absence: going to an
exhibit of Greek statuary, a convention of stamp collectors,
CPA meetings, and the like. Harry calls up the judge and
insists they take Blanche. The judge suspects a trick and
refuses, then realizes he's desperately in need of jurors and
vows to take the very next prospect. It's Gracie, of course,
and, convinced her dumb answers are an act, he immediately
accepts her.
  AFTERPIECE: "World Traveler and Lecturer."

#289 AIR DATE: APRIL 28, 1958—"GRACIE AND THE
  JURY"

While on jury duty, Gracie examines the evidence in a counter-
feit trial and accidentally switches a fake twenty-dollar bill
for a real one. She gives the bogus bill to Blanche so she can
get to the hat sale before it ends. Harry takes the bill from
Blanche and gives it to George. George knows via his TV that
it's a phony and gives it to Harry Von Zell, who is arrested.

He's brought before Gracie's jury, where the mix-up is finally explained.

The repeat of this episode, on September 22, 1958, was the final prime-time "Burns and Allen Show" to air.

AFTERPIECE: "The Forest Ranger."

#290 AIR DATE: MAY 5, 1958—"RONNIE MAKES A
       RECORD"

George is elated after a record-company executive signs Ronnie, but Gracie thinks George was the one who had been hoping for a contract. When the president of the company calls at the Burns home, Gracie tries to pass off Harry Von Zell as Ronnie, but it doesn't work. George enters and explains the situation, and everyone goes down to the studio to watch Ronnie cut his record.

Fred de Cordova directed this episode.

AFTERPIECE: "The Farmer."

#291 AIR DATE: MAY 12, 1958—"RONNIE'S ROYALTY
       CHECK"

Ronnie's first record royalty earns him $160, and he and his new girlfriend go shopping for a dress for Gracie. But Gracie thinks the girl's a gold digger. She decides to introduce her to Harry Von Zell so she'll leave Ronnie alone. Before she can, however, she finds the dress Ronnie bought her, and thinking it's intended for the girl, she takes it back. She gets Ronnie's money refunded, then buys the dress for herself—charging it to George!

AFTERPIECE: "The Lifeguard."

#292 AIR DATE: MAY 19, 1958—"A VISIT FROM
       CHARLES VIDOR"

Movie director Charles Vidor (Hans Christian Andersen, A Farewell to Arms) asks George if he can get Jack Benny to emcee the annual Directors Guild dinner. Gracie tries to encourage him to use Bonnie Sue in his next film, but Vidor says he's looking for someone well known. Gracie calls the newspaper and announces Bonnie Sue's engagement—to Harry Von Zell. Vidor isn't impressed, so Gracie plants a new story. The Von Zell engagement is off—now the young starlet is engaged to Charles Vidor! George agrees to get Vidor off the hook with his wife if he'll let George emcee the dinner.

AFTERPIECE: "The Jewel Thief."

#293 AIR DATE: MAY 26, 1958—"RONNIE GOES INTO THE ARMY"

Ronnie is set to go into the Army and Gracie plans to take an apartment near the base so she can visit on weekends. She thinks he's being shipped to Alaska and goes to see the general. The general agrees to send him to Fort Ord, near San Francisco, which is where he was going anyway. Finally George ends it all by calling them and saying Ronnie can't go into the Army because he still has a year of college to complete, and the whole thing happened because they needed a story for this week. The general agrees, and says how much he's enjoyed working with Gracie, Bea, Larry, and, of course, Judy Meredith.

AFTERPIECE: "The Plainclotheswoman."

#294 AIR DATE: JUNE 2, 1958—"LOCKED OUT"

George and Gracie have a dinner party to attend, and Ronnie has a date. Before they can all leave, Gracie takes a call for George from a man with the BBC. Unaware the man was calling from Beverly Hills and not London, George refuses to leave the phone until he hears from him. George sends Ronnie and his date to the party with Gracie. Still no call; George finally goes to the party. When they return, Ronnie takes the keys to drive his date home and the Burnses are locked out. The Mortons offer to help and they also get locked out. A

locksmith arrives and locks his tools in the house. At last
Ronnie returns and lets everyone in. Then the BBC man
shows up in person, since no one answered his calls. They
couldn't—they were all locked out.

AFTERPIECE: "The Moving Man."

#295 AIR DATE: JUNE 9, 1958—"THE WEEK IN NEW YORK"

The Burnses are taking a trip to New York, and Ronnie plans
a big party at the house while they're away. The Mortons
decide to go to Hawaii so Harry can get as far away from the
Burnses as possible. When George and Gracie hear about the
great party Ronnie has planned, they cancel their New York
trip. Harry Morton is the last to hear the news, as he arrives
in his Hawaiian outfit complete with ukulele.

AFTERPIECE: "The Summer Resort Owner."

#296 AIR DATE: JUNE 16, 1958—"THE JUNE WEDDING"

When the hotel mixes up honeymoon reservations for Ronnie's friends, George and Gracie decide to let the newlyweds
stay with them. The young couple casts a spell of love over
everyone. Bonnie Sue wants to marry Ronnie, and Gracie
convinces her that marriage can be unhappy. Then Harry Von
Zell wants to marry Gloria, so Gracie tells *her* marriage is
wonderful. Finally, the hotel calls and says the bridal suite is
available. George and Gracie take it, and Ronnie's invited
along, since he missed the first time.

AFTERPIECE: "Amusement Park Manager."

#297 AIR DATE: JUNE 23, 1958—"SUMMER SCHOOL"

Ronnie is making plans to have a "Ronnie Burns Entertainment Troupe" at Big Bear Lake during his summer vacation.
But when George finds out what Ronnie's college grades

were, he decides his son should attend summer school instead. Gracie manages to persuade the professor to hold classes out by their pool. George finally relents and lets Ronnie go to Big Bear.

AFTERPIECE: "Baseball Team Manager."

#298 AIR DATE: SEPTEMBER 8, 1958—"THE GRAMMAR SCHOOL DANCE"

Ronnie's romance with his latest girlfriend runs into a snag when he's coerced into escorting his teenage fan-club president to a grammar-school prom. Gracie manages to straighten her out by turning the girl's young boyfriend into a sophisticate, and Ronnie gets to take out his new lady as originally planned.

AFTERPIECE: "The Sailor."

#299 AIR DATE: SEPTEMBER 15, 1958—"THE EXCHANGE STUDENT"

A visit from a foreign exchange student throws the Burns household into a turmoil. Ronnie fears Bonnie Sue will desert him in favor of the handsome young Frenchman. Gracie can't think of a polite way to evict the boy on Ronnie's behalf. But when the Frenchman's girlfriend shows up and takes an interest in Ronnie, the student packs and leaves immediately.

AFTERPIECE: "Robinson Allen on the Desert Island."

This was the last "Burns and Allen Show" filmed (June 4, 1958) and the second-to-last episode to air. The final episode of the season was a repeat of #289, airing September 22, 1958.

INDEX

295